SIMPLE HABITS FOR COMPLEX TIMES

SIMPLE HABITS
FOR COMPLEX TIMES

Powerful Practices for Leaders

JENNIFER GARVEY BERGER

AND KEITH JOHNSTON

STANFORD BUSINESS BOOKS

An Imprint of Stanford University Press
Stanford, California

Stanford University Press
Stanford, California

Special discounts for bulk quantities of Stanford Business Books are available to corporations, professional associations, and other organizations. For details and discount information, contact the special sales department of Stanford University Press. Tel: (650) 736-1782, Fax: (650) 736-1784

Printed in the United States of America on acid-free, archival-quality paper

Library of Congress Cataloging-in-Publication Data

Berger, Jennifer Garvey, 1970– author.
    Simple habits for complex times : powerful practices for leaders / Jennifer Garvey Berger and Keith Johnston.
        pages cm
    Includes bibliographical references and index.
    ISBN 978-0-8047-8847-2 (cloth : alk. paper)
    ISBN 978-0-8047-9943-0 (pbk. : alk. paper)
    1. Leadership.   2. Management.   3. Complexity (Philosophy)
I. Johnston, Keith, 1955– author.   II. Title.
    HD57.7.B4697 2015
    658.4′092—dc23
                                                                    2014033654

ISBN 978-0-8047-9425-1 (electronic)

Typeset by Newgen in 10.5/15 Minion

*For our friend Nicki Wrighton, whose vibrancy in life and
grace in the face of a volatile and uncertain future
will live on in all who knew her*

What is usual is not what is always, the day says again.
It is all it can offer.

Not ungraspable hope, not the consolation of stories.
Only the reminder that there is exception.
—*Jane Hirshfield*

CONTENTS

FIGURES AND TABLES

ACKNOWLEDGMENTS

A book that intends to help people transform their relationship to the future requires a lot of relationships, and quite a bit of transformation, to make it into the world. We began working on this book in 2005, and at first we thought we'd create a leadership development theory on which we could build a leadership program. It turned out we needed to experiment a lot on the way, and so there were years of leadership programs, reading, researching, and talking with leaders that transformed our ideas as we worked to help transform organizations.

We are grateful to the long line of theorists—in complexity, communication, adult development, leadership development, organizational change, and more—who have thought hard about what it means to live and lead in an unpredictable future. Those of you who write about and teach adult development have been models of our growth and thinking about what is possible. Particularly important to us are our ongoing relationships with the ideas and practices of Bob Kegan, Bill Torbert, Susanne Cook-Greuter, Marcia Baxter Magolda, Bill Joiner, Steve Josephs, and Michael Basseches. Perhaps even better than your ideas are the conversations and confusions we have shared over the years. We are grateful to be learning from and growing alongside you. Complexity theorists Eric Beinhocker, Peter Coleman, Gerald Midgley, Dave Snowden, Ralph Stacey, Brian Walker, and Robert Woog have stretched our minds and challenged us to not only see the world in a new way but also to actually see a new world, with new relationships among people and ideas and causality. We aren't there yet, but sometimes we tip into the basin of attraction that contains these ideas with the wholeness each of you seems to hold. Barry

Jentz and Joan Wofford continue to inspire us with their practical ways of dealing with the complexities of interpersonal communication and the development of new ways of listening to learn.

Our safe-to-fail experiments have often been in relationships with coaching clients and participants in our leadership programs around the world. We have hidden your names and details here, but your stories have taught us more about what it means to lead with heart and mind than any theory ever could. Your experiences are woven through with ours, and you make us better even as you work to make those around you more capable and to make the world a better place. It has been an honor to work with you. We are grateful for the opportunities that our clients have offered us, especially those complexity-based leadership programs we've created and cocreated and re-created alongside Al Morrison, Felicity Lawrence, and Angela Geerts at New Zealand's Department of Conservation; Gary Wingrove, Susan Ferrier, and John Somerville at KPMG Australia; Carole Brown and Paul Atkins at the Australian National University; Gayle Karen Young at Wikimedia; Nisha Agrawal at Oxfam India; Kirstin Dunlop and Felicity Nelson at Suncorp; and Sally deWitt and Lori Homer at Microsoft.

We have been clear all along that leadership—and leadership development—is a team sport. To lift our game, we have sought out a remarkably impressive team. Our partners Carolyn Coughlin and Jim Wicks at Cultivating Leadership have endured our writing and rewriting of our leadership curriculum to fit our emerging ideas, have pushed us around when we got too comfortable, and have made our ideas both richer and more practical. We are grateful for the ways we have felt safe to fail with you—and the laughter helps a lot, too. Our associates, Patrice Laslett, Geoff Mortimore, Sue O'Dea, Tim Pidsley, Ingrid Studholme, and Karen Waitt, have taught these ideas alongside us, prodded us when we were theoretically (or practically) mushy, and taken over details with clients so we could retreat and spend just a few more minutes writing. Joey Chan and Jade Yi have opened us to the vastness and nuance of China and offered us multiple perspectives on culture and complexity. Diana Manks has kept us sane even when we threatened her own sanity with our growing ability to forget things, move dates around, and attempt to find just one more venue possibility.

Those of you from the Growth Edge Network have tugged at our thinking and changed how we make sense of the world. You were a great safe-to-fail experiment, and we are amazed and delighted at how successful our mutual learning and enjoyment has become.

While many of you fall into at least one of the overlapping categories we've already talked about, we are most grateful to the early readers of this manuscript. Your questions and marginal squiggles, the pieces you remembered and the pieces you didn't—all of these made us better. Robyn Baker has read each chapter with the thought and care we've come to expect, and she never lets us get away with under- (or over-)thinking something. Al Morrison, while in violent disagreement over pronoun usage, has helped us see the ways our ideas resonate with leaders in complex and intractable fields. John Somerville's challenge to be more practical and less frustrating with our suggestions was a source of inspiration and mirth. Rosheen Garnon's thoughtful efforts at not just reading but "doing" the book, and the stories she shared after her work with each chapter, were inspirational. Gayle Karen Young always reminded us of the delights of the possible. Zafer Achi combined an incisive (and not always gentle) read with a reassuring certainty that these ideas would change the world. Craig Smith and Rachel Smith (not related) provided helpful perspectives on child protection issues, and Ewen McAlpine was a rapporteur on leadership qualities at large. Michael Cavanagh and Bill Torbert, our peer reviewers, took enormous time and care, and we hope you'll see your ideas reflected on these pages. Thanks also to Kelly Garvey Satcher, our test leader in a child protective services agency: your thought and care with these ideas is overshadowed only by your thought and care with the families you serve; Jennifer is proud to be your cousin.

Book writing probably takes its biggest toll on the folks who happen to be closest the authors. Keith's wife, Trish Sarr, has been his companion in leading many crusades over many years and has inspired him to always look beneath the surface of things and to be present with the full range of thoughts and feelings that arise from moment to moment along the way. Keith has also been shaped on this path by his experience as the global chair of Oxfam International and the web of committed leaders in Oxfam and other development organizations he has worked with around the world.

Melissa Garber kept Jennifer sane (and fit) with daily walks through a beautiful landscape in a difficult time. Jennifer's dad, Jim Garvey, offered encouragement to step off the trail of the typical business book and combine business and fiction in a safe-to-fail experiment. She is grateful for the support and for the genes. Her mom, Catherine Fitzgerald, might have the ultimate mother's revenge from the days when teenage Jennifer found all of her mom's ideas boring: in addition to seeing Jennifer follow in her footsteps as a coach and as her collaborator on an earlier book, she also coaxed her into the complexity field. Now mother-daughter outings are more likely to include the latest books on applied complexity rather than family gossip. Jennifer's kids, Naomi and Aidan, have taught her much about what it is like to grow up in a world unprecedentedly complex and uncertain for leaders in high schools, as well as organizations. Thank you for being the teenage field testers of some of your mom's wacky ideas. Jennifer's husband, Michael, continues to be a source of unending support during book writing and the unexpected twists and turns life offers. Life on the beach in New Zealand is awesome; cancer not so much. Jennifer can imagine no better companion for all of the twisty, sparkly, and unexpected detours on the path.

Finally, we'd like to thank each other, which is kind of weird but also really matters. In the years since we've begun building ideas together, Keith has gotten his doctorate and Jennifer has gotten her New Zealand citizenship. As we've formed a firm and developed a set of theories and practices, we've also grown a complex and pretty beautiful friendship. Meeting each other nearly a decade ago from opposite sides of the globe was just barely probable, but now we're wandering into the unscripted world of the possible. Just like life, really. What's next?

INTRODUCTION

If you've picked up this book, you've probably noticed that things in your world are a little more complex—maybe even a little more overwhelming—than you'd like. You might be finding that you have to balance the needs of more people than you did before and that there is more volatility of perspective than you used to notice. Or maybe you're finding that the pathway that used to look clear is murkier than you'd like. Or maybe you think you would be a better leader if you could just find a way to slow down all the changes in your team or organization or sector so that you could catch your breath.

We know what you mean. While we have taught leaders around the world and researched, read, and written about leadership, we have found that this rise in complexity, ambiguity, volatility, and uncertainty is not just lingering around the edges of our workdays: it's everywhere. Coping with these changes requires whole new ways of making sense of the world and of taking action to make a difference. Some of these new ways are about how we have conversations and learn from one another, others are about how we solve intractable problems, and still others are about how we plan for an unknowable future.

We have been motivated by many good books on complexity and on leadership that explain carefully how the world is changing, how our ways of understanding it are changing, and how leaders must change to be more effective. But once you're convinced that you need to be different, what then? Leaders tell us they want to learn more about what can they do to begin to make these changes. What steps can they take? What equipment would help them on their journey? How might the pieces come together to enable them to thrive as leaders? We've spent the past decade trying to answer that question. Here's what we've found.

As you might guess, learning to thrive in this new world is no simple enterprise, no quick trip to a theme park about complexity. Instead, it's a long and scenic hike through the wilderness, wading through rushing rivers that might unsettle you and going into forest so deep you can't see what's coming next. To thrive in this wilderness and come to love it, you'll need new muscles and new ways of making sense of the world around you, new practices that will augment your current approach.

We have organized our expedition to first explore the habits of mind you'll want to develop en route, the habits that will shape your thinking and action over time. We use those habits to explore the various terrains we'll encounter as we learn to thrive in complexity: the way we think about and interact with people, the way we think about and solve problems, and the way we lead ourselves and others into a better tomorrow. In each case, the complex conditions of the world create the practice, which we support with habits of mind that you'll develop as you read. Our companions for the journey are a set of leaders, all of whom are working with their own complex challenges—their stories will unfold as we travel together.

Chapter 1 introduces what we mean about these shifts in complexity, volatility, ambiguity, and uncertainty that seem to be growing in our workplaces and our families right now. We also begin to explore the habits of mind that will accompany us through the other chapters. We meet Yolanda and Doug and learn about the tragedy that has marked their day.

Chapter 2 reminds us that while the world is complex, some things are still simple, and it pays to know the difference between the two when it comes to how you might think about and work toward the solution of an issue. Yolanda and Doug learn about complexity and why it matters to them.

Chapter 3 looks at how feedbacks flow through systems and relationships, and it offers a way to use feedback in a complex space. We meet Jarred and see in action the little miseries we inflict on one another in our quest not to hurt each other.

Chapter 4 takes on the question of how to create and spread a vision even when you can't know what the future will hold. Jarred attends a strategy workshop and ponders his role.

Chapter 5 debunks the idea that we are logical creatures, because simple, cold-blooded logic, in addition to being out of our grasp, is also limiting the face of a complex and nonlinear world. Instead, we can delight in our particular quirks and build organizational practices and perspectives that help us as we are instead of as we imagine ourselves to be. Yolanda conducts a study and has to remind herself not to jump to unfortunate conclusions.

Chapter 6 addresses the question of how a leader can communicate all this complexity to others, and how doing so is different from communicating about something that looks simpler and more predictable. Jarred hosts some people at his house for a weekend strategy session to support his mom.

Chapter 7 focuses on the ways we change over time to become better able to handle complexity and ambiguity, and it highlights the benefits of both thinking about that change and also doing it. The leaders of Jarred's organization meet with board members to understand what changes in them personally might be necessary to support the changes the organization requires.

Chapter 8 brings these ideas together into a model of how a leader can use a complex approach to create change in an organization. One year later, we get a sense of how things have worked out for our characters and where they might go next.

In all of the chapters, we offer tools, approaches, and new questions to ask that leaders around the world have told us are the most helpful ones in facing this more complex world with grace. As you try out these powerful practices, we think you'll find that the complex world will become less of a problem to be solved and more of a landscape to savor and discover.

Welcome to the trail.

1 LEADING THE POSSIBLE

"Damn!" Yolanda Murphy, director of the statewide Family and Children's Services (FACS) Division, slammed her fist on the keyboard, inadvertently closing the email window she had just been reading. In her first 18 months on the job, Yolanda felt she must have seen more tragedy and mayhem than the previous director had seen in his seven years in the role, a notion never omitted in front-page news stories about the miserable series of misfortunes that still seemed to be unfolding.

Now that she was 56 years old, this was supposed to be the apex of her career—her first stint as a chief executive. While many applauded her as a no-nonsense, competent manager who knew the agency and the state government, some had thought that she lacked the frontline social work experience to do the job well. But not even a career social worker could have anticipated all of these different pieces breaking down, she thought. Six children dead and four hospitalized in 18 months, children that FACS was following, was supposed to be protecting. And here, today, another case of abuse from a foster family.

"Jamie!" she called. "Will you bring me whatever the review has got so far on the Proucheford office? And will you get Doug in here?" She ran her fingers through her hair and pushed away from the desk. She walked to the window, looking hard into the city as though the answers to her questions were some-how out there, as though she could save children at risk if she just stared hard enough.

"This is about the kid in the Proucheford County Hospital, isn't it?" Doug, Yolanda's next-in-line, had come in without her hearing him. She turned and nodded. Sitting and shuffling through a set of papers, Doug looked as terrible as Yolanda felt. Doug had been with FACS for 20 years and knew the system inside and out. A career social worker, Doug had moved up the ladder to the No. 2 position and until he wasn't willing to be promoted any higher. Before Yolanda took the position, some had told her that Doug liked the No. 2 spot because there was power without visibility, but none of that rang true for Yolanda once she met him. And none of them in FACS could avoid visibility now, with their names trending locally on Twitter and on the front pages and editorial pages of every newspaper in the state.

Doug was coordinating the several investigations to figure out where the fault was in the system, and he had gathered thousands of pieces of data and found no clear conclusions, no smoking gun. Many of those pages of paper were organized into a series of neat files now in a thick stack on Yolanda's desk. He found the paper he was searching for and began to read aloud. "Ten year old kid, lived with this foster family for eight months. History of starting fires, last one burnt down the foster house where he was last placed. Current foster family on probation because of reports—never proven—of abuse of a kid in their care 18 months ago. This kid was the first placement during the probation, and he was placed there after six—no, seven—families turned him down as being too dangerous to placed with them. Got in a fight the day before yesterday with his foster mother's boyfriend and got beat up, head trauma, broken leg, a wide variety of bruises." Doug pushed a picture of a little boy in a hospital room across the table.

"What the hell is going on, Doug?" she asked, staring into the little boy's vacant eyes. "Why am I looking at another picture of a kid hurt while we were supposed to be protecting him? We've got more reviews running than we've ever had before, more people are looking under rocks than we've ever had, and we're still placing kids with foster parents who we suspect of beating other children? Is this a failure of a couple of links of the chain, or is this a failure of the whole damn organization? And who do I have to fire or promote or train up in order for this to stop?"

Doug, holding a close-up of a series of bruises on a child's back, said, "I would give anything to know the answer to that question. I have been through these documents a thousand times and . . ." His sentence was interrupted by Jamie, who had walked into the office, pink message slips in hand.

"Yolanda, you've got calls from the regular local press—but also there's someone from the *New York Times* who wants to talk with you."

"Tell them we're investigating and there will be a press conference at"—she looked at her watch and then at Doug—"three o'clock." Doug nodded. Yolanda sat down at the table and began to page through the largest file marked "Proucheford." "So, Doug, we have three and a half hours to figure out what's wrong—and how to fix it."

THINKING ANEW

A leader, reflecting on the growing needs for a new way of being, offered his ideas about the leadership challenge he—and his people generally—faced. He explained to his stakeholders:

> The dogmas of the quiet past are inadequate for the stormy present. The occasion is piled high with difficulty, and we must rise with the occasion. As our case is new, so we must think anew and act anew.

You've probably faced a situation that made you think something like this, too—as Yolanda and Doug are thinking of their terrible situation. No matter how good leaders are, they find themselves dealing with problems—and opportunities—more difficult or complex than anything they've known before. Superb leaders have long known that they need to find ways to "think anew and act anew," especially as their plates become "piled high with difficulty." This challenge to think in new ways about a novel situation has been with leaders always, and each time, they have pushed at the edges of what we know in order to grow more capable of handling the challenges that seem impossible. Abraham Lincoln was speaking to more than just to the US Congress about the "quiet past" and the "stormy present" in 1862. The truth is that leadership requires ways of thinking anew no matter what era you're in; it's probably true that the first Neolithic leaders were pushed to the edges of their capacities as farming and stone tools created conflict and opportunities for their people. Leadership by its very definition is about taking people and ideas to new places.

The problem for leaders today is that as the world changes so quickly, the future becomes far less predictable, the options become exponentially increased, and the way we need to think about those options shifts.[1] Imagine if Lincoln had had to tweet about his plans (and his breakfast) as well as being Facebook friends with the senators on both sides of the aisle. Lincoln needed to make decisions with small amounts of aging information, a hard thing to do. Leaders today need to make decisions with endless amounts of emerging information, which might be even harder; it is certainly more complex, and it makes our need to "think anew" different from what it's ever been before.

This is the rise of VUCA: volatility, uncertainty, complexity, and ambiguity. You can hardly open a leadership book without this discussion, so we'll speed by it (increasing the speed of change even in talking about the speed of change). We know that even though we generally live longer and in greater safety and have much more stuff than our parents and their parents, people and ideas and organizations are also more complex because there is much more information available and things are much more interconnected. We know it's more uncertain because as those variables intersect, new possibilities get created. These are possibilities no one ever thought about in advance: they just emerged from the current context as one new idea bashed against another new idea (or against an ancient one). You also know that those interconnections—of ideas, of people, of conflict and congruence—are more likely because there are so many more of us around. There are billions of us: more than twice as many people now than there were in the mid-1960s, and at least those people in the developed world consume vastly more resources. This increases our volatility at a global scale because now our planet is having to do things it has never done before, and there is no possible way to predict what happens next. It is also the case that many of the issues we face in society, such as climate change, will affect communities over a very long term in unpredictable ways, even as organizations and news outlets still seem captured by the very short term, preferring black and white to ambiguous gray.

Our awareness of the fact that the world is changing irrevocably also puts pressure on the way we think about the present and the future. Serfs in the 1600s probably had something like a "Kids these days!" expression, but they didn't look at their children and wonder what they would be when they grew up; even 50 years ago, there weren't that many choices. One of our clients recounted her deep frustration in high school when her teacher asked whether she wanted to be a nurse, a teacher, or a secretary. "I was so frustrated to have only three options—none interesting to me," she told us. Less than 40 years later, Jennifer's then 14-year-old daughter, Naomi, came home frustrated because the teacher told her that the job Naomi would do when she grew up had probably not been invented yet. "What does she expect me to do about that?" Naomi asked. "How can I prepare for something that doesn't exist?" Indeed. This might in fact be the key leadership question of our time.

Abraham Lincoln faced a world of rising volatility, uncertainty, complexity, and change. And so did Franklin Delano Roosevelt. And so did Keith's grandfather as he was making the decision to leave his home and travel around the world to New Zealand to begin a new life. So it would be easy to say that this is just part of the human condition and move on from there. In our work with leaders around the world and our work leading global initiatives ourselves, though, we've been convinced that the thing that is happening in the world now is unlike any other time that humans have ever faced before, and we've been convinced that the rules for leaders are different now.[2] And there's no handbook about how the rules have changed or how you need to change to meet these new requirements. We're trying to change that with this book, which while not a handbook, is a kind of a guidebook to this new land and to the strange way things work here.

Here's one of the most unsettling and distinctive features of this new land: it operates from a different set of choices, and because it is more untethered from the constraints of the past, it lives more in the set of options about what is possible rather than the set of options about what is probable. This sounds like an easy change that might be on a motivational poster: FOCUS ON THE POSSIBLE! It actually requires more than just attitude, though. A focus on the possible requires changes in the way we think, engage with others, and take action. Moving away from our own belief in a predictable world is a major effort indeed.

See, our minds love categorizing and learning from the past in order to keep us safe into the future.[3] And that has been great for us. Without this capacity to predict and determine risks, we'd be just a stunted branch on the evolutionary tree. We carry with us a kind of a bell curve of possibilities, and depending on our background and knowledge (and, unfortunately, on what we ate for breakfast and which magazine headlines we happened to see as we waited in line at the grocery store[4]), we are constantly making decisions about risk and reward. That internal judging system has done pretty well to protect and keep us for tens of thousands of years, but it's beginning to short out now. And one of the key ways our system misfires is as it considers the difference between the probable and the possible.

Let's take a few examples. We tend to make decisions based on what we think is most probable. In this way, our brains are like the actuary tables—judging the future by what we've seen happen in the past. We add new kitchens if we think it's probable that the new kitchen will increase the value of the house in five years when we sell it, or we do a wilder, more idiosyncratic renovation if we think it's probable that we'll stay in this house for decades into the future. We choose Aruba as our holiday destination from among the ones we think are most probable to make us happy (based on the criteria we've decided is best for us). We choose "be more customer centered" as a strategy for our division at work when we think it's probable that the old strategy constrains our growth and effectiveness and this new one is the most enabling of the future we want to create.

What we don't notice is that because we are using the past as a kind of measure of what's likely, we have sharply constrained the set of possibilities when we made our decisions. We didn't consider whether an earthquake would roll through our house, making our new kitchen (and indeed, the neighborhood) less attractive to potential buyers. We picked Aruba because it was so much more off the beaten path than Jamaica, but still we've had friends that have gone there. We didn't select Réunion in the Indian Ocean, because we'd never heard of it—it was possible but not probable. We choose the customer-focused strategy out of the ones that were relatively familiar to us because we can see the problem (we're too internal) and being more customer centered looks like the best way to solve it. It might be that our internal focus is a symptom of some entirely different problem (our remuneration system creates perverse incentives for us to manage internal politics rather than customer relationships), but we picked from what looked like the most probable a cause to us (or the probable cause that was most attractive to us). As you read, you might be thinking that it would take all of your time and be paralyzing if you had to think about earthquakes and every tropical island in the entire world. You would never renovate anything, never lie on a white-sand beach again. We agree that these would be bad outcomes, and we're not suggesting that at all. You can carry on planning your holidays and your renovations as before, because the rise in complexity and holiday options is less material than the rise in options leaders need to consider in their work. If you choose an island that isn't as perfect as it possibly could have been, the difference is mostly irrelevant because you'll have a good time anyway (even if the sand is whiter, the water warmer, and the fish more beautiful somewhere else). But if you put your eggs in the "customer-centric" basket when really the thing that's about to change your industry is the new phone app that replaces you, the change is very material after all. Part of the battle is knowing when to let the rise in VUCA change the way you work and when to just simplify things. We'll help with that distinction as we go.

The future has always been unknown—the serf in the 1600s didn't know, Lincoln didn't know, your parents didn't know. As Marshall McLuhan said, "We drive into the future using only our rear view mirror." Because there's no way of knowing what's next (that's the uncertainty and volatility part), we are always walking forward with our hands out in the dark, waiting to bump in to things. And because things are changing, we have lost much of the ability to predict what will happen next from what has happened before, to pull out the memories from other dark rooms we have bumped through in the past. Complexity is about getting our heads around what is possible (because anything could happen) rather than what is probably going to happen (which is determined from what has happened before).

This shift—from trying to get your head around what is most likely to trying to get your head around what is in the field of possibilities—is much bigger than it sounds. As research has shown in study after study, our brains just don't like this. Our general pattern is to prune and simplify. We need to work at it if we are going to create new patterns of behavior for thinking and acting in this new world. We need to talk to one another differently, gather information differently, build strategies and plans for the future in new ways. We need new habits of mind that stretch and expand us to deal in more thoughtful ways with the complexity the world offers.

HABITS OF MIND FOR COMPLEXITY TODAY AND A MORE COMPLEX TOMORROW

All the leaders with whom we have worked have had some seriously impressive qualities. They are a smart bunch with good analytical facility and clear-mindedness. They are able to take apart problems and come up with solutions, quite quickly and often when the data are still emerging. They have been very good at the core business they are managing, whatever that might be. They have natural skills, and because both organizations and individuals know the power of continuous learning, many of them have been to additional schooling and/or have had coaching to help them get even better at the leadership tasks they face. And nearly all of them, when we finally put away all the barriers, admit that they are stressed and overwhelmed and concerned they're not up to the task. They are overwhelmed by their email, by their growing and diverse stakeholders, by the impossible demands on their time, by the increasing scale and scope of the challenges they face. They do not all have a language about volatility, uncertainty, complexity, and ambiguity, but they all have a felt reaction to it.

It's probably true that they're not up to the task; it's totally possible that this task of leading in times as complex and volatile as today is a bigger stretch for us humans than anything else we've ever had to do. That's the bad news. The good news is that there is a way to grow more able to handle the complexity in the world around us: three habits of mind that stretch your thinking capacity and help you grow more "complexity of mind."[5] The better news is that while growing that new capacity, you can also be understanding your work and its demands in an entirely new way at the same time that you are creating new possibilities for those with whom you work. In other words, as you grow to be a better leader over time, you can also be a better leader right now.

This means as you exercise the habits using the tools and approaches in this book, you may find your thinking changed about key issues you struggle with at work. And as you're solving difficult work problems, these habits are also an exercise routine for your mind; they stretch you and help you become more capable of dealing with complexity. Once they become your habits, they'll expand the way you can think, and they'll change your ability to deal with those things that are now overwhelming.

These habits of mind are deceptively simple:

- Asking different questions
- Taking multiple perspectives
- Seeing systems

So what makes them so powerful, and how can you benefit from that power?

ASKING DIFFERENT QUESTIONS

In our stereotypes, the thing leaders do is answer: they craft a vision, get others to follow them, make decisions purportedly at the drop of a hat. Our images of strong and successful leaders are filled with people synthesizing large and disparate pieces of information, making tough calls, getting others to band together and follow, and triumphing as they win out in the end. Stereotypical leaders have vision, charisma, and brilliant minds. They also tend to be male and, oddly, tall.[6]

Of course, all these images of leaders have been questioned in the past several decades. Now research tells us that charismatic leaders are more likely to leave the organization in a mess; that even when we think we're making decisions with clear heads, we're actually responding to unconscious thoughts; and that all-powerful leaders often go all-powerfully wrong. No matter how many articles you might read about the death of the charismatic leader, however, it doesn't actually change the fact that we like our leaders to look and act and lead in particular ("leaderly") ways, and that those people who lead in this way are more likely to get promoted and groomed to step into leadership positions, even as people know that perhaps leaders should be focusing on different things. You, whatever kind of leader you are, are likely under pressure to act in particular ways, and you may have found that those ways make you hide some of who you really are as a person while you're wearing your leader hat.

One leadership skill that you might not even see as a leadership skill at all is the power of asking different questions, which pulls against the stereotype of leaders having all the answers. Asking genuine questions (not Socratic or leading questions to which you already know the answers) has only recently been highlighted as a core leadership skill, and now there are some books and articles devoted to this task, both for leaders and also for people in other professions, like doctors, lawyers, and airline pilots. What those who study a variety of topics (e.g., neuroscience, decision making, leadership, medicine) are all learning is that the questions we naturally ask tend to lead us down a path we feel most comfortable about, a path whose destination is already familiar to us. In fact, most of us ask questions to confirm our hypotheses, not out of any deep curiosity or doubt. This is shown in study after study when people ask questions they think they know the answers to, and—if they don't get the answers they assumed would come—they carry on as though they had gotten the expected answer, often not even noticing the difference. Our brains, which determined the question in the first place, had already determined the (correct) answer, too. This is not much of a learning stance, although it offered our forebears protective advantages for tens of thousands of years.

In a time of consistency, this pattern is probably pretty helpful. You know what to look for, you ask questions that have proved helpful in the past, and you collect and sift through a very limited amount of information to choose from patterns that you recognize from experience.

In a time of complexity and uncertainty, though, this pattern is unhelpful. You don't know which data might be more important or where the novel solution to an emerging issue might be hiding. Your old patterns constrain you, and your old questions keep you in familiar territory. It is new and different questions that open up new and different possibilities.

The way to break this pattern and actually begin to learn is to ask questions you wouldn't have asked before, or to figure out what you really don't know and to ask those questions. At first, this can feel to leaders like a waste of time ("Why would I want to know the answer to *that*?"). Or it might make leaders feel uncomfortably vulnerable. One leader took us aside privately during a leadership program and shut the door behind us. "Are you really saying I should ask questions I don't know the answer to?" he asked in a hushed voice. "If I do that, won't everyone think I'm stupid?" As you go on, though, you'll discover with many of our clients that asking different questions helps you become a different leader, and that this different way of being a leader is more effective, more thoughtful, and tends to get better results. It is a side benefit that while these different questions help you get better results, they also grow your perspective.

Just now, though, Yolanda is stuck in her same old questions.

Looking around at the now-empty conference room, Yolanda ran her fingers through her short hair. The gray streaks through her black hair were still feeling "distinguished" to her, but the way the pressures on in this job were going, soon she'd start to just feel old, and she would have to make the decision all her friends were making about coloring her hair. She wondered why something as insignificant as her looks was running through her mind, and noticed ruefully that that's what happens when you've just spent the past hour in front of reporters with cameras. The door opened and Doug walked in. "The last one's gone now," he said, sitting heavily at the big rectangular table. "I hardly think they'll be satisfied, though."

"How could they be satisfied when we don't know what the hell is going on?" Yolanda asked, her exhaustion and worry sounding edgy and irritable when she spoke. "I don't know what to do about it. I have been circling around these issues for so long, and I feel like I keep coming up empty. Not only do I not know what the answers are—I don't even know what questions to ask any more!" Doug gaped at her for a minute and then smiled, having seen a possibility in a bleak time.

"That's it—we need a set of different questions!" he said.

Yolanda looked at him, frustrated. "Thanks, Doug, but it's answers we need more of, not questions. That last hour of a barrage of questions we couldn't answer should have shown you that."

But Doug had gone to the supply closet and pulled out chart paper and markers. "Are you up for this now, or shall it wait until the morning?" he asked, uncapping the markers as though he knew what she would say.

"I'm not up for anything," Yolanda admitted, "but I also can't stop thinking this through. And I keep asking the same questions over and over in my head: Who is responsible? Is it the system breaking down or just a series of horrible coincidences? Where will my influence most matter?"

Doug was listing the questions as Yolanda spoke. "OK," he said, "those are totally reasonable and important questions to be asking. And we keep asking them over and over again and getting nowhere, so it's time to try something else." He pulled the paper off the sheet and hung the questions on the wall.

Doug has just pointed to a leadership skill fundamental in dealing with complexity. Trying to figure out what questions you're asking and making an intentional shift to different questions opens up new avenues for exploration in an uncertain and volatile world. These different questions are mindset-shifting questions, and they involve noticing the mindset you're currently in and then—with full intention—shifting it or putting another one alongside it. Because most leaders get stuck when they're dealing with intractable problems, or with problems so murky that every answer leads both somewhere and also nowhere, they tend to find themselves, like Yolanda, asking simple questions about solutions and next steps. Asking different questions is noticing what kind of question you usually ask and taking an intentional move to ask a different sort of questions.

You might think about the questions you always ask. You can run your mind over a current issue and just gather questions that you're asking about it. Now step back and ask questions about the questions. Group them; try to figure out what they have in common. For example, the questions Yolanda is asking are things like: Who is responsible? Where in the system is the problem? What can I do to be more powerful given this set of circumstances? Yolanda might say that her questions are mostly about responsibility and action and where to focus attention.

Yolanda's next step, like yours, is to see if she can get underneath the questions themselves and identify a mindset (see Figure 1.1). The questions you ask will tell you a lot about the way you're seeing the world at that moment in time. A mindset of abundance or a mindset of scarcity? A mindset of threat or a mindset of opportunity? A mindset of curiosity and openness or a mindset of judgment and action? A mindset about what *is* or a mindset about what could be? Notice that all of these mindsets are the right ones to have in certain circumstances. They're only problematic if you *are* the mindset rather than *choosing* it—in that case it would be most accurate to say that you don't have the mindset—the mindset has you. Your mindset determines your behavior, determines what is or is not possible in a given situation, including what questions you think to ask.

Yolanda's mindset is one of threat and of narrowing to decide. Both of these are totally legitimate. Narrowing to decide is key for someone who needs to take action quickly. Threat is an important mindset to have at times (it has kept our species alive). The combination of these two is important when the situation is relatively simple (or chaotic and with a need to move very fast to stabilize the system). It's not very good for coming up with innovative solutions to complex problems. The chemicals for learning and neurogenesis, the

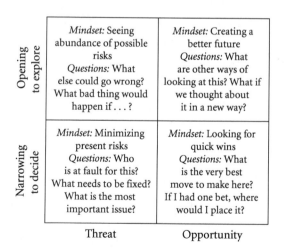

		Threat	Opportunity
Opening to explore		*Mindset:* Seeing abundance of possible risks *Questions:* What else could go wrong? What bad thing would happen if . . . ?	*Mindset:* Creating a better future *Questions:* What are other ways of looking at this? What if we thought about it in a new way?
Narrowing to decide		*Mindset:* Minimizing present risks *Questions:* Who is at fault for this? What needs to be fixed? What is the most important issue?	*Mindset:* Looking for quick wins *Questions:* What is the very best move to make here? If I had one bet, where would I place it?

FIGURE 1.1   Questions and mindsets

growing of new brain cells, shut down in times of stress and threat, and the blood rushes to the muscles that help us flee or fight. Although, as leaders, we often use threats and stresses as powerful prompts to action, there is a cost in this: it is much harder to learn when you're faced with threat.

Asking different questions is about shifting the mindset, and it is a reciprocal move: your questions can shift your mindset and your mindset can shift your questions. If your questions are about finding accountabilities for some perceived threat, you might shift that and see if you could imagine accountabilities for something that would be better, that would be the ideal way you'd want it to be. If your questions come from a mindset of narrowing to decisions, you might shift them to see if you could open the boundaries wide and see how you could create a big list of possibilities. Similarly, if you're always opening to possibilities, you might want to try narrowing questions. And so on. The little matrix in Figure 1.1 is just one of these that we could helpfully explore together; there are many ways to ask different questions.

Yolanda might begin to ask herself questions that don't seem to immediately solve the problem at hand but that shift her mindset. She might see that she is operating under threat and wonder, "What if all these terrible things were an opportunity for me to do something radically different with the department? What if we could reinvent systems or structures because of the failures we're seeing now?" As former White House chief of staff Rahm Emanuel might have counseled her now: "Never let a serious crisis go to waste." She could ask questions that shift her mindset away from narrowing to opening and ask, "What are the many different pieces that this problem might touch? What is the largest number of systems and people and relationships that might be at play here?"

It turns out that finding different questions to ask is a skill, but it is relatively fast to learn, and it can be applied quickly too. We'll go into much more detail in the chapters to come, and we'll give you a large selection of different questions to ask during times of complexity, ambiguity, and change. The biggest barrier to the transformational nature of asking different questions is simply to remember to try to do it. The second major barrier comes from our fears that these new questions will take lots of time or confuse us with additional ideas. As we progress through the book, we hope that you'll see enough value that you'll begin to incorporate asking different questions into your habits, and so get their full transformational benefit.

TAKING MULTIPLE PERSPECTIVES

Yolanda kicked off her shoes and wandered around the room, reading the different set of questions they had asked as they brainstormed together. Doug had been right, and things were somehow more expansive after that exercise. "Now we still need to figure out what to do next," she said, "but I know that now I'm seeing many more options than I saw before!"

Doug smiled at her, the first real smile she'd seen in at least a week. "This shifts things for me, too," he told her, glancing at the clock on the wall.

Her eyes followed his to the wall. Six thirty. "I think I can sleep tonight, too," she said. And I think it's time to call it a night." She gathered together the papers from the press conference several hours before and slipped her shoes back on, when Jamie walked in, scowling. "Jamie, what's up? What are you still doing here?"

"I stayed to watch the press coverage on the news at six," Jamie explained. "And it just seems to be getting worse." She sat down heavily in the chair. "They did a series of interviews with important community voices around the state, and of course they've picked the ones with the very strongest opinions. There were some lovely ones talking about how hard this work is and how you can't blame FACS for the failing economy. But they also talked to a couple of influential folks who were most critical. One of them," she glanced at her notes, "a Reverend Welcher who presides over a huge church in Mountainview, is calling for your resignation, Yolanda, and saying that the corruption in FACS goes all the way to the top."

Yolanda's café-au-lait skin blanched to gray, and she sat down heavily. "My resignation," she said, softly. "If I thought it would save a child, I'd have resigned already."

Doug had the opposite reaction. His face flushed to a deep red, and he jumped to his feet. "I can't believe that our partners in the community are the ones coming down on us! They should be getting their own sorry act together before calling us names. And they have to come out with a term like corruption? Nobody has ever even hinted that there's anything like corruption in this! And why the hell should Yolanda take the fall for this? And why is a pastor in Mountainview even being interviewed about this? Jamie, let's get this Welcher guy on the phone and give him a piece of mind!"

Jamie looked at Doug as though he had lost his mind but left Yolanda to actually say that. "I think this is jumping the gun a little, don't you, Doug?" Yolanda said gently. "What we all need is to get a little distance on this and cool off."

"I don't want distance," Doug growled. "I want to kill someone." Looking at normally mild Doug's face flushed and angry somehow made Yolanda see the absurdity in the situation, and she started to laugh. Jamie, reacting to both Yolanda's laughing and then Doug's expression of bewilderment, began to laugh too. "Will you mind telling me what the hell is going on?" Doug roared.

"Doug, I've seen you respond to child abusers with more compassion than I could ever muster, and now that someone says something mean about me on the six o'clock news, you want to kill them?" Yolanda said, still laughing. "You look like a white version of my big brother when he heard that Adam was kissing me after school."

Doug smiled sheepishly, his face still flushed. "OK, little sis, I'll back down. But if you think we're going home now, you're crazy. We need to figure out a counterattack right now and get it out by the newspaper's press deadline. Jamie, get the current news reports from the TV and newspaper websites and let's see whether this is a localized call for Yolanda's resignation or whether it looks like there are particular geographies or sets of constituents behind it." Jamie glanced at Yolanda, who nodded her assent to the plan. "Could you please order some dinner for us all, too, Jamie?" Doug called off to her as she hurried off.

"Doug," Yolanda said, seriously now. "I wasn't kidding when I said that you looked like my big brother that day. He was the most gentle boy you ever saw, too, until he found out that someone was messing with his little sister, and then he wanted to break his face. I don't have your psychological training, but what is it that happens to people when they turn into totally different people under some kinds of stress?"

"Well, I can't be held responsible," grinned Doug. "It is the fight-or-flight chemicals—they are cutting off the blood supply to my neocortex. There can be no executive functioning in my brain until normal service is resumed."

"And then gentle, mild-mannered people begin using warlike metaphors about counterattacks? Is your brain back yet? I mean, have your executive functions returned?"

"Probably enough to be useful," Doug offered. "Although I might froth on at the margins for a bit longer. It takes an astonishing amount of time to get those chemicals to flush out of your body."

"OK, so I control the pen for a little while. I'm worried you might have been sniffing it," Yolanda said, taking the pen Doug had uncapped out of his hand. "It seems to me that we don't need to defeat the enemy here, because the pastor in Mountainview isn't our enemy, whichever brand of God he worships. We're on the same side. We just need to figure out why he might have said what he said about corruption, and then what we can learn from it about what to do next."

Yolanda doesn't know it right now, but she's just suggested the use of the second key tool: taking multiple perspectives. Multiple perspectives are easy to take when everyone is on the same side. They are variations on a similar theme and usually with shared values and beliefs. The farther apart the sides move, though, the harder it is to imagine the other person as anything but an enemy that needs to be defeated. The very best leaders don't think in terms of us and them; they don't think in terms of enemies. There are people who want different things, but each person tends to act from a place that she considers an honorable and rational approach, no matter how horrible it seems to you.[7] There is power in knowing the other perspective, not just to use it against a person in some way but also to learn from it.

When we reflect back on the most superb leaders, we find that they were masters with this tool. They are so widely quoted that we hardly need to do more than mention their names: Gandhi, Mandela, King. These were people who didn't just try to speak louder than those who opposed them or to outwit their opponents with more sophisticated language or arguments. All three were driven to work for radical transformation in their worlds, transformations that were deeply threatening to those in power and to many others in their society. These leaders knew that to make any real progress in the world, they needed to fundamentally change the dynamics between them and those who held power. Yet they also understood that they would need to work alongside those who seemed to be their enemies, understanding them and ultimately building relationships with them. They would need to see a three-dimensional picture of the motivations and fears and dreams of those who were oppressing them.

Leadership—whether at a global scale or on a small cross-functional team—is not about standing on either side of a river shouting at each other. That tactic might win you an argument, but it's unlikely to make any real progress. Leadership is about gathering people together—even people with quite different goals and understandings—and helping them build bridges that take everyone to a new place. Understanding other people's perspectives is a central tool in bridge building, because until you know how others see the world, you'll have little opportunity to influence or learn from their perspective.

Yolanda's crisis offers her an opportunity to revisit the people she thought were players in the drama that is unfolding in and outside of her agency. She thought she had a grasp on who the players were in this system—the heads of the area offices, the frontline caseworkers, the press, and of course, the children and families her office was supposed to serve. She had never guessed that someone from the largest church in the state would have a role to play in the drama as well. With this new player, Yolanda will have to figure out how to deal with him and which category the person might fit in. Right now, if she's not really thoughtful about it, Yolanda is likely to lump the Reverend Welcher into the category "enemies of FACS."

Just getting the players on the table is incredibly helpful. If you think about an issue with which you're struggling, you can imagine for a minute the variety of people and perspectives involved. There are likely people who support your cause or hope and people who oppose you. There are likely people you believe to be the good guys, people you believe to be the bad guys, and others whose perspective just mystifies you—maybe they seem flighty or confused or confusing in some way, or maybe they are motivated by factors you don't understand. You could probably map them together, watching for the ways the players intersect with one another, the way they hold or give away power or information, the way they seem to cluster around a variety of different primary interests. From this relationship map, you might begin to notice interconnections and outliers, and you might begin to get a sense of the perspectives you deeply understand (perhaps because they're like yours) and the ones that seem most foreign to you (or that you think you understand but maybe have just caricatured). Now you might begin to wonder what was really going on for those people whose behavior is so unsettling to you. And you'll be curious about it from their own perspective rather than from your perspective as someone who was thwarted by them.

Taking into account multiple perspectives simply involves remembering that whatever other people do, they tend to do it because they think it's the right thing. The odds are good that Reverend Welcher's primary motivation in suggesting that Yolanda needed to resign wasn't wanting to hurt her. He probably also wasn't thinking that he could manipulate the situation to turn it his way for some diabolical reason. Maniacal villains—those who clearly want to do harm in the world for harm's sake—are mostly found in action movies. Often we believe someone did something mean or cruel or bad intentionally when it was just an accident. Despite many of our own plans being disrupted by unforeseen consequences, things not working, or other mishaps, we often assume that others are competent and acting in a well-organized conspiracy. Sometimes it helps us to understand the range of possibilities if we can just assume that someone made a mistake or that things did not work out as a person expected.

One way we can make sense of this is to remember that in real life, each person is the hero of her own story, and those who would try to thwart her look like the villains to her. No matter how odd or obnoxious someone else's behavior may seem to us, the odds are good that that person sees her behavior as reasonable and quite possibly heroic. For example, as far as Reverend Welcher is concerned, he was being the good guy when he spoke to the press—

highlighting a flaw, or protecting vulnerable kids, or pushing a perspective he thought was the right one, or seeking accountability from a faceless bureaucracy. Or maybe he was speaking to the press on another issue and his deep sadness and hurt about the latest abuse case slipped out, unbidden.

This hero mindset helps us take multiple perspectives, and it helps us have more productive conversations. Any time you come toward someone who thinks she is being heroic with a story about how she is being villainous, your odds of success are sharply diminished. If you can get access to the heroic story someone else is telling about herself, you have a renewed understanding of that person, a new set of ways you might interact with her, and a way to keep your own story as just one of many possible choices in the world.

Yolanda needs to make sense of Reverend Welcher as someone who is trying to do the right thing by publicly calling for her resignation. To do that, Yolanda needs to switch perspectives. She needs to ask, "If I had just done what that person did, and I thought my actions were perfectly reasonable, what story might I be telling myself?" Because Yolanda isn't inside the head of the other person, she cannot be sure that the story she constructs is actually the one the reverend himself might tell. Rather than her usual approach of looking for what strikes her as the most probable story, she may have to fight to keep her mind open. So she'll have to construct another possible story, and another, so that she'll have a list of possible rationales that the other person might have. As she constructs possible stories for the various community members, Yolanda may begin to open up to different stories of the players in this system. She may begin to find that motivations she once saw as inexplicable or quite negative, she can come to understand them as logical—and even good—from a different perspective. As she sees these different possibilities, Yolanda's own perspective will enlarge, and she will be able to understand more parts of the system, empathize with more players, and be in a more powerful position to influence people with a richer set of understandings than she had previously.

As you look down your own lists of players, your first task is to find the one who has always seemed either confusing or bad in some way, someone whose motivations you question (because he seems out only for himself or because he sees things in ways that are "too" something—too logical, too emotional, too financial).[8] Try to see what story you can construct from that other person's perspective so that his arguments and obstacles make perfect sense. It does not count if you allow your own perspective to shape the arguments (e.g., "I think he's obstructive and stupid, so here's a stupid argument that he might believe."). It has to come out in a sentence that the other person might feel good saying, one that is both consistent with what he has said in the past and also has the other person looking good—at least in his own eyes. The first time you try to construct such a story, you may get stuck and find that the entire exercise seems impossible—how could you make a logical story out of something that is so stupid or self-serving or blind? But if you keep at it, like an exercise program, you will find your mind getting more limber as you are increasingly able to take another person's perspective—even if it's quite different from yours.

Once you are able to construct several stories that make sense for you with someone who is difficult, you'll be able to construct several stories about nearly everything you see. When someone nods off in a staff meeting, it won't be an obvious insubordination or a clear sign to you that you're totally boring (although Keith, who tends to narcolepsy himself, says it was especially unsettling to have a cabinet minister doze off once when Keith was in the middle of giving a one-on-one briefing). There will be other perspectives you can take that will open up the stories you tell yourself about other people and their motives (maybe your somnolent staff member or Keith's cabinet minister just got a new puppy, or maybe there was a fire last night in the house next door). This has the effect of making you both more creative and more compassionate—two characteristics in shorter supply for leaders than we might like. Leading with creativity and compassion—as well as the increased scope of vision that a range of perspectives might bring—helps widen your perspective to improve your relationships. As Yolanda and Doug are about to learn, however, taking multiple perspectives also helps widen your scope to improve your problem solving.

SEEING SYSTEMS

"I'm just on the edge of seeing something new—just outside of my vision. I keep thinking that if I turn my head fast enough, I'll catch it," Yolanda said, looking at the walls covered with chart paper. "Do you think one of these has the secret piece we've been missing?"

Doug put down his chopsticks with a sigh that might have been the frustration of a wicked problem, or the contentment of a good dinner. "I don't think we've found enlightenment, Yolanda—I think you're having some reaction to the MSG in the moo shu pork."

Yolanda gave him a distracted look, and began writing on another sheet of paper. "OK, so let's look at what has caused all these in the first place. So we've got two kids in homes currently under investigation who die suspiciously— one in Proucheford, one in Mountainview, but we don't know what the cause of death was yet and can't tell whether it was negligence, violence, or just a horrible accident. There are two who die in household fires in foster homes right here in the capital; one who runs away from a foster home and is found dead a week later across the state line; and a Proucheford toddler who looks like he was shaken to death, mother and her boyfriend already in the court system." Yolanda murmured as she drew out the problem with blue ink. She frowned at the paper. "It never gets any easier to think about these six kids," she said. She picked up a blue pen. "And we've got three kids in hospitals because of injuries they got in foster homes—one in the Proucheford hospital, one here in the capital, and one taken into Kentucky to recuperate near his grandparents. Oh, and the new boy from today—where is he?" She picked up the boy's folder from the table, piled with folders and takeout containers. "Proucheford again." She put down the pen. "These ten incidents—and these are the ones we know about—in the last 18 months, and in five local bureaus involving seven different caseworkers, all caused by accident, neglect, or rage."

Doug pointed a chopstick at another set of pages on the wall. "You've already got this stuff up there, Yolanda," he said. "We're going in circles again. You've got a page for each incident already."

"Those pages didn't help us figure out what's going on, though," Yolanda said. "Those pages just made me lose my appetite."

"So why is your page any better?"

"I'm not sure. I thought by seeing it all together it would be easier."

"I think seeing it all together is harder. I think it's easier to deal with this case by case. You said yourself that it was five bureaus and seven caseworkers. There's no pattern here, Yolanda. You know we've looked at that. The incidents—other than the house fires—are really different from one another, and those two house fires are likely just the bad luck of substandard wiring or heating systems in our foster family population. Fires are just more likely in that kind of housing. You can't find a silver bullet because there is no silver bullet. Maybe this is a run of bad luck combined with an election-year high profile and a long economic downturn from declines in the coal and paper industries. Sometimes bad things happen that just aren't attached to any one single cause."

"Maybe so, Doug, but my job is to do more to reduce those sorts of strings of bad luck—if that's what it is. We need systems and structures in place to make it so that these types of accidents won't happen again. Who was it who said, 'Every system is perfectly designed to get the results it gets?'[9] Somehow our system is designed with little holes that are creating the opportunities for the abuse and neglect of these already-at-risk children. And we have to redesign it so these things don't happen again. We made this thing in the first place, and now we can remake it to work better."

Thinking about making and remaking something is the way we tend to make sense of the world. Generally, we make sense of things through relatively simple cause and effect—and we believe that we can control the cause and/or the effect. Complexity theory teaches us that cause and effect are like sleight of hand in a magic show—distracting enough to keep our attention away from the millions of other things that might really be going on. Perhaps one of the most important and difficult ideas related to complexity is that of *emergence*. One the one hand, emergence sounds simple: when the nature of the thing is something that emerges; it is when things are more than the sum of their parts. We say sentences like that all the time.

Emergence is actually a challenging concept, though, because it unsettles our notion of cause and effect. Hydrogen and oxygen molecules do not on their own create a particular sensation, but put lots of them together and *wetness* emerges. Trading my services for your goods might make things better for both of us; when thousands of people do that, an economy emerges. Keith spends a lot of time in India, and he knows that when you put a whole lot of vehicles on the road with no clear adherence to traffic rules, a new kind of order emerges. Hydrogen and oxygen don't cause wetness, trades don't cause an economy, and having few rules of the road does not cause order—at least not in the simple way we tend to think of cause and effect.

You can see this when you think of teamwork. We often say that teams are more than the sum of their parts, and it's true that when you put good people together under the right conditions, teamwork emerges and great things happen. But put those same people together under hostile or difficult conditions, and gossip and gridlock might emerge. So it's not that teams *cause* brilliant teamwork any more than teams *cause* gossip and gridlock. Teams form into a small, complex adaptive system, each member working and relating and thinking and feeling and influencing the others. Depending on how that goes, you can get spectacular teamwork or a spectacular waste of time and energy. Understanding the various factors that led to the emergence of the good stuff (teamwork) or the unhelpful stuff (gossip and gridlock) would help a leader think in new ways and create new solutions for improving this team or launching a new one.

Similarly, none of Yolanda's policies or people *caused* the violence to these vulnerable children—the violence emerged from a complex system of policies, people, relationships, experiences, and histories. As Yolanda and Doug search for the "silver bullet," they are looking for a simple cause rather than focusing on what the system is currently producing. Instead, complexity theory urges taking a look at the current system and how it operates in order to create the conditions that are emerging—so that leaders can strengthen the conditions they want and weaken the ones they don't. But what leaders are really trying to influence is emergence, and no one person or group can control that. Even though Yolanda and Doug are at the very top of the FACS leadership, they cannot control the forces that are putting these kids in harm's way. They can influence the way the system works, but only if they get their heads around that as a task.

In addition to cause and effect, the human brain also naturally seeks narratives; we live our lives thinking about linear stories (this is one of the reasons Yolanda and Doug and others are your companions in this book). When there isn't a straightforward narrative, the brain creates one by filling out the missing bits—often without our even knowing it. Taking multiple perspectives is one way to help make that filling-in process conscious. Thinking about what we call non-Hollywood flow is another way. We go to movies where we know just what the plot will be, and we appreciate the several twists and turns which lead to an utterly predictable Hollywood ending (Jennifer once went to a scriptwriting workshop where the successful screenwriter-teacher laid out the plot structure for 98 percent of all Hollywood movies). The reason Hollywood endings are just that is because other sorts of endings—unpredictable ones, or endings in which the plot threads don't tie up in a bow at the end—are panned by viewers. We like having everything work out in the end.

Life, however, is far messier than any movie could ever be, and the plot threads don't tie up in a bow. Our brains can't function without any order, though, so our brains tie knots for us that we didn't know about, and they make us believe in straight, linear patterns where really there are just wandering paths. In our actual lives, events tend to be *nonlinear*, another key concept from complexity theory. In real life, you can do something 26 times with no effect, and then do exactly the same thing a 27th time and have it turn out differently (think of speeding on the highway). In real life, you can make a big change that results in little difference (like when you spend millions of dollars to study, create, and run a companywide culture-change initiative that is supposed to break down silos), and then make a small change that creates a big difference (like moving the development and the marketing groups into a single space together instead of having them at different ends of the building).

Take Yolanda's puzzle. She may be drawn to a big, sweeping change; this makes sense as the response to a big problem (and it makes public relations sense, too, as the agency puts forward a major change initiative to prove that it has taken the issue seriously). But it may be a more subtle change that actually makes the difference in the end. In a non-Hollywood situation, it's not always the star of the show who saves the day.

It turns out that thinking about the world as a complex system rather than a simple cause-and-effect story challenges most of the easy assumptions we make about the world, and it challenges many of the approaches we take to solving problems, talking to people, and building a better future. But we've also found that once you begin to understand the new rules and approaches of the complex world, new possibilities emerge—and then, as our clients have discovered, solving problems can become more creative, more inclusive, and even more fun.

POWER HABITS

We are conscious that this book offers habits of mind as powerful practices for leaders, so we'd like to turn our attention briefly to the practice of power.[10] We believe these habits are power enhancing in particular ways, although as you begin to form them, you may also reimagine what power is and who might have it.

There are occasions when you may enjoy (or dread) considerable power. These habits will help you use that power in more effective ways, particularly in the face of uncertainty and complexity. When the way is not simple and predictable, one of the core requirements of those in power is likely to be to cede some of the control to others and let the system itself begin to come into a new pattern, guided but not controlled by those in power. At other times, you may have very little power of any kind, either because the power is highly concentrated with someone else or because it is distributed among so many people that it's hard to find at all. Here these habits help make a different sort of change from the side, which can be indirect but unexpectedly effective.

Bill Torbert describes how this journey may evolve from what he calls unilateral forms of power, such as that derived from coercion, position, or personal charisma, to "mutually transforming power," which derives from paying attention to one another in vigilant and vulnerable ways and working together to create visions and find ways forward.[11] In a simpler world, perhaps unilateral power held by a single, smart, capable leader could rule the day. In a complex world, as we'll explore together, it takes a collective sharing of power, creativity, and perspectives to become agile and nuanced enough to lead into the uncertain future. As we work together to explore the new practices needed in these complex and ambiguous spaces, power becomes a new kind of force to be wielded and shared.

MAKING A START

This introduction to the habits of mind was meant to give you a sense of where we're going, and we hope you'll now come along for the ride. We're off to explore some of what we think are the most useful ways you can put these habits of mind into practice in your complex world while making progress on some of your key leadership challenges. We know that most of what you are doing is working for you already, and we don't want to disrupt that. Rather, we hope that however you think about or do your work, you'll find ways to expand that thinking, to have more choices, and to grow a bigger perspective when faced with uncertainty or ambiguity. We have worked with leaders in deep trouble, and we have worked with leaders who were soaring to the top of their companies at lightning speed, the golden men and women of the organization. What our clients have in common is the experience of being in over their heads in a world so complex that old rules don't seem to help anymore. This book will help you understand and thrive in those new rules.

You'll see that many of the ideas we offer in this book have a paradoxical feel, and that's because being a leader under conditions of complexity is dripping with paradox. As you try to ask different questions to grow your curiosity, take multiple perspectives without losing your own, and influence the system even though you'll never be able to see the whole thing, you are always trying to keep your head above the paradoxical waters of leadership. This book is meant to be a flotation device. Remove it from its package, place your arms through the straps, and tighten them around your waist.

2 ENGAGE WITH COMPLEXITY, BUT KEEP IT SIMPLE

Yolanda walked in to find Doug in her office, flipping through files on the Ikea couch next to the window. "Not another problem!" she said as she saw him.

"Lovely to see you, too," he said, looking up briefly. "Nothing new has happened as far as I know. Did you get any rest?"

"I called both of my kids last night to just check in and be sure they were doing OK with me getting slammed in the papers."

"And?"

Yolanda smiled. "You know how kids are in their 20s—way too busy with their lives to think much about mine. My son has to deal with his first performance reviews this week and my daughter's preparing for a big conference presentation, so I just gave them each a virtual hug and fell into bed. You?"

"Yup, we are not trending much yet on social media, I am told, so I suspect it would hardly register for a 20-something. I got away from this mess by sleeping well enough and then taking the dogs out for a run this morning. That always gives me a new perspective," Doug answered.

"I could use a good night's sleep. The thing I keep coming back to is this: why didn't we see all of this coming? The press keeps talking about how obvious it all is. They have dug up new dirt on the boyfriend that makes us look like morons for letting him care for a troubled kid," Yolanda tossed a page torn from the local paper on top of Doug's pile of files.

"Ah, Yolanda, the wisdom of hindsight," Doug said, running his eyes over the article. "It's always easier to trace the causes afterward. That's when everything becomes crystal clear. Trying to figure out what's important in the moment is a much harder task—you know that."

"I do know, but the paper paints a pretty damning picture of our processes and systems if we let this man with a record in a house with one of our most at-risk kids."

"Yes, but I've seen the report that was done on that house. The boyfriend isn't even on the list. He didn't live there—he was just one in a long list of friends and acquaintances who occasionally visit, if people were telling the truth. We can't do background checks on each person our foster families allow into their houses. It's hard enough getting people to take some of these kids in the first place. And the ones who might be best for our kids still struggle to open up and describe their family relationships to officials like us."

"But Doug, that makes it sound like it's not only not our fault, but also that we'll never be able to protect these kids. If we can't know which things to look for and if we can't look at everything, what should we do? How do we build a strategy that takes us to a better place in the future? And how do we assure the public that it's not corruption? Sometimes it feels impossible."

"I'm stuck, too," Doug admitted. "I feel like we're back at the same place we were last night. We didn't see this coming, so how are we going to see the next one coming?" Doug and Yolanda paged through the files silently for a few minutes looking for some detail they had missed. Then Yolanda stood, suddenly.

"You know who might help us with this? Curtis. Let me see if I can get him in here."

"Curtis? The IT guy? What does IT have to do with this?" Doug called after her. He was still puzzling about that when Yolanda's head reappeared in the doorway.

"Let's head to the conference room—he's on his way."

Curtis was one of the most recent hires at FACS. He had retired twice so far—first from the navy and then from a start-up software company. On the surface, his was an odd CV for a child protection agency. He hardly needed the meager salary FACS could afford to pay him, but he wanted to make a difference in a field that was of vital importance to him. As a young kid, he had been in foster care while his single mother struggled with her health and with money. He thought it was his foster parents who really put him on the track to be the person he was today, and he always wanted to go back and do something for disadvantaged kids. Even though being IT director at FACS was a job he could have done in his sleep, Curtis was still thrilled to have it, and he was fascinated to be in an organizational culture that was so different from that of his past work lives.

Curtis walked around the conference room, looking at the pages of data Yolanda and Doug had posted the day before. Ten pages for the ten kids physically abused or killed over the past year, arranged chronologically. Dates, names, events printed on each page. Doug walked in with the files and Yolanda followed, with three cups of coffee precariously balanced in one hand and her laptop in the other.

"OK, let's figure this thing out," she said, grimly. "Curtis, I figured you have all this systems and complexity theory experience and you might be able to help us pick out what's going wrong here. We know there's probably a pattern, but we've only been able to gather evidence afterward. We want to stop these events before they happen. How can you help us learn from this so that we can figure out the next tragedy before it happens?"

Curtis sat down in one of the worn chairs and pulled out his tablet computer. "I can see you've done a lot of thinking about each of these kids in a case-by-case way. That seems like a good beginning, but no obvious patterns?"

"Nope," Doug said, sipping his coffee. "There seem to be way too many moving pieces. It's not like a single bureau or a single caseworker is implicated in all of these. I guess that's why Yolanda was interested in your perspective. I didn't even remember that you had a background in complexity."

"Yeah, both from the navy and from the agile software development approach we used at the start-up. As an engineer and mathematician by training, I got really interested in the ways things work when they're not predictable and are pretty much outside our direct control. Like this I guess. It is kind of offensive to an engineer to have things seem so out of control, sometimes when you least expect it."

"I don't know that much about complexity thinking as a field," Doug admitted. "Can it help you prevent tragedies like this?"

"Well, we're never going to be able to prevent all cases of violence against these kids—no matter how hard we try. There are just too many factors to believe that we can ever control them all. But I'm totally aligned with you in trying to reduce them in any way we can, and I'm guessing you're right that a complex adaptive system like this will require new ways of considering the issue. We see that mostly good things emerge from this system. Mostly it works like we want it to—we have more than a thousand kids in our care in one way or another and very, very few of them end up in worse condition. But there are these terrible things that emerge from the system, too. Rarely, but significantly. And I've seen from my perspective that some of what we do here seems to be just wasted work."

"We've tried to cut down the bureaucracy in every way we could while still maintaining standards," Yolanda explained. "I bet you're right that there's still wasted work, but surely that's not what's causing these problems."

"There's that notion of *causing* that can get us into a lot of trouble," Curtis said, smiling. "Let's look at that whole idea of cause and effect. Now, let's see what we can learn about the future from looking in the rear view mirror, peering at the present and imagining the future."

We have been talking about a VUCA world—one filled with volatility, uncertainty, complexity, and ambiguity. The complexity piece bears some extra thought because it's attached to an entire branch of research and theory that has implications for leaders around the world. There are a couple of important distinctions that give rise to new ways of thinking and acting during times of complexity, and there are some counterintuitive approaches to practice using the habits of mind.

There has been a backlash against what people call complexity, and leaders have been urged to simplify their messages and their approaches. We have a lot of sympathy for that view. We often see organizations create complicated strategies to solve problems. Say that the senior team realizes that there aren't

enough senior leader candidates and assigns human resources the task of fixing that problem. The HR department works away on the problem by instituting a talent management system that requires training, meetings, and new
forms for managers to fill out. Eighteen months later, managers complain that
they have so many forms to fill out and new processes to manage that they are
spending less time developing their people than they were before. The solution actually makes the problem worse, as the managers make their data collection and form filling and talent review meetings a lower priority because
of all the hassle. Often, what happens next is another layer of complicated
procedures on top of the first: for example, a checklist to make sure managers are meeting their people development requirements as well as the talent
management procedures, or a set of requirements that all the procedures have
to be followed before the target staff can be considered for promotion. No
wonder we're exhausted!

And at the same time, lots of what leaders are called on to think about and
lead these days isn't simple. It isn't the straightforward piece-by-piece tightening of an assembly-line process. Things are complex, and that complexity is
growing. There is a huge difference between simplifying your message or processes and believing in a simple world. Leaders ignore that difference at their
peril—and their organization's.

We like many of the complexity frameworks (we'll cite some of them in the
notes and put up more information about others on our blog for those of you
who are, like us, complexity geeks), but we're going to begin with the one that
has shaped our thinking most: the Cynefin framework, by David Snowden
(see Figure 2.1 later in this chapter).[1] The reason we like Snowden best for our
purposes is because he helps us think about simplicity and complexity, and he
does so with a quick and compelling look at cause and effect.[2]

SEEING THE SYSTEM: GETTING AWAY FROM
A SIMPLE IDEA OF CAUSE AND EFFECT

One of the great discoveries little kids make is the connection between cause
and effect. If you've ever been around an 18-month old who keeps dropping
her cereal bowl on the floor and watching it go splat on the floor, you've seen

how interesting simple cause and effect can be. (Plus there's the extra delight of what happens to Daddy's face as she drops the bowl again and again!) Human brains are great at picking up cause and effect: so good, in fact, that we do this without even really considering it.[3] This is one of the reasons we've been so successful as a species. (Scientists don't think that any animal other than the primate has a sense of cause and effect.)

At the same time, because this idea of cause and effect is so automatic, we tend to overuse it in a couple of ways—and this tendency can get us into trouble.

One key mistake we make is to fill in the connection between cause and effect with very little data. We dislike knowing about an effect without a sense of cause—it offends our sense of story. So we take whatever data we have and create a causal story. It doesn't matter that the story is missing pieces—as long as we can tie the pieces together (and our brains will fill in the missing bits), we'll be able to make a satisfying story we can believe in. The Nobel Prize–winning behavioral economist Daniel Kahneman shows how our brains are attracted to creating missing data with a tiny little story: "After spending a day exploring beautiful sights in the crowded streets of New York, Jane discovered that her wallet was missing." When Kahneman gave readers a surprise recall test, "the word *pickpocket* was more strongly associated with the story than the word *sights*, even though the latter was actually in the sentence while the former was not."[4]

Do you notice how weird that is? People thought this was a story about a pickpocket because it took place in the crowded streets of New York. It's much more likely that Jane left her wallet behind somewhere (because more wallets are lost than stolen), but our brains pick out particular words and create a little bridge between them. This is a marvelous quirk of our brains, the way we jump to conclusions and solutions, and it's probably a key piece of what has made us so effective as a species. In times of complexity, though, it is much less helpful, because we have a hard time remembering what actually happened, with missing bits and all. Our brains have remembered (or created) a causal loop that we don't think about; we just believe it.

Another thing we're great at is *retrospective coherence*, a fancy term that means that when we look back at something, we can make sense of it all. You can see Yolanda and Doug wrestling with that now. Of course they should have looked into the boyfriend's background, because now we see that the boyfriend's background is of prime importance to the way the story has turned out. But there are millions of pieces of data that aren't of prime importance to the story, and we can't always (or even usually) know which pieces of data will turn out to have been important. Notice Yolanda and Doug aren't kicking themselves for not examining the foster mother's brother-in-law; he didn't turn out to be important to the plot of this particular story. But because it looks so coherent looking back at it, we believe we should have been able to see the patterns looking forward, and we believe we should be able to know what's important. This sense—that we should have been able to predict the future because the past looks so clear to us—is a core reason we blame people for things they couldn't have known, search for villains in stories about tragedies, and believe that a careful study of the past will help us be more certain about the future.

The thing that makes this even trickier is that lots of times we do know what's important, even looking forward. That's why we have safety inspections of airplanes and health inspections of restaurants, quality control in production lines, and signs in bathrooms reminding us to wash our hands. We know from past experience that safety and cleanliness and quality control matter in these areas. And developed societies have become much more stringent about health and safety issues because the gains in well-being and comfort are clear. The modern, Western world has much higher expectations about living longer, driving safer, and making industries and governments take responsibility for the safety of the services they provide.

The issue is that the past isn't always a good enough guide. We live in New Zealand, which is a country in the Pacific Ocean's Ring of Fire where the landscape is changing and alive. When a volcano blew up unexpectedly a few months ago, the newspapers were full of interviews with volcanologists (Jennifer, a newer arrival here, had never even heard that word before) who were tracing the history of the eruptions of this or that volcano. But that isn't really what people wanted to know. What people were curious about were questions like, "When will the next eruption happen?" "How violent will it be?" and "Will I be at risk?" To these questions scientists can make a guess, but volcano activity cannot be predicted from the past because nature is a complex adaptive system, in which an enormous number of variables combine to create storms and droughts and earthquakes and volcanic eruptions.

So the tricky thing is that sometimes we can use the past to put in place systems that will solve problems in the future and sometimes we can't. You wouldn't want to eat at a restaurant whose management believed that there was no predicting the future, that just because one bunch of people got sick from eating food that wasn't refrigerated, you couldn't assume another group would get sick too. But you also wouldn't want to invest in the tech firm whose chief technology officer believes that because people used CD-ROMs in the past, they'll keep using them forever. That's why seeing the system and trying to make out what kind of issue you're facing is such a help.

SEEING THE SYSTEM TO GET A HANDLE ON COMPLEXITY

Seeing the system allows us to step back from our patterns and habits about thinking about the world and instead be more intentional and explicit about the way we approach a problem or situation—especially when it comes to the complexity of the situation. We have patterns of beliefs about the world that our brains naturally go to, and trying to see the complexity of the system is a little like brain yoga—unnatural, sometimes painful, and great for increasing our flexibility and reach.

Snowden's framework is called the Cynefin framework—pronounced "Ken-ev-in" (it's Welsh, like Snowden, and a little quirky).[5] The core distinction Snowden makes is between those issues or events that can be generally predicted and those that cannot be. Those things that can be generally predicted live in the land of the *probable*, where we can make a high-reliability guess about the future from observing and understanding the past. Those things that cannot be reliably predicted live in the world of the *possible*, where the future rests on too many unknown variables to predicted from the past. This is a powerful way to understand your decision making, and it's one we should think a lot more about. So one of our different questions to help you see the system is this:

> In what ways is the issue you're dealing with in a predictable space, and in what ways is it in a not-predictable space?

A key question to ask yourself is about whether the part of the situation you're dealing with is a thing that happens the same way each time (spring always follows winter in parts of the world with four seasons), or whether the part of the situation you're dealing with is uncertain, ambiguous, or rests on enough variables that the past doesn't help you know what will happen next (last year the azaleas were in full bloom on April 15, but that doesn't mean they will be this year).

There are a few more helpful ways to judge how simple or complex something might be. One is to ask about how much disagreement there is about project goals and ways to achieve them. Another question is whether the knowledge and capacities needed to work on the issue are located in one organization at one place or whether they are spread across different places, organizations, and sectors.[6] If the answer to these questions is "goals and process agreed, and with the skills locally held and readily to hand," we will call this domain "simple."[7] Lots of important work gets done in the simple domain, including getting food to market and making our planes and trains and buses run on time (most of the time). This is the land of the probable, where managing the obvious risks is enough to keep the system running well over time.

Some things in Yolanda and Doug's world at FACS are predictable, agreed, and with the skills and knowledge readily available. There are payroll systems and key forms to log. There are yearly budget cycles and semiannual performance reviews. You could look five years ahead and believe pretty accurately that you'd know what the various procurement and review systems might be. Everyone who knows the systems would agree about what comes first in line and what comes next. There is little ambiguity, uncertainty, or disagreement. You don't need to research something or consult an expert unless you think you can run the processes a lot more effectively. Standard procedures, project management, best practices, and business-process reengineering are all approaches that work well in this space. Here your agenda will be to just get the system working as well as you possibly can, to monitor it for key risks, and to be sure it doesn't fall over (because when simple things fall over, very big problems can occur).

There is much of the work at FACS that isn't simple at all, though. Some of the work has been researched (and continues to be researched) as adults work hard to create the conditions that will support troubled families and help vulnerable kids to thrive. For example, there are certain markers the social workers at FACS know to look for as they place a foster child. They have checklists about housing, the way the foster parent interacts with other children, the food and clothing the kids have access to. They do criminal checks on the relevant adults, they do drop-in checks once the child is placed, and they talk to teachers and social workers at the schools the children attend. These checklists of things they know are of prime importance (because research has shown this over time) and are a key part of getting their work done well.[8]

The elements on the checklist might be more uncertain, though, and then there's more potential for disagreement (is the tone a foster mother uses angry and potentially violent, or just stern?). Over time, experts can research these things and know what's most important to put on the checklists, and they can get more specific about what it takes to make a good place for kids to live. Snowden would call these things complicated. They are researchable, and experts can provide advice. Different experts might provide different advice, and they might even all be right. These specific things might not yet be known, but they are knowable. In this domain, too, you're tracking what is probable, though there will still be dispute around the edges: sometimes an event that wasn't probable still happens.

A key issue facing child protection workers and communities (and people in most other risky situations) is how do you sift out the weak signals and take notice of them before they become destructive? We beat ourselves up for missing the small signs that seem obvious only after the event. Yolanda is frustrated, looking back, that they missed that the boyfriend had a record. How could we have missed that? How do we see so many of these things only in hindsight? Note that we can also miss so many positive little shoots of growth that might have blossomed into something spectacularly beautiful, but we tend not to dwell so much on opportunities missed as on the little things that cause things to go wrong.

Spotting these little things, or "weak signals," is a critical skill both in building stronger organizations and in acting against family violence. Perhaps understandably, child protection agencies have usually put most of their focus on incidents of physical abuse. There are two problems with this: a focus on incidents misses patterns, and a focus on physical abuses misses the role of mental abuse. Family violence that causes serious harm is usually part of a cumulative pattern of physical and mental harm.[9] The challenge for businesses is to spot the weak signals of change or disruption in their cultures or markets. The challenge for those struggling to protect families is how to spot the weak signals of controlling behaviors when the violence and intimidation may not yet be apparent.[10]

The question isn't about how to *predict* all these things, because we simply can't. There are too many variables in these situations. The question is first how to recognize the markers of a situation that may indicate the beginnings of a pattern or glimpses of an existing pattern of control, violence, and intimidation. A second question is how to take action to block these patterns from developing or taking hold, or how to undo existing patterns.

Snowden talks about situations such as these, in which there are so many variables and so many things that might happen, as "complex." They require not only a different way of *acting* in the world but also a whole different way of *seeing* the world. Here we are in the world of the possible rather than the probable. Remember that coping with the probable is what humans and human systems are most oriented toward. Dealing with the nearly endless number of things that are possible is beyond our easy reckoning and requires new approaches.

Two more domains are useful in the Cynefin framework (see Figure 2.1). One is the unpredictable chaos domain.[11] This isn't a lasting state of a problem or issue but a temporary dissolution into a random state in which things need to be stabilized and moved into another domains for longer-term work. The other domain is what Snowden calls disorder. This is when we don't make a thoughtful decision about what sorts of actions the situation might require and we instead just act out of our preferences. And as you've seen here, and as you'll see more in chapters to come, our intuition and our current habits mostly take us into the realms of the simple and complicated, and rarely into the complex.

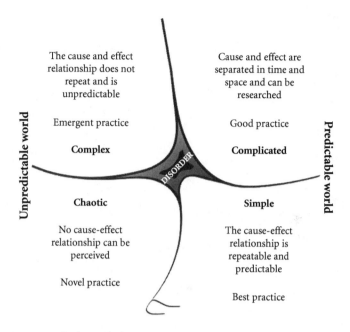

The cause and effect relationship does not repeat and is unpredictable

Cause and effect are separated in time and space and can be researched

Emergent practice

Good practice

Complex

Complicated

DISORDER

Chaotic

Simple

No cause-effect relationship can be perceived

The cause-effect relationship is repeatable and predictable

Novel practice

Best practice

Unpredictable world

Predictable world

FIGURE 2.1   Cynefin framework
SOURCE: Used and adapted with permission from Cognitive Edge.

"OK, cool model," Yolanda said, looking at the curves Curtis had drawn on the board. "But what are we supposed to do about all this knowledge? Do I just go out and stand in front of the cameras and say that raising kids—especially vulnerable kids—is unpredictable work and they need to cut us some slack? Maybe I could draw them these squiggles and they could photograph me pointing to chaotic. That would make the front page!" She smiled to show that she was being lighthearted, and Curtis smiled back at her.

"I'm not sure we want that kind of cover girl around here, boss," he told her with a twinkle in his eye. "How about if we look at the different steps we can take to make sense of these different kinds of issues? I think that a series of practical ideas might fall out."

SEEING COMPLEX SYSTEMS

The rules in complex systems are unexpectedly simple. It's actually harder (or, er, more complicated) in a complicated system. If you're in a system that you think can (or should) be predictable, then you have to work to predict it. You have to get experts in and make decisions about exactly which outcome to work toward and which of the many possible paths is the best to take to get there. This seems fairly straightforward to us because there are so many organizational systems that do this: we create key performance indicators and quarterly goals against which we are judged; we focus on business targets we have decided are optimal; we create business plans to justify our new product line or approach. We live in organizational systems designed (or at least pretending) to shape and predict the unpredictable. We also want to hold others to account, and we are prepared to be held to account ourselves because we want to be seen to be doing good, delivering a service; we want to know that we can make other people happy, make the world a better place, and/or make a million dollars or two. We usually have the best of motivations for *making sure* that things work out.

Jennifer has been fortunate enough to sit on research grant committees in a few different countries, and during a meeting, committee members would watch carefully the connection among the budget, the methods, and the questions being asked. And then, over cups of tea and store-bought cookies, everyone would chat with one another about their own research, about how unexpected a turn it had taken, about how the questions or the methods or the budget (or all three) had changed fundamentally once the investigation had started. Then everyone would brush off the cookie crumbs and doubts, and go back into the meeting to make decisions about the grant proposals, pretending that in these cases, at least (though never in their own), the proposals could predict the future, and the quality of that prediction could be judged.

Let us be clear here that there is an important connection between the success of a project and the quality of its proposal. There is some important connection between the success of a skateboard shop and the quality of the business case that convinced the investors to fund it. It is not that these things are meaningless, just that they mean less than we hope they will. That is the bad news. The good news is that there is another way, and you can choose it only if you can see it.

In a complicated system, we search for likely cause and effect. We try to understand the variables and figure out which are most important. We try to create processes and procedures that are repeatable and scalable, and that lead to predictable outcomes. This is hard work, often because we make judgments of success or failure based on whether things go just as we predicted they would. If they do not, we deem the system or procedure to be flawed, and we try to replace it with a better one. We do not tend to wonder whether our basic assumptions about the predictability of the world are themselves flawed.[12] Working in the complicated space is filled with complicated steps. Systems need to be analyzed and mapped, future paths plotted, scenarios described and weighed, and strategies drafted. The search is on for the points in the system at which interventions will give the greatest leverage.

In a complex system, we actually have a more straightforward time of it, if only we can get our heads around the different—often simpler—rules. Here we're not looking to predict or control the future because we have no idea what that will be like (it's unpredictable). Instead, we look at the present. Underlying the complexity of the present are a series of patterns, ones we tend to be blind to because we are so much part of the system, too. But if we gather enough perspectives and try to see the system, we can identify some of the patterns and see which ones are keeping the system stable (either in a way we like or in a way we don't) and which are creating the conditions for potentially massive change (again, either to a better place or to collapse). This gives us a way to make some changes, but it's not the typical way we go about solving problems.

It might be that the hardest part of this work is to prevent ourselves from racing along to a solution as soon as we've looked at a problem, because we'll nearly always want to put in a simple or a complicated solution. The rules are different in a complex world, remember, and they fight against our reflexes. Recall the example we gave earlier about the organization that needed a better leadership bench and the new processes and meetings and checklists the HR department implemented? This is the typical way we solve a problem in organizations. We see a current problem (not enough leadership-bench strength), we see the hoped-for solution (more leaders), and we connect a fairly simple cause-and-effect line to get us what we want (a talent management system that we have seen in another organization with great leadership-bench strength). Our resources get poured into the solution, and soon enough implementing the solution becomes its own challenge.

This sort of problem definition and solution creating is not helpful in complex situations. There's too much emphasis on the narrowing of the problem and the implementing of a crisp and clean solution. If things weren't so interconnected, if they weren't so volatile, if they weren't so messy, this might work. But as it is, these sorts of cause-and-effect solutions rarely work for complex problems.

This is because in the complex world, often the solutions are not in a straight line to the problem. Theorists talk about this as "oblique,"[13] but we think of it as "neighborly," meaning solutions that live in the next neighborhood over from the problem. You can't find them if you hone in too tightly on exactly what you think the problem is or if you are looking for leverage points and racing ahead to an obvious (to you) solution. So you want to collect a whole lot of ideas about what's going on in the system, ideas that open up new possibilities, ideas that are stories unattached to particular solutions. This is not the typical "innovation" brainstorm in which we harvest solutions from many different areas. This is a "rich picture of now" brainstorm in which we seek to understand in as full a way as possible what is going on today. We want to know as much as we can about now without yet narrowing. Which things are working and which things are broken? Instead of focusing on a strategy for tomorrow, wrestle your solution-impulse to the ground and just be open to data about the present. As they say to trainee ER doctors: "Don't just do something. Stand there!"

"OK, so what do we know?" Yolanda asked as Curtis furiously made notes on sticky notes. Curtis had expanded the boundaries of the conversation beyond the current crisis points to look across the whole system, and he also narrowed Doug and Yolanda's gaze by pulling them back to the workings of the present system. Yolanda summarized their conversation: "We know that our system mostly works. Nearly 100% of the kids we're protecting end up safe in their foster homes until, ideally, they can be returned to their families. We have created several innovative ways of working with families to increase the chances that the families can be reunited, and we've watched as those systems seem to have the result of decreasing the amount of processing time and increasing the amount of time social workers can spend with at-risk families."

"I think we're also doing a mostly good job at identifying which at-risk families have the lowest potential for violence," said Doug. "I've noticed a trend that I think would be hard to spot without this poking around I've been doing. As a department, we're investigating more families overall, and unfortunately there are greater numbers of injured kids than we've had in the past. But when you look at the data, you see that we're visiting and investigating a large number of families we ultimately decide are not at high risk. I've gone back to look at the results of what comes out of those families, and it turns out we're right about those families in just about every case. When we decide a family is not high risk and we put small processes in play to monitor and train the parents, we do not see injury to those kids in the future, and we haven't had injury in those circumstances in three years. That's really different from the past, when we got it wrong much more often and said that families were safe when they later proved not to be."

"Wow. That's really interesting," said Yolanda, surprised. "So we're making really good decisions about who isn't at risk, but maybe we're making not-so-good decisions about who is at risk." She paused to jot down an idea. "But then there are the budget cuts. We have watched our budgets shrink and the number of caseworkers shrink, which means that even with process improvements, the caseworkers are juggling more cases than they ever have before. So even when we reduce administrative time, caseworkers don't have more time with each family; they just get more families on their books."

Doug nodded. "And the economic climate has also worsened, and that puts pressure on families already at the margins and that pressure flares up in unexpected ways so that while our numbers of case workers shrink, the total number of cases increases." They paused as Curtis started putting the sticky notes on the big whiteboard.

Curtis handed the pen to Doug. "Here's what I've seen. The internal systems at FACS for things like IT, HR, and all kind of back-office support—which I hear were a real shambles when Yolanda came in—have improved dramatically, and people tell far fewer stories about the bureaucratic nightmares of working for the government. Employee engagement, which was very low, is steadily rising."

"True enough, though I fear that this latest incident is so demoralizing that engagement will take a hit," Yolanda added.

"We also know that there have been ten cases this year when kids in their care have ended up hospitalized or, worse, dead," Doug said, and they watched in silence as he wrote each child's name on a different sticky note.

"Yes," Curtis said somberly. "And my point is that we need to understand some of the patterns in this system in order to figure out what to do next. Not to find a single problem to solve, but to look for the areas or neighborhoods where sets of solutions could be attempted."

Doug stared at all of the sticky notes, now spread out across the whiteboard. "OK, so your point is that we've got a complex system and we need to understand the present in a new way before we can figure out what to do next. But we've got the data up on these cases, and it's impossible to figure them all out. There are so few patterns that seem really helpful—ten cases is way too many when you think about the lives involved, but it's too few to find helpful patterns in the data. We can see that about a third of the cases of all varieties this year happened in the kids' families of origin; two-thirds in foster families. But half the *fatalities* happened at the kids' families of origin. One of those wasn't even in the family court system at all, but the parents were in the criminal courts; the other two were under investigation in our system but without a conclusion about whether the kids were at risk enough for us to make a move. So we have cases that should have been ours but weren't forwarded to us yet, cases that should have been judged to be dangerous that hadn't made it through the system yet, and then a set of foster-care issues. What other patterns do you see in the present?" Doug asked the group, making notes on the whiteboard.

"Well, there's the location issue. We have five different local bureaus involved, with the capital and Proucheford both appearing multiple times—the capital has four of these cases, and Proucheford has three. The rest are scattered around the whole state," Yolanda added as Doug moved sticky notes around, making and remaking clumps of data.

"And even though Proucheford is a much smaller region than the capital, we seem to have a disproportionate number of cases there," Curtis continued. "What do we know about that bureau?"

Doug grabbed the file from the table. "We've noticed this trend, too, and have followed up a little, though I have to say that Proucheford wasn't really on my radar as a problem until this latest incident. Relatively new bureau chief, went in to straighten up the office. She's met with some resistance as you might imagine but nothing really alarming."

"We want to not just look right at the location of the problem, remember," Curtis urged them. "What about the community? The patterns of interaction between the community and the bureau? We want to find as much about the present as we can."

Doug glanced up from his phone, which had been buzzing on the table. "While we're trying not to narrow down into a solution, the *Proucheford Chronicle* has just realized that the city has a disproportionate number of cases. Now the local paper is calling for the resignation of the bureau chief."

Yolanda sighed and sat down heavily in her chair. "I had been worried about that. Ramona isn't going to be that good in front of the cameras either—she's a call-it-like-she-sees-it manager, a little firm, a little black and white. It's what we needed to fix the disorganization of that office, but not ideal in the middle of a political firestorm, and, as I'm learning from you, Curtis, it's totally unhelpful in the middle of a complex problem. How shall we handle this new wrinkle?"

SEARCHING THE SYSTEM TO FIGURE OUT
THE INCLINATIONS

Yolanda and her colleagues were starting to trace the patterns of their system and explore what it is currently *inclined* to do. This is a counterintuitive move that can feel like a down-market form of leadership for those of us schooled to be visionary leaders focusing on lofty strategies and plans for shaping the future. And yet in a complex system, paying attention to the inclinations of the current situation is of key importance. The point here is that systems organize themselves, and they organize around particular patterns of behavior and interaction. These become habits, and those habits shape the way the system works. You've experienced this in your own work life, we're sure. Perhaps at one organization you found that it was relatively easy to have access to the supplies—the technology, equipment, and so on—that were necessary for you to do your job. At your new place, there is such a mass of confusion and red tape around procurement that you can hardly get a basic laptop issued, much less the specialty apps you need.

What sense do you make of this? You might wonder if it's a personality problem. Maybe the head of procurement is such a stickler that now people can't buy anything without a notarized request. Or maybe your attention is drawn to the procurement policy, which might have been written ten years ago, when computers weren't such an enormous part of our work lives but were more expensive capital items. Or maybe you'll think it's an industry issue—when you worked in the IT field, people understood technology but here in the financial sector, no one gets what a difference good technology can make.

In any case, our pattern is to notice the problem (i.e., that the system makes it hard for you to get the tools you need to do your job) and then to attach a causal guess to figure out *why* it is so (A personality issue? A processes issue? An industry issue?). We are on a quest to satiate our cause-and-effect hunger.

In a simple system, you might just ask around about what caused the problem, and if it's really simple, everyone would agree (although they might not do anything to change it). In a complicated system, you could investigate and discover what makes an excellent procurement system, what makes one less good, and then compare your situation with the ideal to find out how it's broken and how to fix it. Researching the pathways other organizations took to solve this same problem would point you toward a selection of likely answers.

In a complex system, the key is to try to stay away from causal conclusions—remember, our brains are more naturally drawn to linear cause and effect, and in a complex world, that's often the wrong neighborhood. Instead, we want to resist that pull and understand as much about the inclinations of the system as possible. We can do this through thoughtful feedback and other sorts of data collection conversations with people in which we try together to make sense of a situation. We seek out as many perspectives as possible that will give us as full a sense of the inclinations of the system as we can get. If you are struggling to get the IT you needed at your new job, you could begin to collect data to understand the system in which this problem takes place. Is the system inclined to limit access to resources to new people? To IT resources but not other ones? To requests they don't understand or value? Thinking about the inclinations gives you a broader set of questions to ask and ultimately a much bigger solution set to pursue.

At FACS, they're now asking that core question: what is the system inclined to do? They have looked for the simple patterns, the ones that might be in the space of leading to particular solutions (about whether it's a certain kind of case that is getting missed in the system or a single office that is off the rails). When they find that neither of those things is true, they need to look at a deeper level of system inclinations. Doug has pointed to the inclination of the system to understand what it means for a family to be a safe place to raise kids. This is an exciting discovery, and while he doesn't quite know how important it might be at this point, he knows that it's something to highlight. They also see that the economic downturn, particularly tough in this state, has created pressure on families but also a pressure within a resource-tight state agency that means that caseworkers are inclined to have less time per family than they did before. This won't be true in every single case, but it's the way the system is pushing the caseworkers to behave. It also seems like the system is inclined to have FACS take the blame for anything that happens to a vulnerable child, whether or not FACS had anything to do with the child. On Yolanda's list of ten kids are cases in which the families weren't even in the FACS system yet. It is as though the larger system of the public and the press expect that FACS will find and save each potentially vulnerable child in any part of the court system or even before they come into the court system. This might highlight an inclination of FACS and its employees to take on too much responsibility for issues outside their scope. If, on your good days, you imagine yourself as the caped crusader rescuing the vulnerable children of the community, it is hard to draw boundaries around such a sense of mission and to not feel that you are always responsible in some way: leave no child unsaved!

After you have played around with what the inclinations in a system might be, ask an even harder question: what is the system *not* inclined to do? This will take more data and more perspectives to be able to get a handle on it, because it can be even harder to find what isn't an inclination than it is to find what is. Right now the FACS system seems not inclined to overreport families as safe when they are not safe. They might take too much time to decide whether or not a family is safe, but once that's decided, FACS seems to be in the right place. They don't seem to be inclined to pass their responsibility over to others or to spread blame around. They don't seem to be inclined to coordinate well with other agencies either or (this is just a guess from the data we've seen) to coordinate well with community members like Reverend Welcher, who was so upset in Chapter 1. They may be challenged to work with other agencies or community groups whose values or procedures may not fully align with those at FACS.

Once you have a sense of what the system is currently inclined to do (and not do), resist your desire to push toward a particular outcome. Instead, ask questions about what inclination you wish the system had: What sorts of stories are people telling about this issue now? What sorts of stories would I like them to be telling a year from now? What sorts of activities do people here spend most of their time doing? Which activities would I like them to cut back on and which ones would I like them to expand over the next eight months?

See, the focus isn't on the particular outcome (like the performance management system); the focus is on the inclinations of what happens in the system (growing more leaders). This means that you do not invest your energy in finding the single best solution to the problem you've defined. Instead, you invest your time in understanding, which gives you the chance to find a much larger neighborhood to explore and offers you the opportunity to create a much larger portfolio of solutions.

SEEING THE SYSTEM TO ENGAGE, PLAN, AND LEAD IN NEW WAYS

As you'll see as this book unfolds, making sense of the inclinations of a system is the first way to begin to change those inclinations. Whereas in a complicated situation you want to study and come to conclusions that you can roll out at scale, in a complex situation you want to understand the current situation and then try some things in order to iterate, to learn more about the current system, and eventually nudge your way toward success. To enable this change to happen, though, you'll need an organization in which it is safe to learn—and that may mean that you'll need some significant changes in the way people talk to one another and think about their work. We find that most of the organizations we spend time in talk about learning but reward perfection and certainty, which pulls in exactly the opposite direction.

The key lever in a complex system is learning; the key methods are conversation, discovery, and experimentation.[14] In a complicated case, you have distinct times for diagnosing the problem, coming up with the solution, and then implementing that solution. In a complex setting, the problem definition, data collection, and experimentation are all part of a continually repeating cycle, each piece of which is meant to lead to learning, and each piece of which might lead to changing the system as well (because even asking questions and gathering data about an issue has the potential to change people's thinking and action about it).

In practice, what this means is that people in safe-to-learn organizations need to stop pretending that they're working toward some kind of unified plan of what the future will look like (we are continually amazed at how many people know this is pretense and yet don't talk about how the emperor is naked). They need to admit that they don't actually know exactly what the future will look like but that they're going to try like mad to influence the uncertain future anyway. This is a radically different way of talking about leading into the future.

We know this is counterintuitive for smart and successful leaders. We once sat in a meeting of high-level company directors on a sunny afternoon on a porch overlooking the sea. The directors were trying to narrow down which would be the very best way to change an inclination in their own system (which seemed to be preventing people from learning). They went around and shared their ideas and pushed around the possibilities, each of them thinking that his idea (in this case they were all men) was the best. None of them was particularly listening to the others except to reload, as each sought to use the ideas of the others to strengthen his own argument (while dismantling the arguments of his colleagues). The conversation was polite and friendly, but it seemed to us to be going nowhere. We asked whether this conversation and these ideas were appreciably different from ideas and proposals they had put to the group at their last meeting four months earlier. No, they weren't. Which ones had been tried? None, because they still hadn't come to conclusions about which one was really the best. What would happen next? They'd try again at the next meeting in four more months and maybe at that time come to a decision about what was the best approach to try. Ouch. And these smart, successful leaders are not the only ones chasing their tails as they attempt to solve a complex problem in a complicated way.

We asked the group what would happen next if they moved away from a pursuit of the very best idea and went instead with a couple of smaller ones that might be good enough. There was both a sense of great relief in this pursuit and a collective angst: What do you mean we would be working toward something that might not be the best? If it is not the best, by what decision criteria do we judge? How do you make a strategy for making a change if you don't even know what the best outcome might be?

We introduced them to the idea of a new way of talking to one another in a way that made the group safe to learn. First, they were going to have to listen to one another in new ways—to combine and build ideas rather than dismantle and protect them. Then they were going to have to try to come up with a new sort of approach. This issue was not going to lend itself to a single winning intervention, as they were proving in round after round of fruitless conversation. Instead, we encouraged them to try out a new way of operating in complexity. A safe-to-fail experiment (you have to keep saying this aloud to avoid tripping up and calling these failsafe) gives you a new way of building your strategy (as we'll explore more in Chapter 4). It helps you remember to do what is most useful in a complex situation—expand rather than narrow, look at neighborhoods near your problem but not right next door, solve multiple problems simultaneously, and expect the scale of the problem to be very different from the scale of the solution. A safe-to-fail experiment has its focus on trying to change what the system is inclined to do rather than trying to move toward a particular known outcome. It takes what is happening today and tries to change it a little in a desired direction rather than picturing the ideal future and building the steps toward it.

There are a series of elements that can help you wrap your head around what it takes to be safe to fail. For example, it sounds obvious, but the safe-to-fail experiment needs to be doable. The group coming up with the experiment needs to be able to get it done—or at least have access to those who can get it done. These experiments shouldn't be all-of-organization events in any case; they are safe to fail and so live at a reasonable scale. Note that "culture change" programs are not actually doable. They're important, they're complex, but they're also impossible (which might be why they just about never work). But a project to get people to have more positive interactions with one another, perhaps by changing the way meetings are held, or maybe even by clustering sets of couches around the office, is doable by someone, and it might just change the culture. (And it might not, but all you'd be out is the money for the couches.)

It has to be *safe* to fail, so if the experiment fails, no really bad stuff will happen. In this case, you decide what would be really bad stuff, what would not be safe to fail. Obviously no one should be in personal peril, physically, emotionally, or economically. In some industries, staying off of the front page of the local paper is key; in others, shoddy quality control would be dangerous to the future of the company. Think carefully about risk here. There's no such thing as innovation without risk, but there are some risks that are unacceptable. Have a good conversation about this and push against your assumptions about risk. Nearly all the organizations we work with think of themselves as risk averse. If you're in one of those, you might want to get someone outside the organization or group to come in and help test your thinking.

You have to be able to learn from it, so you have to be able to tell how it's going. We are not in any way talking about control groups and comparison studies (those are useful things for researching in the complicated space, but they're not generally helpful for the safe-to-fail experiments we're talking about here). We are talking about gathering data and stories about the way interactions are shifting. If you want to move the quality of conversation from bordering on the insulting to being more productive, your experiment should include some way to measure the quality of people's interactions. Don't get weighed down by objective, quantitative criteria; look for qualitative early signals that might arise before real quantitative data might show a pattern. Before you even begin the experiment, you should have a sense of what improvement would look like. Would it be a week without a group email that slams someone? Would it be that more people said hello to one another as they walked the halls? Have some guesses about some things you can look for. And then look. But you also have to look for things that are going wrong—especially for perverse and undesired outcomes. What would help you know that it was going wrong? Maybe there ended up being no emails at all because folks were too afraid to put anything in email anymore, which meant that some important communications were not recorded. Maybe you found the number of small groups talking urgently together increased, and their conversations stopped as you approached. Again, brainstorm the many different ways you might recognize an experiment gone wrong, and watch out for them. (This is particularly important because humans have a tendency to see data that support their ideas and to not notice data that refute their ideas. You have to actually go searching for discrepant evidence if you're going to find it before it gets out of hand.)

Another key element of the safe-to-fail experiment is that it needs to start small, but if it goes well, you've built in a way to ramp it up. Note that this isn't the same as rolling things out to all, because in a complex world, we just can't know whether that would work or not. But if you try a thing on one team, you want to put in to place some conditions that might make it more contagious to other teams. In contrast, if the experiment goes badly, you want to be sure there's a way to dampen it or shut it down. Because many experiments will fail, you want to know when the moment comes to shut down the experiment and repair early damage (if any), and then learn. Remember, it's the learning that's the most important thing. If you're just throwing pebbles into a pond and walking away, you're not doing safe-to-fail experiments. Each experiment needs to be one that increases the amount of knowledge you have and that increases the data or feedback you can share with others. This means it's at least as important to talk about and share learning from the failures as from the successes. The point is to learn like mad.

A lovely example of a safe-to-fail experiment comes from the book *The Power of Habit*, by Charles Duhigg.[15] He tells the story of a US Army major in Kufa, a small city in Iraq, in 2003. The major noticed that the number of gatherings of Iraqis that became violent was increasing in the city, and he wanted to reverse the trend.

The US Army doesn't have to think in safe-to-fail experiments. It could go in with guns blazing or round up the usual suspects. But this major wanted to try another approach. He studied videotapes of the riots and watched the way they tended to unfold: crowds would gather, and over the course of a few hours, more and more people would come along. Food vendors would set up in the afternoons to feed the gathering crowd. Then, as Duhigg tells us, "someone would throw a rock or a bottle and all hell would break loose."[16]

You might look for who the culprit is here in this story. Who is the person or group inciting violence? You might ask, how could we offer such a show of force that no one would dare riot again? This major had a different approach. He met with the mayor and asked about whether the city could pass an ordinance keeping food vendors out of plazas. The mayor was puzzled but agreeable. The ordinance was created.

The next time a crowd gathered, the pattern repeated: a few people turned into a larger group. More people came by to see what was going on. The crowd got restless and started to get angry. Then they started to get hungry, and with no way to get a meal nearby, they went home for dinner. Problem solved, with a solution in a neighborhood many of us wouldn't connect with riots. But like all who use the safe-to-fail approach, there were multiple experiments running at once. Duhigg concludes, "In addition to removing the food vendors, [the major] had launched dozens of different experiments in Kufa. . . . There hadn't been a riot since he arrived."

We hope this gives you just a sense of the different ways of thinking and approaching issues in the conditions of uncertainty and ambiguity. In the complicated, predictable world, it's appropriate to research to find the very best solution to defend your perspective heartily. In the complex, unpredictable world, the best approach is to leave aside the idea of the best answer and reach toward the idea of creating safe-to-learn conversations, strategies, and action plans. To do this, we'll begin at the beginning—people giving and receiving feedback from the system.

Doug stepped back from the whiteboard. "Have we gotten any farther than we were?" he asked, scanning the many questions and data points that covered the board.

"I think so," Yolanda said, noting the hope in her own voice. "We know that we have been so busy focusing on the past and the future that we haven't really got a clue what's really going on in the present in Proucheford. And we have to check to see whether the simple or complicated pieces we have in play are really working. Like, are the checklists really a good guide for our caseworkers?"

"And we need to get way more feedback from a whole diverse group of people so that we can make sense of things," Curtis reminded them.

"And I guess finding out more about Proucheford is not only an investigation but also an experiment in its own way, right?" Yolanda mused aloud. "For example, does the attention of the executive director alter the system so much that we can't really learn what's going on? Or does that make things better?"

"The real experiment there," Doug said with a twinkle in his eye, "is how your son will take the news that his mommy is coming to stay for the week in Proucheford."

Yolanda smiled up at her colleagues. "Let's go learn stuff!"

---

3 SAY WHAT YOU THINK, LISTENING TO THE WAYS YOU MIGHT BE WRONG

Jarred left the meeting room unsure of whether he was going to put his fist through a wall or dissolve into tears. His boss should not be allowed to talk to him that way! Jarred had been at Actualeyes five years now and had recently been promoted from senior programmer to manager of one of the emerging software lines. He expected this, his six-month review as a manager, to be a celebration of sorts, not a reaming. He grabbed his coat off of his chair and headed outside for a coffee and a walk around the block.

The feedback Murray gave him was totally unfair. Sure, Jarred was new at this managing thing, but the charge that he didn't support his people was absurd! And the accusation that he had been unprofessional and juvenile? Jarred was spending at least an hour more at work each day as a manager than he had as a programmer, and this critique left him shocked and totally off balance. How should he respond? Who could he even talk to about this?

As he drank his latte in stony silence, his phone buzzed a reminder. Damn. He had forgotten he had a performance review with one of his team members. He was hardly in the right frame of mind for it, but she had flown in to the office from the Midwest for this meeting, and he couldn't put it off for another time; his calendar was totally filled for the next week or more. He swallowed what was left of his coffee as he rushed back to the office, determined to do a better job than his boss had.

On his way back, Jarred reflected on what he wanted to tell Michelle. She was a high performer who was, it must be admitted, a source of humming anxiety for him. She was argumentative and disruptive to the work of the team, and often late with her projects or explaining why they weren't worth doing anyway. She worked remotely after having gone back to her childhood home to care for her aging mother, and he felt he knew her the least well of all his team members. Plus, she was 20 years older than he was and seemed to think she had the right answer to everything. Still, even with his negative impression of her, there was no way he was going to make her feel as low as Murray had made him feel. He took a deep breath before he walked into the room. It had been a terrible day so far.

Fifteen minutes into their conversation, Jarred knew his day was actually getting worse. Michelle had responded to his initial questions by telling him all the things that were wrong with *his* performance, not seeming to notice that this meeting was supposed to be about her own performance. He had gone in softly, intending to gently open her eyes to the way she was acting in the team, and instead had gotten muddled up in the way she felt he was keeping her in the dark about things. His question "Have you noticed the way some team members seem to get more airtime in our meetings?" had turned into a download about what a waste of time the meetings were and how the others seemed to be disengaged. Jarred's zinger "How is it going getting your deliverables in on time?" had somehow ended them up in a conversation about the future of Actualeyes and what their strategic direction needed to be if they were going to stay in business. He was lost and bewildered and knew he needed to try another approach.

"Look, Michelle," he said, interrupting her strategic recommendations. "You know how important it is for us to all work together, right?" She nodded, silent at last, but wary about where this might be going. "And you know how we rely on every team member to get his or her piece in on time and to the specs we agreed on so that we can all do our work, right?" She nodded again. "Great! I am so glad we agree on these things!" Jarred told her, relieved they were on the same page at last. "Now let's get back to work!" Jarred quickly gathered up his papers and fled from the conference room, delighted to have this terrible day behind him.

Giving performance feedback is on every leader's must-do list, and yet every leader we've ever worked with reports giving performance feedback to team members is one of the most stressful parts of the job. Studies show that providing feedback is one of the most important things a leader can do well, and that leaders rarely do it well enough. It's so constantly a complaint that we wonder whether the human brain is actually wired to *not* give feedback particularly well.[1] Even in a time of certainty and clarity, having good feedback mechanisms in place is vital for the benefit of individual leaders and their teams. We've all seen examples of leaders who don't give good feedback and thus have more performance issues than they should. Or leaders who don't listen to feedback and instead limp on, making the same mistakes again and again. We asked emeritus business school professor and developmentalist Bill Torbert about the most important feature of a high-performing team in conditions of change or in conditions of stability. He said that, in study after study, one thing was more clear than anything else: a team's excellence rested on its ability to give and receive very high-quality feedback, constantly.[2]

So feedback is always important. When the context is ambiguous and changing quickly, however, the need for more people to have more access to feedback is the difference not only between good teams and great ones, but also between those that can rise to the changes in context and those that get swept under. This is because in every complex system, feedbacks are the lifeblood, the way that evolution and change begin and spread. We see this in systems from professional services firms to coral reefs. Those systems most attuned to changes in the context and able to respond in careful, agile ways to a changing world are the ones most likely to survive. Those that have too narrow a range to respond to changes or whose feedback systems don't connect to the capacity to change in response to the feedback are the ones that fail. Without good feedback mechanisms and without feedback given and received in ways that enable real learning (rather than defensiveness), people can't learn, and the early and weak signals of coming change are lost. We strongly believe that in a complex and uncertain context, creating a feedback-rich, safe-to-learn organization is the first thing for a team to get right (which is why we start with it here). Doing this well is so foundational to the success of leaders, teams, and organizations that it may seem like Management 101. It is. It is also

Management 201, 301, 401, and so on. It is central to what leaders have to do, and, in practice, it is really hard to do well.

The problem is that it's counterintuitive to offer and receive feedback in the most helpful ways. It seems to be more natural, ironically, to create ways to avoid or ignore feedback in a system. To understand this, we've put many hundreds of leaders on video with the simplest of feedback scenarios and carefully watched what they say as they have tried to give performance feedback to another person. These leaders have been from all over the world—from private, public, and community organizations—and they have ranged from middle managers to CEOs to professional specialists such as scientists and IT consultants. They generally fall into some very human patterns. Some shoot the person between the eyes with their feedback; they tell us they're calling it exactly as they see it and pulling no punches. Murray might have been in that camp; certainly Jarred felt attacked. Some seem to wander in circles for quite a while before getting to the point, leaving both parties dizzy and confused. Some, like Jarred, rely on a 20-questions approach to try to get a person to give herself the feedback that the manager seems sort of afraid to say aloud. Some people ask seemingly open questions in the hopes of funneling the other person to the preferred answer.[3]

We've also watched as leaders are given a piece of unexpected feedback. We've watched them deny it, argue with it, ignore it entirely, or (maybe just as worrisome) accept it entirely without much question. We generally do not see people having a thoughtful and measured response in order to learn deeply from unexpected and ambiguous context. Instead, people leap to either throw it away or accept it, mostly using just their reflexes (rather than their minds) to make that decision.

In all our work, although we've seen some (rare) examples of people giving and receiving feedback really well, we've never seen anyone who had a *natural* inclination for this. Those who were the best at giving feedback had always worked hard at overcoming their natural impulses and pushing themselves to take a new approach, and they had needed advice and practice to get better over time. Having difficult conversations well is a skill to be learned, not a personality feature with which people are born.

We think difficult conversations are difficult because of the thick braid of skills and mindsets required: you have to have skills for offering the feedback, skills for listening to others, and the mindset that holds those skills together. Let's talk about the mindset first.

ASKING DIFFERENT QUESTIONS TO SHAPE
YOUR FEEDBACK MINDSET

The mindset of the person giving feedback has the greatest impact on what comes out of his mouth. Check yourself for a minute—think about your own mindset as you give feedback. Generally, it looks something like it did for Jarred, earlier:

> Michelle is a real problem because she is argumentative and disruptive to the work of the team. She's often late with her projects (or explains why they're not worth doing anyway), and she seems to think she has the right answer for everything. If she could just save the time she invested in arguing and put it instead toward getting more work done, things would be a lot better.

What strikes you as Jarred's mindset here? Barry Jentz and Joan Wofford talk about the "people as problems" mindset; Robert Kegan and Lisa Lahey talk about the "supervisor with super vision" mindset.[4] In both cases, there's a sense that the feedback givers have access to something like the truth (Michelle is argumentative, disruptive, and late) and also to the solution (turn your arguing time into work time).

Jentz and Wofford write about noticing the ways you take a problem-solving approach to giving feedback to another person—as though you have all the data you need to diagnose the problem and suggest a solution. But really you have only half the data you need (at most), because you know only what you know and you've seen only what you've seen. Unfortunately for you and all of us members of the human race, it doesn't feel as though you have only half the data. It feels as if the data you do have are all the data necessary. That's not just your quirk, though. The human brain has an enormous capacity not only to not see the whole picture but also to not notice that it hasn't seen the whole picture. Daniel Kahneman calls this the "what you see is all there is" phenomenon.[5] In study after study, he shows that humans have the uncanny ability to race into problem solving or decision making with only the data in front of them and, worse still, to not notice that they have raced ahead. What you see is all there is. No wonder we don't go into feedback sessions thinking about what we need to learn from the other person. We are so focused on telling our own message as well as we can (because giving feedback makes many of us nervous) that we can hardly expect to notice that we are walking in with a maximum of only half of what we need.

In addition to this idea, Kegan and Lahey unpack the enormous responsibility in being the supervisor with "super vision." You, as the supervisor, have control of the most important thing—the truth—and you need to wield that truth in a way that will be supportive and informative for the person you're dealing with. You might have to cajole or convince or compel that person in some way to see the world that you see and to take the steps you know he should take. The hardest part is to really think about your approach: how will you get this person in the right frame of mind to hear you? A little conversation about the weather or the weekend, or perhaps some really positive feedback to begin with so that he can listen to you well? With this mindset, giving feedback is a hard job, and the responsibility rests squarely on your shoulders.

You can take on this responsibility in a noble way (as Jarred does as he struggles to get Michelle to see the world he sees without hurting her feelings) or in a less noble way (as Jarred thinks his boss Murray does). No matter which way you hold this mindset, the conversation you're creating is designed for one person to learn: in this case the other person. This makes the conversation less of a feedback loop and more of a message-delivery service.

If you were correcting a simple mistake—say, a series of clear grammatical or calculation errors—you'd know what the problem was and how to fix it. You wouldn't need to worry about the whole feedback loop. The issue is that the flaws of others often appear to us as blatant as a series of simple and obvious errors. But in a volatile and uncertain world, when dealing with the complexity of people, odds are good that while you're treating the problem like a math problem, it's really something else entirely, and you need a new approach, a new mindset. You need to pay attention to the return journey of the feedback loop and be sure that you've gotten both a clear set of data out and allowed for a clear set of data to come back in.

To that end, we'll begin with one of our key beliefs about what it takes to thrive in a complex world: Everyone should be learning, every day, at every chance they get. Even (or especially?) you. This makes sense when you think about a fast-changing environment. If you're not learning constantly, you're left behind. The loop part of the feedback loop is pivotal.

While this doesn't sound so mind blowing, it is an idea that is easily blown off in organizations. It is a radical idea, and it has pretty significant implications. It is a key gift of the habits of mind, though, to create the conditions that enable learning, and not just for other people—but for you, too.

So here are the different questions we want you to ask:

- What if this person weren't a problem for me to solve, but a key knowledge holder for me to understand?

- What is it this person knows about the situation that could shift or change my mind and how might I find this out?

In short, the question we want you to carry (here and elsewhere) is this: what do I have to learn here?

Imagine the changes in behavior this might invite, if you were to carry this question with you. Jentz and Wofford call this the "people as sensemakers" (rather than the "people as problems") mindset, and they show that it shapes every interaction you might have with another person. Notice that in Jarred's whole time of reflection and conversation, he never wondered (even for a minute) what he could learn from Michelle. Even when Michelle was trying to help him learn (by giving him some feedback he absolutely wasn't ready to hear), Jarred was unable to learn from her. The question in his mind wasn't "How could I learn something here?" but "How do I get her to stop being off topic and start learning what she needs to?" And we can't blame Jarred for this, because we've probably had this experience many times ourselves.

Asking a different question enables a whole new set of thoughts and behaviors, and that enables two things at once to happen: (1) it helps you give feedback so that other people can hear it and (2) it helps you learn more so that you can be a better leader. Both of these create the conditions for success in a complex and volatile environment.

ASKING DIFFERENT QUESTIONS TO SHAPE YOUR FEEDBACK BEHAVIORS

So, now that we've begun with mindset, let's have a look at the way you might actually act in a feedback session. If you have a "people as problems to be solved" (i.e., simple) mindset, you just think hard and unilaterally decide what sort of conversation you need to have with the person and how to get him to come over from his (wrong) way of thinking and acting to your (right) way. We've seen lots of models for this; they're often even taught in leadership or management programs. Each of these models has some really good things about it for acting in a simple world (that's why they're so commonly taught), so let's look at them:

- *Don't come to someone with feedback (or a problem) unless you have one or more solutions*—In this approach the responsibility lies with the person giving the feedback to also come up with the best solution for acting on the feedback. That sounds totally reasonable and helpful: you're telling people about the problem and the solution in one bite.

- *The feedback sandwich*—You know this one. You open with good news, slip in some bad news, and then close with good news. That way, the person in front of you is opened up for the bad news by hearing the good news and still likes you in the end because you've closed with something good.[6] And we're supposed to give more positive feedback than negative feedback (the best ratio is at least 3:1[7]), so this puts us well on our way to that.

- *Socratic questioning*—Here, you leave people to draw their own conclusions by simply asking a set of helpful questions to take them to the realization that there's an issue (and the hope is that they'll then ask you for a solution or even stumble on your solution and offer it up as if it were their own). This, we're told, increases ownership of the issue because the other person—the person needing to change—came up with the idea himself.

Our trouble with each of these approaches is that every one of them heightens the feedback giver's sense that she has access to the truth and needs to use an approach or tactic to illuminate that truth for someone else. Each of them sits squarely in a simple world in which it is clear and unambiguous enough for one person to have enough data to be sure about both the problem and the solution. Notice how these approaches fall apart if you live in a world where things have too many moving parts for you to be certain about what is going on. Instead, you can ask different questions: What if this person weren't a problem for me to solve but a key knowledge holder for me to understand? What is it that this person knows about the situation that could shift or change my mind—and how might I find out? Let's look at these simple feedback approaches and see how they look in the face of this different question:

- *Don't come to someone with feedback unless you have a solution*—If you need to learn from the other person, you can't come up with a solution on your own. You don't know everything you need to yet. Coming in with problem and solution would be like coming up with an answer after ignoring half the data set.

- *The feedback sandwich*—If you're interested in learning from another person, it doesn't make sense to try to bury the bad news or coat the feedback in good news. You're not trying to make it palatable, you're trying to test it out, wonder about it together. You'd still want to share both good news and bad news with the other person—and still in a ratio that leads to better relationships and collaboration. You wouldn't want to share either good or bad news in such a way that it would preclude the other person from sharing his or her perspective on that set of ideas. You might, in fact, want to purposefully and explicitly separate the good and bad news so that the person you're talking to can react in different ways to your different sets of assessments.

- *Socratic questioning*—This one is trickier, because it often *looks* open and curious. You're asking questions, so aren't you already doing what this different-questions approach suggests? Our experience is that generally people who use this approach are not actually curious about something new they might learn from the other person. (This lack of curiosity starts, we're sorry to point out, with the great Socrates himself, who was a smart fellow who might be forgiven for thinking he had the solution concealed inside his cloak.) Instead, the questioner leads the person down a familiar path (designed by the questioner) and entirely inside familiar (to the questioner) territory. We can spot this in our videos with leaders because they will generally ignore any new information that comes their way and continue their set of questions. When someone gives an unexpected answer to the question, the leader looks more exasperated than confused—because the other person is missing the point. The leader is using questions to search for particular answers, not to get more information on the table.

So now that we've deconstructed all the techniques you might rely on, what do you do?

"It was a total ruin of a day," said Jarred, draining the last of his beer and smiling ruefully. "But the good news is, I can ask my mother for management advice."

Yolanda smiled back. "I haven't had the most stellar week either—my name is still in the state papers and all over local cable news shows. But I am happy to think with you about your dilemma and see whether my years of experience would be more useful to you than they seem to be to me; it's pretty lovely for me to help my only son in this way."

"Maybe lovely for you. It's just that I didn't want to be a bastard like Murray was to me, but I'm not at all sure Michelle even knew what I was talking about. I'm not sure in the end that I communicated what I wanted to say any better than Murray did."

Yolanda sighed. "What I am in the middle of is plain ugly, but there is a way what you are trying to do, giving—and, if I'm honest, *taking*—feedback has always been one of the hardest parts of my jobs. I still don't think I'm great at it, but I have taken a lot of workshops and gotten a lot of coaching over the years, and goodness knows, I have screwed it up hundreds of times. I'm certainly better at it than I was, though. Let me ask you a different question: what did you learn from Murray and Michelle?" Jarred looked puzzled, so Yolanda tried again. "I mean, you said Murray tried to give you lots of feedback today, and then it sort of seemed like Michelle was trying to tell you some things, too—when you were meaning to give a clear message to her. Is that right?"

Jarred nodded uneasily. "Hmm. I haven't thought about this. It's hard to remember. OK. Murray told me that I wasn't doing a good job supporting my people—that they were confused about what they were supposed to do and whether they had done a good job or not. And, maybe worse, he told me I was 'acting like I was still in college,' and that it was unprofessional to go out for drinks with my team after work. He has never even seen me in a meeting with my team, and he acted like he knew everything about me!"

Yolanda nodded. She wasn't surprised to feel her maternal defensiveness rising at what sounded like an unskilled conversation. She tried to keep her tone in check with the next question. "And Michelle? What was she complaining about?"

Jarred needed to think even harder about this one. "Honestly, Mom, I wasn't really listening," he said, a faint color rising to his mocha-colored skin. "Let me think. There was something there about our strategic direction and how the company was going to go down the tubes. And something about how her colleagues seemed checked out. And a zinger in there about what a waste of time my meetings were. There was more too, but I was so busy thinking about how to get her back on track, that I wasn't really paying attention to her points."

"So you got some tough messages from Murray that seem unfair to you, and you were thrown by that, and you were so focused on the message with Michelle that you were not listening to her." Taking her son's hand in hers, Yolanda smiled. "I sure know how hard it is to listen to negative feedback. I think maybe that's what I've learned most over the years—and it hasn't come easily. I have to force myself to go into these conversations—whether I think I'm supposed to be giving a clear performance message or taking one—with a real focus on listening to what I can learn from the other person."

"I get that I am supposed to do that with Murray, but Michelle was supposed to be listening to me!"

"It is not all one-way traffic in organizations, although, God knows, I often wish it were. It turns out that we always need to listen in a feedback conversation—if we do, we'll find it always goes both ways. Let me tell you that as executive director, none of my staff would tell me anything if I didn't go after their views and show them how hard I was listening to them. Now there's heaps of feedback from the public, the papers, the families we support, and that's helpful in its own way, but it's not really good information about how I'm doing as a people leader because it is not coming directly from the people I am leading."

"But it's so hard to listen when people are slamming you!"

"Tell me about it. The papers today were calling for my resignation," Yolanda told him, her voice heavy with sadness. "I've learned that when you don't want to listen, you have to listen harder. You have to be able to listen into the wind. But it's not just about listening; it's also about what you say back to people. What did you tell Michelle?"

"You mean when I could get a word in edgewise?" When his mother smiled and nodded, Jarred went on, "I told her the truth, only in a gentle way, not in the mean way Murray had told me. I told her how she was disruptive in meetings and that needed to stop, and how she needed to get her things in on time. I didn't say anything about how hard it was for me that she always thinks she's right. I couldn't think of a nice way to say that."

Yolanda tried to decide whether to be a supportive mother or to be a thoughtful leadership mentor. She decided to ask which Jarred wanted. When he told her he wanted her advice not as a mother but as leader, she took a deep breath. "OK, here's my approach."

ASKING DIFFERENT QUESTIONS TO BUILD A LEARNING APPROACH TO GIVING FEEDBACK

With your "people as sensemakers" mindset, there is a whole new possible approach. It comes from the paradox that you have to believe that what you've observed (the particulars of it and what it meant to you) is important. At the same time, you have to believe that what you know and think, no matter how much that feels like the truth, is only part of the story. What other people think is important, too, and you might be really curious about what they think and believe. Kerry Patterson and colleagues talk about this as "filling the shared pool of meaning."[8] It's not enough for everyone to hang out by their own particular truth pools: we need the largest shared pool possible. If you want to learn and you want the other person to learn, you can have a different kind of conversation, the kind in which you're each asking different questions.

The first step is to know what you really believe in the first place and to see whether you can separate out different pieces of it. Our opinions and observations come to us all tangled together, and if we don't do any work with them, we just hand over the tangled mess to other people (and they don't much like that). Generally, the tangle comes with a lot of judgment and abstraction, and it is often filled with gunk that feels true to us but is mostly just clutter to the conversation. Rather than handing all that mess over, it is useful to ask different questions to separate out different pieces:

- *Data*—What actually happened in this situation? What evidence do you have? What are the facts everyone would agree upon?
- *Feeling*—How are you feeling about this? What is the strength of the emotion you're feeling?
- *Impact*—What is the impact of this behavior on the workplace? How do you know this?

These questions are harder to address than they look, so let's take each idea in turn.

Data

Here we want just the facts, ma'am. You want to lay your cards on the table clearly and without judgment so that the person you're talking with can see the picture you paint—and maybe even agree with it. A sentence that starts with something like "When you got angry at me" is likely to create disagreement; "When you were so nasty to Heather" is just about guaranteed to ramp things up. Murray telling Jarred he was acting like "he was still in college," and the fact that Murray found it unprofessional to go out with his team for drinks certainly wound Jarred up. But "When you buy five rounds of shots for the team on a Tuesday night" might let Jarred see something of what Murray sees rather than just getting defensive. See if you can get as close to the raw facts as possible, a sketch that would be allowed in a court of law without any objections from a lawyer.

This sounds easy, but it's actually pretty hard. Facts don't come into our brains separate from opinions and judgments. What enters is often an emotion that gets linked to a couple of examples, and those tied together with a story about why the whole thing was objectionable in the first place. We had a client once who took a stab at this by starting, "When you were so disrespectful of our collective norms." When we called him on that, he tried again: "When you prioritized your directorate over the work of this executive team." That wasn't much better. We got him to actually think about the data—what had happened—that created that meaning (disrespectful, not a priority) in his head. Turns out he was referring to a team member's being late to the team meeting one day—which occurred to him as obviously the same as being disrespectful of their collective norms and prioritizing other work. He saw little difference between the different sentences as far as the point he was trying to make. If he had stayed with his meaning rather than the data, not only did he risk making his colleague defensive; she might have also been bewildered about what he meant in the first place. Without data, the other person might have been both angry and confused.

As we've already begun to explore, in a complex and rapidly changing context, data about the present really matters. Data offer the core material for our change in the future. The higher the quality of data, the better.

Feeling

This is often the most controversial of these steps. We ask leaders to think about the emotion associated with this issue and see if they can put a real name to it. "Why would we bother to talk about our emotions when really people should be professionals and not bring their emotions to work?" people often ask us.[9] It's because all of the leaders we work with are human, and they cannot avoid bringing their emotions to work; humans bring emotions with them everywhere. As Douglas Stone and colleagues explain, "Difficult conversations do not just *involve* feelings, they are at their very core *about* feelings."[10] We talk about our "emotional baggage," but there are no left-luggage lockers for emotions; it is more like our emotional second skin.

Even when this is granted, why would we talk about them? We urge leaders to name the emotion that arises for them in part because emotions are contagious and leaders' emotions tend to be the most contagious of all.[11] And because humans tend to fill in stories where they have a vague sense of what's going on but no words to put to that sense, we urge leaders to take control of that empty space and put a name to it. How many of us have had the sense that a boss was disappointed with us, only to later find out that he was in the middle of a difficult family time? Or how often have we taken a boss's feedback as a sign that she's angry at us (as Jarred does)? A boss who yells, "I am not frustrated!" is not convincing. One who growls quietly through clenched teeth but never names an emotion is no better. One that says, "Look, I'm super frustrated and even a little scared about this incident," is on the way to a much more helpful conversation. Feelings are vital data, too, and they need a place in our data collection.

Impact

The final thing it's important for the other person to know if you're going to have a collective learning conversation is about the impact of this event on you or others. This one seems obvious, too, but it turns out to be as lost in the tangle of our thoughts as the others. Something might happen that has the impact of making you frustrated—but that's a feeling, not an impact. Why were you frustrated? What was the consequence of this behavior? What negative thing happened as a result of this incident? And how do you know it was connected? Look back at the data and be sure the pieces fit together well.

So now you have a little set of unbraided strands. Jarred's frustration about Michelle's behavior might get parsed out more helpfully. Instead of "argumentative and disruptive," you might get something more like this:

- *Data*—"In the last few team meetings I've noticed that you seem to have a different perspective from other members of the team about what work needs doing and why it is (or isn't) important, and I've noticed that you often express that perspective with some force and urgency, on several occasions interrupting your teammates to add your perspective."

- *Emotion*—"This has left me frustrated and concerned."
- *Impact*—"I've noticed that now the team seems more hesitant to talk through an issue, and I worry that it's because they don't want to create more conflict among us."

Here's the thing, though. Even if you get this feedback piece smooth and clear and perfect, with a set of perfect data, crystal-clear feelings, and well-defined impact all laid neatly on the table in front of you, you still haven't fully created the conditions for a learning conversation. You may have done a good job offering the feedback as you understand it, but *you* still haven't learned very much. We're trying to enable the looping of the feedback loop, remember. To do that, you have to stop talking and make yourself actually listen.

ASKING DIFFERENT QUESTIONS TO LISTEN CAREFULLY

The human mind, as we've seen so far and as we'll continue to explore, is designed for simplicity. To do well in uncertainty and ambiguity, we'll need to dial down our reflexes and dial up new habits. One core survival habit for complexity is listening, and the habits of mind can help here, too. The thing is that if you're going to learn, you have to actually hear what the other person says. This sounds easy, but as we have all discovered at one point or another, it is shockingly hard. In fact, listening might be the hardest thing we can do for another person—and, maybe more important, it might be the hardest (and most rewarding) thing we can do to increase our own learning.

Just as we have discovered that humans seem to be built with an almost-perverse inability to give feedback well, we have discovered (as have many others) that we have at least as strong an inability to listen. This is perhaps even more distressing than our inability to naturally give feedback well, because nearly all of us love being listened to and don't get that enough. What an ironic design we humans have: to be constitutionally drawn to that thing which we are also constitutionally unsuited to do. Getting out of this quandary requires practice and intention.

Here's the different question that is at the core of really excellent listening: "What is this person's purpose, intent, hope in delivering this message? What does this message mean to him?" This is as opposed to everyone's normal question: "What does this message mean to *me*?"

If you could remember to ask this different question even 5% more of the time than you do now, you would be an unusually good listener (because most people never remember to ask it at all). You would also be a better leader because listening is powerfully connected to leadership. In fact, in some key competency measures, the most important compensating factor is listening. That means that research has found that listening is the best thing of all at making up for all the other competencies you might not be good at.

That makes good sense to us, because listening has several totally different and important benefits. First of all, people enjoy being listened to. Listening builds trust and relationships. It makes people like you better. Inasmuch as leadership is about relationships, listening is a great positive. Second, listening is contagious. It is an uncanny experience of those who learn to listen well that others begin to listen just a little bit better to them. As mediators and diplomats know, often listening to someone else is the only possible way to get her to listen to you—this is why listening is stressed as so pivotal in such professions. Third, and finally, listening has one more special benefit to you. It makes you better able to actually learn early from a changing context, because it knocks you out of your own perspective and opens you to new data, allowing you to see new patterns. When you listen—really listen—you inevitably learn things that you didn't know before.

Now ironically, this third reason (which is our personal favorite) is also a key reason *not* to listen. When we ask clients what prevents them from listening, one key issue that always comes up is that if they listen, they might learn something new and might have to change what they were planning to do. They might become less certain about the direction they're taking. They might have core ideas unsettled. They might become confused. Or, if they really listen hard, nobody will be minding the store of their arguments, rebutting the opposition, and they will lose the debate.

The dislike of confusion is not only something that is idiosyncratically our clients' (or our own); it's built into our brains. If someone gives you a question you don't know the answer to (especially if it's a question you could never really know the answer to), you're more likely to simply substitute it with an easier question than to puzzle over the very difficult question for long. Daniel Kahneman gives study after study showing this strange (and unsettling) phenomenon. He talks most particularly about the way we have a kind of automatic, fast thinking system that substitutes easy questions for hard ones before even letting the slower, intentional thinking system have a go at the question. Our brain is working to save us the effort with a kind of paternal oversight. "There, there dear," you can imagine your brain saying gently, "Don't you even trouble your pretty little head with that hard question. Here's a nice easy one for you instead."

What does this oddity of our brain have to do with listening? Well, if our brains are trying to protect us from difficult questions we might not know the answers to, imagine how much more difficult grasping a complex perspective might be! Our brains will be working as hard as possible to save us the energy of listening carefully and of potentially being unsettled. Listening doesn't happen by mistake; it is hard to do well, and it costs us energy. Unless you purposefully invest the energy, you're unlikely to listen well enough to learn something really unexpected.

This is especially true if your head is filled with the message you're trying to tell someone else. You have probably been engaged in a difficult task at some point or another (navigating through a strange city or putting together an Ikea dresser) when someone has been talking to you. You're in the same room, and you're not listening to music or the TV or anything else, but when your partner (or roommate, or child) says, "Are you listening to me at all?" you realize with a shock that you weren't. You can't remember a single thing the person was telling you.

Listening when you have something to say is just like this. Your head is full of your own message, your own anxiety, your own words, keeping all your ducks in a row. There's too much in there for you to be able to hear anyone else. We've found you actually have to carry a different question with you on purpose and make it a key piece of your whole plan if you're going to be able to listen to someone else. In fact, even if you have it as a key piece of your plan, you're still likely to struggle with listening. We've been teaching and practicing listening for a couple of decades between us, and we still struggle daily with the practice.

Keith, as a leader in a big international organization, had to give a tricky piece of feedback to a key stakeholder. Seeking to practice what we preach, he prepared well for the conversation, carefully following the steps here, untangling the data from the feeling from the impact. He even wrote *listen* a number of times in capital letters on the sheet of paper with his notes on it. And still, it took him several back-and-forth exchanges with the other person before he noticed that he was just trying to convince her, not trying to learn from her. As he remembered to ask the key listening questions ("What is this person's purpose, intent, hope in what she is saying to me? What does this message mean to her?") he found that the conversation opened up and they could both learn from each other.

And just today, Jennifer was working on this book at her dining room table as her 11-year-old son Aidan told her about his day. She smiled and made all the right noises, and so was surprised when Aidan said, "Mom, don't you teach listening? Or do you just teach fake listening?" That made her close her laptop. We're learning. You get better and better at listening, but you never arrive.

The story we are telling here of the conversations between Murray and Jarred and Jarred and Michelle is about one-on-one feedback conversations. These are often difficult conversations in which the other person (and you) may not want to hear something. Here, the approach of offering data, feelings, and impact, and of listening really hard to the other person's responses, is especially useful. But these skills are also applicable in other conversations: in leading your team, in negotiations, in working through critical issues as part of a group. When matters get heated in a group discussion, it is very helpful to check out what you are hearing from another person, to be clear about the data you have and the sense you are making of it, and to be curious about which data other people have and the different sense they are making of the situations. These are skills that help the group be curious together and to go deeper into the underlying factors that may really be driving an issue.

Jarred shuffled his notes again. He felt more nervous this time than he had the first time he talked to Michelle. This time it was not the lack of preparation he was feeling but the *presence* of it. This was a hard conversation and he knew that a key piece of what was hard about it was that he would have to learn some things about the way his relationship with Michelle had broken down that could be painful or unsettling for him. Still, he was willing to try.

"Hey, Jarred, what's up?" Michelle looked confused, and who could blame her? Yesterday when they had talked, Jarred had assured her he was too busy to see her again during her visit; that had been true before he moved some things around to make this meeting possible.

"Hey, Michelle. I want to say sorry for yesterday. I don't think I was listening well to you, and I don't think I was speaking particularly clearly either. I'd like to try again and see whether I can do a better job of telling you what's on my mind and listening to what's up for you. I have the sense that things aren't as good as they should be between us, or between you and the team in general, and I'd like to understand that better and maybe we can work toward a solution." Michelle looked surprised at Jarred's serious tone. He realized that he usually tried to diffuse a conversation like this with humor, and he was resisting the impulse now to crack a joke. Jarred shuffled his papers and looked awkwardly at his notes. "I'm afraid this is uncomfortable for me and I'm not likely to do it gracefully, but I'd like to tell you about how I'm seeing things and see how you're seeing things. I've set aside an hour for this conversation—does that work for you?" Michelle nodded. "Would you like to start with what these past six months have been like for you, or shall I begin?"

Michelle, who had interrupted Jarred at every opportunity yesterday, was now perplexed about where this might be going. She was quiet for a minute. "Why don't you begin?"

Jarred laid out his feedback on the table between them, carefully unbraiding the data, the emotion, and the sense. He stammered more than he'd like, and twice he had to circle back and try again when he heard too much judgment creep into his voice. But Michelle listened and took some notes about what he said.

"I don't think you understand what's really going on in the team," she told him when he had finished.

Jarred opened his mouth to tell her that of course he understood the team—he was the manager; he had an overview of their work; and he, unlike her, was in a room with them every day. But halfway through the sentence, his eye caught the word *listen* written in red capitals on his paper. The sentence died in his throat. "It sounds like I don't understand the team the way you do," he said with effort. "Why don't you tell me how you see it."

Michelle looked surprised and somewhat taken aback. It's hard to give feedback clearly when someone asks directly for it. "The team has changed a lot since you've come on board—in fact, the company has changed a lot in the past few years in general. We used to be so small and scrappy, all engaged in building and marketing this product we believed in so much. It was a world where if you had an idea, you could just run with it. No one told you what to work on, and no one ever made you do a stupid assignment simply because his boss had said it might be a good idea."

"I don't do that—" Jarred began, but then he remembered this part of the conversation was about Michelle and how she saw things. "Or at least I don't do that on purpose," he continued.

Michelle gave him the half smile he tended to find totally patronizing, but today it almost struck him as sad. "I know you don't do it on purpose. You're part of the new management layer put in place to help us be more efficient. And I know you're just trying to do the things Murray wants you to do. But we don't really make good decisions about our work together anymore—we just take orders. And the team is going nowhere."

"You just don't understand because you aren't here!" Jarred blurted out. "We have a great time and people are really happy here!"

Michelle looked at him. "Are they? I know you have a good time after work and you go out for drinks and all that. But do people have a good time at work, I mean when they're actually doing the work itself?"

"Who has fun doing work? It's *work*! You just get through it so that you can go out afterward."

"But there's the difference. Here the work used to be fun, and we used to be able to see our ideas through to the very end. Now it's just a job." She paused, and Jarred tried hard to actually listen to what she was saying. "I guess it wasn't that it was fun all the time," Michelle admitted. "There was tons of grunt work to do then—we had to type up everything ourselves and do all the testing of the software and that got tedious for sure. But we were doing it for a piece of the program we believed in and cared about, so it didn't feel so much like work."

Jarred shook his head a little as if to clear it. "So what I am hearing is that you're frustrated with the whole way Actualeyes is working these days, and with me and the work I am assigning you. You think we're on the wrong path. Wow. And I'm just guessing at this one, but maybe you think I'm too young and inexperienced to get us back on the right path." To his horror, Michelle started to cry.

"It's not that you're too young or anything," she said, "although I do think you'd be a better manager if you paid more attention to the big picture. Still, you must know that I really like you. But I was a part of building this company when there were only seven of us, and I hate what it's becoming—just a software company like every other software company. And you can't know the difference because you weren't here then. And it feels like the company is losing its soul and everything is going in the wrong direction!"

Now Jarred was at a total loss. He was confused by what Michelle was saying, and he had no idea what to do in the face of her sadness. He had the sense that this was a much better conversation than the one he had had yesterday. He was even beginning to notice a connection between a couple of things—in what Murray had said (badly) and in what Michelle was saying now—about the way he was too light with things, too focused on making the team happy after hours, and maybe not focused enough on using the team to create the best possible solutions to customer problems. The sense that there might be something in what Murray was saying was a blow, but there was probably something he could do about all that, although he didn't quite know what. But now he was also hearing things that were way outside his scope, about the whole company and not just about his division, and he had no idea what to do with that. He mentally groaned when he remembered what Yolanda had told him as she helped him prepare for this conversation: "When you really listen, sometimes you get knocked right off your perch." This is what he got for following his mother's advice!

As he blinked in his confusion, Michelle snuffled and smiled at him. "I am sorry I lost it there. That is sort of embarrassing to cry like that. But I think that might be the most honest conversation we have had since you have been on the job. Maybe we can make some changes to the ways we do things."

---

4 CREATE A CLEAR VISION FOR AN UNCLEAR FUTURE

Jarred had heard talk of legendary "lake-house sessions" in his five years at Actualeyes, but he'd never actually been to one. At first he was excited to be invited, then curious, then anxious, and now, having arrived, his first reaction was relief: he got the right level of casual, relaxed in a plaid shirt and chinos but still a little bit crisper than the boss's frayed jeans. He had wondered whether he was coming to some kind of mansion, but the lake house looked about as well worn as Squint's knockabout clothing.

Squint—CEO and founder of Actualeyes—cleaned his glasses on the tail of his rumpled shirt as he peered around at the group, assembled on old sofas and cane chairs on the deep veranda of this weekend house that had been in Squint's family for three generations. "Welcome to the lake," he said, smiling. "Let's see if we can knock off this whole strategy session by lunch so we can take a swim!" Squint pulled his glasses back on, making Jarred wonder again about the coincidences that brought them all together on this lovely spring day.

Squint's nickname had stuck with him since middle school. What could you expect the other kids might call a nerdy boy with glasses named Stephen Quinn Thomas? His classmate and best-friend-to-be, the similarly spectacled Arlen Stefansky, was the unoriginal "Four Eyes." In middle school they were the subject of nasty jokes; now the two of them were multimillionaires. Squint was the software genius; Arlen was the financial whizz and CFO. After college (accounting and an MBA for Arlen, engineering for Squint), the friends made their shortsightedness a brand of honor: Actualeyes. They chose the name as a joke between them, and to have the last laugh on those sports jocks and their groupies, who had mocked them through high school.

Arlen, both his nickname and his spectacles long since forgotten, handed around a small stack of papers. "You're all here because we think each of you has an important part to play in this strategy session—which we're guessing will take us the better part of our three days away to sort," he flashed Squint a little smile to show how sympathetic he was about the lost hope for an afternoon swim. The two had spent hours in that lake as kids and teenagers, and three years ago when Arlen bought a piece of land just two properties away, they had fitted it up with comfortable but small bunkrooms so that they could blend work and play by having sessions like this here. "We know that some of you have been with Actualeyes since the beginning eight years ago (he smiled at Hannah, who made the third in the founding troika), and some of you have only been here a little while (he smiled at the communications manager who was sitting next to Jarred—he was so new Jarred couldn't even remember his name). Let's just look very quickly at where we've been so that we can get a better handle on where we're going."

Jarred had heard this story before. 4Eyes, 4All, and now 4Sight were all decision support and relationship management tools. Rumor had it that at one point, when they were considering a dating software program, Squint was keen to call it 4Play but they decided, even for them, the name would be a tad too sophomoric. People assumed the real force behind that decision—and many others—was Hannah, who in many ways was the firm's conceptual and strategic anchor. It was her work doing qualitative research, market research, and focus groups that Squint first managed to build into software: first 4Eyes, then 4All. Hannah met Squint in graduate school while she was working on her PhD, and he was trying to decide between a PhD in computer engineering and a company launch. One of their mutual professors saw a possibility for a great collaboration and introduced the two; they might never have found each other from inside their separate disciplines. Squint's first efforts were to build Hannah a qualitative research tool that was easier than doing her analysis with highlighter pens. As she began work in market research, his work went with her. Two weeks after she turned in her dissertation, she took the plunge with them when they created Actualeyes.

"So our niche in the market, as you all know, is to combine tools that support and require human engagement alongside thoughtful relationship management and decision support tools," Arlen was explaining. Jarred looked around at the others gathered there. In addition to the three founders and the new communications manager (Stephen? Kevin? Nathaniel?), there was Jasmine, the strategy manager, and Kelly, the head of people. Jarred's boss, Murray, the head of engineering, was there, and Jarred met his eye sheepishly. After the disastrous performance reviews, Jarred had talked to his people about the concerns Murray and Michelle had raised and had found some significant dissatisfaction with his leadership. He was on a better path now, but it was still hard to forget the humiliation of the artless conversations that pushed him in this direction. He pulled himself back to the present and smiled at the managers of the other key product lines: Chris ran 4Eyes, the biggest and oldest product line, and Minh was responsible for 4All. Jarred himself was responsible for the new product, 4Sight, which had been launched in beta for the small number of clients who were testing it out.

Arlen continued, "So here's our challenge. Our new vision is about combining our excellent software tools with services that help us solve more of our customers' toughest problems. We've had this vision in place now for nearly 12 months, and according to our metrics—which Hannah will tell you about in a minute—we have almost not moved the dial on our service line at all. Services have moved from 10% of our revenue offering to 13% in that time." Squint let out an audible sigh, and those near him glanced anxiously to judge his disappointment over these numbers and then stifled a laugh at the longing on his face as he gazed out across the lake. Arlen smiled and cleared his throat. "Not only do we have to figure out how to take this vision and make it breathe; we have to do it in a way that is so compelling that we don't lose our CEO to his fishing tackle and rowboat."

Squint turned back to the group and smiled. "OK, OK, I get it," he said. "I guess there's part of me that's still a little boy wanting to play in the lake."

Hannah snorted, which made Squint smile again. "OK, maybe a big part." He turned his back firmly to the lake and faced them with the intensity for which he was known throughout the business. "Here's the thing. I think our vision is really clear—we are and have always been a software company that makes human connection better. Now we just also want to build our business to take more advantage of that and to serve our customers better. We are a software *and* services company now, a direction we picked because we were finding more of our time was being spent on delivering services to clients—a natural extension of our work. It seems weird to me that when we called it out as an intentional vision, it didn't increase our service offering much at all. I'm puzzled about why that vision is so hard to live in to. Clearly something we have done is not helping our people move, not helping the organization move.

"It used to be when I had a vision of what I wanted to create, I could just work long hours and build it. If there was a piece of a program that wasn't working, I could just isolate it and fix it. That strategy is harder to enact these days. Now I spend most of my time talking to money people, or marketing people, or big clients. Even our clients and our bankers want to know where we're going, and they're not totally clear what I mean when I say 'Software and services for better human connection.' So I need your help trying to find another way forward. After all, Hannah is always teasing: 'Anyone named Squint needs a clearer vision.'" The group laughed appreciatively and Squint smiled at them, his glasses glinting in the sun. He wouldn't be 35 until September, but sometimes he felt like a much-older man. Looking out over his familiar old porch, into the faces of just a handful of the nearly 500 people who worked for him, he felt the weight of his responsibility to them. He would be so frustrated if these three days just ended up with a rewording of the vision into a vague strategy and a couple of new posters to stick on the wall. He wanted his vision translated into the most productive next steps. He wanted to identify the levers that they would pull to really get this change to happen. He wasn't at all convinced, though, that this meeting was the right way to find and pull those levers.

Jarred was puzzled, too. He thought back to the conversation he had had with Michelle and her sense that the company was going in the wrong direction. And he thought of the work he was doing with his customers and his programmers on making 4Sight really useful. He could recite the vision—software and services for better human connection—and he knew all of his people were able to recite the vision, too. It seemed like people were always talking about software plus services these days. How could it be that all that effort had shifted the real work they were doing by only 3%?

What had he done to increase service offerings? Well, nothing, if he was honest with himself—services really weren't a key part of his job. Michelle was right on this one too: he was really focused on pushing out the software. Maybe that was the whole problem.

Central to the challenge of leadership is supporting a group of people in having a new and brighter future. To help people move from the comfortable familiarity of now toward something mysteriously new requires some sense of where you're going and why. Thus, leaders are often told that they must develop a clear vision or a strategic direction or a business model. In times when the economic and social context is relatively stable, choosing the best direction is difficult, but it might well be possible if smart people have access to good information, can research similar moves made by others in the past, and use their analysis to point to the most likely outcomes. Even in a time of stable predictability, it's still often difficult to get others to change direction (for all kinds of reasons we'll explore here and in the next few chapters), but many leaders (and leadership consultants) offer a relatively linear process: research to find the best direction, settle on it, communicate it, and implement it.

There is a paradox for us as we make a shift from a predictable world to an unpredictable one. In the face of uncertainty, people need enabling processes to be able to cast a wider net into the future (because there is more chance that any single decision might be wrong). But we cannot get too attached to any one way of moving (because there is more chance that a single decision might be wrong). Ironically, in a world where there is no right answer, there are also fewer wrong answers. This can be very empowering for leaders and also very frightening. If there is no right answer I need to find, then there is no right answer others in my team need to find. While this is liberating for me and is liberating for others, as a leader I lose one of the key competencies that brought me into this role: my ability to find the right answer and support others in implementing it. A leader in a world marked by volatility, uncertainty, complexity, and ambiguity needs to have a new set of practices to rely on that keeps an organization changing enough to be following a clear and compelling vision, grounded in its past and aligned enough to be recognizably itself, and yet also with enough agility so that an unexpected and significant change in the context doesn't bring the whole place down.

So there's the paradox: you need to understand that the future you're moving toward is so ambiguous that you couldn't possibly know what will happen, yet you have to be clear enough about what it is that you can get people off the course to which they have become accustomed. The clarity part feels almost impossibly paradoxical: how could you be clear about uncertainty? Yet as decision and change experts Chip Heath and Dan Heath compellingly find in their research about successful change efforts, "ambiguity is the enemy" of change.[1] Ironic, since ambiguity and change are such close companions. What the Heath brothers mean, though, is that being ambiguous about a change you want people to make significantly decreases the odds that people will be able to make the change. In study after study, researchers find that if people are unclear about where they are going, they'll just default to their old patterns and habits. We see our clients in organizations across the world struggle to create the sort of strategic direction that is specific enough to create change and yet does not strangle the multiple possible directions in which the change might go. "Be more client centered" is too difficult a change to mandate (or perhaps it's too easy to believe you're already there). Yet mandating that everyone must make one appointment to meet in person with a client each week sounds too much like micromanagement.

So all this leaves us with a quandary in the complex world. It turns out that a leader in a complex world needs a vision that is directional without imposing too much (or too little) constraint on people. And a leader needs a strategy that is clear enough for new actions but open enough to allow the unexpected to emerge. You need a guided process of evolution. To enable your vision and strategy to come to life, and to evolve and grow in complex times, you'll need to do the following:

- Shape the vision and draw the boundaries
- Understand the system by mapping polarities and attractors
- Strengthen (or weaken) the attractors
- Create safe-to-fail experiments to learn about the system and live into your evolving vision

USING MULTIPLE PERSPECTIVES TO SHAPE THE VISION

In a complex world, a vision is not a photograph of a future destination, and a strategy isn't the map that charts the course. A complex vision is a compass that points toward a future direction, and a complex strategy is a set of safety guardrails inside which people can innovate and learn. A visioning exercise here is very different than a visioning exercise in a simpler world. (We're not convinced that the world of organizations has ever been simple, but it was easier to pretend that it was in decades past.)

In a complex world, the vision is the place at which the past and the future come together in a way that guides people's action in the present.[2] Leaders need to take a careful look at the past: at the values, history, cycles of change, and core myths and stories. A vision that isn't tied carefully to the shared history of an organization is disconcerting for people and risks that there isn't enough to make the organization familiar to people in the future. Many mergers and acquisitions have failed because the stories of the various organizations' pasts were too different and no one was successful in braiding them together into a coherent whole people could hold as familiar and common. We know of a government agency in which the foreign aid arm merged with the foreign business development arm. The agency is in a rocky place now, not only because the future stories of both arms are hard to merge coherently but also because their pasts are different, neither particularly values the past of the other, and there are very real differences between the needs of combating poverty and business development. Whatever the merits of the decision to merge these agencies, to successfully move into the future, they need to be brought to a higher purpose that contains both their past stories and their futures, as well as mutual recognition and respect for each of these. Perhaps they could all rally around an idea of bringing this country to the world and the world to the country in a way that helps everyone to grow. Without a vision that coherently includes both agencies and weaves together a story of a common set of values for the past and the future, we think they are unlikely to have a productive union.

Of course the vision is about the future as well, but in a slightly different way from how we often consider visions. In a complex domain, you don't set a vision that is about targets or clear objectives (we want services to account for X% of our business in five years). You set a more evolutionary vision that is about a direction you want to move in, and the stories you want people to tell about you—inside and outside the organization. The vision must be connected to the highest purpose of an organization in order to work in the complex space, because this highest purpose will attract the sorts of actions you want to promote (even when you're not quite sure exactly what those actions are). You want to create a guiding purpose that people can believe in and feel good about. Growth targets, revenue goals, and the like do not bring out people's creativity toward nudging and experimenting their way in a new direction. They are too narrow and too unattached to the values that drive people and make them more creative. Growth and revenue targets are more likely to attract competition and patch protection. A helpful vision connects people to their highest values and connects people to one another. In a complex organizational system, the interactions between people are the keys to the organizations success.

For millennia, complex systems have gone through the process of evolution, a brilliant way of making use of the past and nudging toward an uncertain future. Evolution is heartless, though, and brainless, too, in its own way. If a species evolves in a direction that fits with the future, the members thrive. Evolution does not celebrate this achievement, though. If a species evolves in a direction that is inconsistent with the way the world is about to become, the members just become extinct. Someone might be sad about that (as we mourn the absence of many important and beautiful species that have died on our watch), but evolution itself isn't sad about it. Leaders are the hearts and brains of organizational evolution that is intentional at least in part, working to create the conditions that push their organizations toward thriving and away from extinction.[3]

To craft this sort of vision, remember to think about what the current system is inclined to do. Think about inclinations in the system today and how you'd like those inclinations to shift over time. You don't want to focus on what the outcome might look like in five or ten years, because that can become a major constraint on the way your organization evolves into the future.[4] This sort of future visioning is a thoughtful set of nudges that shapes an evolution to a better place rather than a road map that plots a steady course to a single destination. And, because in a complex world your own narrow thinking about the present and the future is likely to be an extra limitation (more on this in Chapter 5), it's important to get as many perspectives as you can to engage in these conversations.

Leading a vision in this way requires listening deeply to conversations about the meaning people derive from their work, about the value an organization adds to its community and customers, about the current weak signals of what the future might hold (well before the signals are strong enough for everyone to see them). You don't want at this point to be future focused in your conversations; you want to be totally grounded in the present condition. For example, one personal insurance company we know of has as its aspiration to be the market leader through its high-quality support of its customers (of course many organizations have a similar aspiration). Right now, though, the value the organization mostly adds to its customers is that its insurance is less expensive than that of the competition. (And of course with those margins the company can't afford a great customer experience.) The talk from the top is all about customer support, but the employees find that focus disingenuous because of the constant cost cutting to keep the customer prices so low. Still, with their eyes on the future, the leadership focuses on rolling out programs that focus on customer experience. A focus on the present—on the real truth of the present market and on the wide gap between where the company is and where it might get to—would help the leaders see what is actually most important to them as they weigh the trade-offs. A look at weak signals in the present can also give them a wider sweep of data that might help them look outside themselves and therefore create more space for solutions to their quandary.[5] Taking honest stock of the present is pivotal for crafting a vision.

Similarly, visions in a complex space are most effective when they are attached to the highest purpose of an organization and grounded in the values of its people. Because centralized control is impossible in a complex system, each person needs to carry a piece of the control inside himself. Each person needs to be the one asking how his actions align with the vision—as Jarred realizes he has not done. Because the vision can't be forced, it must be carried broadly by the people inside (and even outside) the organization.

In the complex world, visions and strategies become the ingredients for those throughout your organization to create safe-to-fail experiments, the primordial soup of the complex organization. Boundaries are the guardrails that both enable and constrain experimentation, drawing the lines of play around areas where thriving is most possible and extinction not such a worry.

USING BOUNDARIES TO CREATE MULTIPLE PERSPECTIVES AND MULTIPLE PERSPECTIVES TO CREATE BOUNDARIES

Boundary setting is an underappreciated part of a leader's role, and yet it is one of the core ways leaders can create new possibilities in organizations. There is power in noticing boundaries, choosing them explicitly, and using them to create the guardrails that are the safe zone of experimentation.[6]

The simple act of noticing boundaries has its own kind of power: it's a means to take different perspectives on an issue. Because leaders often don't see boundary setting as a task to engage in intentionally, they find themselves creating and living inside boundaries in haphazard ways, without being explicit with themselves about which boundaries shape their lives and why and how they're using the boundaries to shape the lives of others.

For example, we ran a leadership program with a set of senior leaders in a large, private-sector organization. They felt frustrated about the ways the organization constrained them from innovation, from collaboration, and from having the time and space to focus more on creating what they want for the future rather than reacting to what they have now. As they discussed these limitations together, they realized they each had a different sense of what, exactly, the limitations were. Each person had created in her mind a set of the limitations that came from outside, and all of them had been acting to ensure that their own staff lived inside those boundaries. Upon collective reflection, though, they discovered that none of them had a really clear sense of what the *actual* limitations were in the organization. Listening to their different perspectives on this day was boundary shattering for them; they discovered that most of what they were railing against was a phantom, a rumor, or other ghostly sense of what was allowed or not. They realized that they, too, had been unconsciously creating these boundaries for their people, even as they disliked them for themselves. Collectively, they began to play with creating new boundaries—with their eyes open and on purpose—that would enable some of the things they had previously experienced as constrained.

Once you begin to notice the ways boundaries play in your world, you can also begin to see the ways leaders are always setting and moving boundaries. They ask or instruct people to take on specific tasks and not to do others: this is your work, and that is another person's work. They write terms of reference and contracts and define projects in a host of ways. They expand the scope of projects or narrow them to cope with issues that arise. Boundaries constrain the limitless possibilities of choice and create the spaces for us to work and relate and live inside. They tell us what is in scope or out of scope, what is covered by the contract, or the role description, by the brief or the terms or reference. Even as they constrain us in some directions, they make other things possible. Even as they separate some people or tasks from others, they create connections between others. They are neither good nor bad—but they are vital, and they should be more thoughtfully considered than they usually are.

Think about the boundaries that exist in your organization—whether you've drawn them or whether you're just drawing your attention to them. These might be explicitly created by the organization (e.g., this is our core business, these are our employees, these are our customers or clients, this is our intranet). They might be the ones you put around your work (e.g., this is my favorite sort of work, I won't work on Saturday mornings, I like to work with Geoff better than Dave). They might be the sort our client discovered: phantom boundaries that no one mentions but that people seem to feel (e.g., Don't screw up or you'll get in trouble; extending work with a client we have is better than expanding into a new service-line to get new clients). To make sense of these multiple layers of boundaries, you'll need to get many different opinions on them. Organizations that have one explicit boundary (e.g., We are a safe pair of hands) might have dozens of implicit boundaries that people create out of that one (e.g., Don't do anything that gets our work on the front page of the paper, don't engage in conflict, don't take risks, don't tell people what you're doing). You'll need help with this because your perspective isn't big enough to make sense of all the boundaries at work, and you're also blind to the boundaries that shape your world without your knowing it (as we all are).

Often it takes careful conversation with a diverse set of people to make the most important boundaries explicit; gathering multiple perspectives is critical because the perspective of any one person or team is just too limited. Boundaries are the creators of culture to a large extent, and we often can't see the cultural rules once we're inside them. Without knowing what people think of as the boundaries today, it's hard to purposefully shape the boundaries of tomorrow. As you pay more attention to these current boundaries and as you gather the perspectives of many others (best if these are both inside and outside your department or organization), you'll be able to see which ones are the ones you want, and which ones seem to wall off opportunity or collaboration or other helpful outcomes. It's only then that you can begin to draw the boundaries on purpose and share them widely. Culture change efforts that don't look at the boundaries in the organization are destined to tread water rather than make real progress. The more explicit and shared the purposeful boundaries are, the larger the pool of new ideas will be and the more the people in the organization will learn.

During times of complexity, one key tool is the safe-to-fail experiment. We'll talk about that kind of experiment throughout the book, but there's a key boundary point before we even begin to play around with the experiments themselves. A core distinction that makes an experiment safe to fail in a complex time is that the leader thoughtfully constructs safety guardrails around the zone of play. The point of the safe-to-fail experiment, as we'll explore, is to enable many people to try out a wide variety of possible approaches, all with their eye on learning as much as they can while also nudging the system in a desired direction. Critical to this is that the leader enables broad experimentation and allows (even encourages) failure (because if you're not failing, you're not actually being particularly experimental). The safety guardrails mean that both the leader and the followers can feel secure in trying out innovative—even wacky—ideas and talking about what success and failure look like.

Leaders in a complex space need to think hard about the guardrails they put around the safe-to-fail zone. In our experience, the first couple of attempts at those guardrails tend to be fairly conservative, as leaders don't want to take any chances at all: the whole idea of experimentation is just too frightening. It often takes a group of people to nudge the boundaries to being big enough to give people room to experiment without so big that there is real risk. Best is if the group advising on the boundaries is diverse in as many ways as you can manage: from different parts of the organization, different ages or backgrounds or tenure. Still, as leaders begin to see the power in intentionally noticing and shaping boundaries—whether safety guardrails for safe-to-fail experiments or other sorts of intentional boundaries—they begin to see a bigger picture and make more strategic choices.

There is one last important point about boundaries that can be confusing. Note that boundaries are not targets. The difference between the two is critical. A target is, as it sounds, a destination point, a single dot for people to organize toward. It is the ultimate guess at the probable that turns away from the possible. The space of a target is too small for experimenting well, and in a complex system doing so can have bizarre and unexpected (and unwanted) consequences. A target is generally the result of a single perspective (or set of unified perspectives) deciding on the single behavior that will change the system to some desired state. But in a complex system, no one can know which single thing (out of a nearly limitless set) might change the system in the desired way. Targets tend to be set because they're easily measured and seem to be connected to the issue at hand, but often there is no real causal link between the hope that the leader has and the target she sets to make that hope a reality. There is ample research about the perverse effects of targets on complex systems.

For example, there were common complaints about a public service department that wasn't meeting the needs of its disadvantaged clients. People were calling and staying on hold a long time and getting very frustrated. To solve this problem, the government instituted so-called service-delivery targets to reduce hold time and to be sure that every person was dealt with within a certain targeted time. Call centers were held to account for meeting those targets. And as they improved in this regard, customer satisfaction scores actually dropped precipitously; simultaneously, the number of calls skyrocketed. Why? Because to meet the targets, the call centers had to start instituting rules about how long each call could last, and to meet those time demands, the employees had to rush people off of the phone—or create rules about how many questions callers could ask in a single phone call. This meant that problems weren't getting solved on the call, leading to significantly decreased customer satisfaction and to more work—extra calls for the call centers to have to answer (within the targeted time). In this way, these narrow targets had the unintended effect of pushing the organization in exactly the opposite direction from the larger goal.[7] Instead of offering a single point (a target), leaders in a complex space thoughtfully create explicit boundaries and share these throughout the organization.[8]

TAKING MULTIPLE PERSPECTIVES TO MAKE SENSE OF A PARADOX OR POLARITY

It's clear that you can't map a whole system—it's too big and moving too quickly to map. Like those geographers who will assert that the only fully representative map would have a 1:1 scale, most systems and complexity thinkers note that there is no way to get your head around both the dynamics and all the interconnections in the system. So instead you have to explore and understand the system, get as many perspectives on it as possible without trusting that any set of perspectives (even if they're diverse) will be fully representative. One helpful way for leaders to begin to gather multiple perspectives when facing polarity or paradox is to make a polarity map. This simple little technique, created by Barry Johnson, is unexpectedly transformational and very easy for leaders to pick up and use in meetings right away.[9] Understanding the polarities and paradoxes of your chosen direction helps leaders draw the right sort of boundary: the boundary that attempts to deal with the complexity inside the system rather than trying to solve it away.

The first step is to notice where you have polarities at play. Polarities are issues that are never solvable in any way that could last (you *solve* problems but you have to *manage* polarities—solutions bounce off or even make things worse). Whenever you think about a pendulum swinging from one side and then overcorrecting to the other, you have a polarity. Each side of the polarity mutually creates the other so they are interdependent; they need each other to exist. If you have a question about how many long-term employees should be staffed on a project team versus new employees, that's a polarity: no single and ongoing correct answer, and the idea of long-term employees is actually created by the idea of new employees, and vice versa. If everyone had been there exactly the same amount of time, the distinction wouldn't exist and there would be no polarity to manage.

Once you know that something is a polarity, you pick mutually acceptable names for each side. When you want to understand multiple perspectives, what you call a thing really matters, so it's not OK to call one side of the polarity something like "sensible solutions" and the other "loopy notions we have to go along with." Whether a name is attractive or not depends exclusively on the perspectives of those involved. So if the people in your organization like the idea of "old-timers" and "new blood" and use those terms themselves, then you might get away with using those on either side of the polarity map. But if one (or both) of those is offensive, pull back and get a descriptive and uncontroversial name for both sides ("less than 5 years with the company" and "more than five years with the company"). Then you're ready to draw.

The drawing begins with that ubiquitous shape beloved of consultants the world over—a two-by-two matrix.[10] On the left, write the name of one side of the polarity, and on the right, write the name of the other side of the polarity. In the top two boxes, write the positive pieces of each side, or, what does this side of the polarity really bring into the world that's wonderful? In the bottom two boxes, write about the shadow side, or, what does this side of the polarity bring into the world that is negative? If the map isn't well fleshed out, or if some of the boxes seem much richer than others, you probably don't have enough perspectives on the issue yet (if it's a genuine polarity, the poles have equal weight and so should lead to equally rich positives and equally frightening negatives). You might need help from folks elsewhere in the organization or even outside the organization altogether. Once the quadrants are fully mapped, though, you have a space that holds a whole variety of perspectives in it.[11]

When any of us is faced with a polarity, we might have the urge to solve it. Most leaders have this reflex. The trouble with polarities is that they can't be solved; one of their defining characteristics is that you can't do without either the left or right side. Often, when organizations try to create a solution to what is really a polarity, they lean too hard into that one side. That tends to end up with the organization falling down into the negative features before pulling itself up into the positive features of the opposite side—often with some kind of change program. And because ambiguity makes change difficult, leaders of change are often advised to boil the issue down into simple propositions: "We need greater clarity about our priorities, roles, and results. This will make us a more effective organization and we will remove the costly churn and confusion that comes from too much flexibility and uncertainty." That is a clear call to arms that the team can rally around, going from the bad present to the better future. The clarity in this messaging comes from dropping the "ambiguity" side of the polarity. It might not be a sustainable change, but it is clear for now. In a year or two, though, the leaders will be declaring the need to slice through rigid systems and procedures and the one-size-fits-all mentality that drives the organization. They'll worry about the way clarity has forced them down pathways that seem opposed to innovation. They'll want to create autonomous units encouraged to innovate. Then they'll swing that way to "solve" the problem of having too much clarity (and this story could pivot back and forth for years). When we treat polarities as problems to be solved, we tend to oscillate back and forth from one side of the polarity map to the other. It is déjà vu all over again as the wizened old-timers in the organization will observe.

We have one client that pivots on the "local autonomy versus centralized control" polarity; there have been more than a dozen organizational reviews that try to solve that one. In our example in this book, FACS has this polarity operating, along with a number of others. Nearly all of our clients struggle to get on top of the "long-term thinking versus short-term thinking" polarity, and most of them feel themselves pulled to the gravitational force of the short-term side (and the dangerous bottom quadrant that goes along with that overemphasis). A related polarity for our private-sector clients is how much to invest in growth, which may take some years to be realized, or how much to focus on shorter-term profitability measures. And in each case, the impulse is to solve the issue rather than see that it needs to be managed purposefully over time. Our human impulse seeks to create comfort by fixing a thing once and for all rather than admitting that we're going to have to live in the struggle of the polarity. This impulse is reinforced by the painful experience of those leaders who have tried to change things over the years and have had their best efforts soak into the sand. They often conclude they need to move earlier and more decisively if they are to get changes to stick. They end up stressing how bad things are now and how much better they will become when the problem is fixed, because only by creating a shining vision of the future and an imminent burning platform will they get any sustained movement from people in the organization.

If you're going to avoid this impulse, the idea is to think of these polarities as a dynamic wave you're surfing all the time, not a platform you can simply build and expect to stay put. You'll never solve it, just as a surfer never solves the wave—she just stays on top of it as it shifts and changes, matching her weight with the rhythm and force of the wave. When she finally gets knocked over, she gets back up and has another try. People love surfing waves. They bob like seals in icy water for the privilege of being ground into the sand when they make a mistake. But when the wave is right and they're on top of it, they are both part of the force of the water and separate from that. They are lifted and soaring. We could love surfing polarities, too, if we could just recognize the ride for what it is and learn from the mistakes we make. But the feedback loops are much longer when we're dealing with organizational polarities, and the forces are never so clear. Still, if we can harness and hold these multiple perspectives, we can watch the patterns and learn.

"This conversation about polarities is interesting," Jarred said, surprising himself with his boldness. He had kept a pretty low profile until now, in part because he was confused about why they were talking about polarities when he thought they'd be talking about strategy and vision. "It seems to me like the whole vision we've been trying to implement is itself a polarity, isn't it? I mean, you don't have the products-services conversation unless you have both products and services. We wouldn't be measuring the percentages of products to services unless there were some kind of polarity, right? They seem mutually dependent and interrelated, and maybe that means that we'll never find exactly the right number, or maybe the numbers will shift and change based on the market and on our internal capabilities and all kinds of other factors we don't even know about yet."

"I think you're totally right," Hannah said, excitedly. "Let's map it."

As the group looked at the polarity map (shown in Figure 4.1), they began to see more clearly some of the things that had gotten in the way. They had such high hopes for what they could become, but they had not been willing to give up much of what they were doing or even perhaps to be different in the ways they did things, and so they were all leaning quite heavily into the software side of the polarity map, and they could see that they were beginning

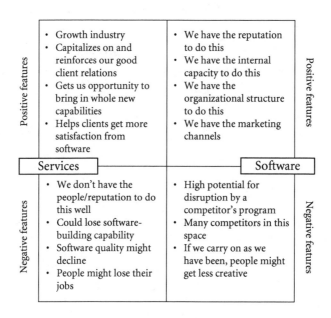

FIGURE 4.1   Actualeyes services and software polarity map

to fall into some of the negative features of that side. The fears in the bottom half of the services line were enough, though, to keep them from rushing into services too quickly. They were afraid of losing their past as they moved into a new future.

"So, Squint," Murray began, and Jarred was surprised to hear the hesitancy in his boss's voice. "If you want to really make this vision possible, we'll have to do a reorg, won't we? Cut back on software engineers and hire consultants that are used to providing services to people?" Jarred felt the heat rise into his face with this question. No wonder Murray was so hesitant to ask that question. As head of engineering, and the most powerful person at Actualeyes outside of the three founders, he had quite a lot to lose in this transition—not only power but also the relationships with his people.

Squint glanced quickly and Hannah and Arlen, and then looked back at the group, his face as serious as Jarred ever remembered seeing it. "I can see where you're going with that question, Murray. And we have certainly talked about it among ourselves a lot. I understand that to make the service offering really succeed we need a significant proportion of our people behaving quite differently in quite different jobs: say, 20% to 40% in two years' time. We will need to be bigger. Some of the people in an expanded service function will need to be new. I hope a good chunk of them will be software folks who can learn to make the transition." Squint offered his shy, rueful grin. "I figure if I can make it on this change journey, then there are lots more capable folks working for us now who will make the change way faster than I have. So we will expand as a company and many of us will get to expand as individuals, too. That seems pretty cool to me." He took a deep breath and continued.

"It is also the case that some of our software specialists may not want to be part of the change. My guess is that will be a very small number in the end, but I'd be interested in your estimate on this, Murray. I want us to work together to try and protect as many of those jobs as possible—and to help people grow to meet these new challenges. But I'm guessing we will lose some folks along the way," Squint finished.

The group was silent for a minute, their minds running over the people they feared wouldn't be able to make the change and wondering whether they themselves might be on that list. Hannah read the apprehension and decided to add another layer. "But this shift can't all rest on structural change and a reorganization," she said. "I also have rarely ever heard of a reorg actually delivering significant behavioral change, and it's behavioral change that drives new possibilities. There must be some way we can begin to bring our vision into the world without dipping too far into some of our worst fears—on either side at the bottom of this map. So we need a strategy that is clear enough to move people, open enough to allow the ambiguity of a changing future, one that keeps the top half of the software polarity map without dipping too far into the bottom half, and that pulls in the top half of the services polarity. Looks like Squint won't get that swim after lunch after all."

"OK, I get it," Squint said smiling. "No swimming in anything other than complexity for a while. But here's the thing—don't we have a clear enough direction by now? Or is it just clear in my head? Here is what I have heard and where I have got to. See if it makes sense to you or how you can sharpen it up. You've all talked compellingly about both the fears and the delights on both sides of the polarity map. We want to hold on in the top half with the best hopes of the value we can add by doing both software and services well. And we want to have as little of what we fear in the bottom half, right? That means building our services as we maintain our software but shifting our energy a little, because I think we're all afraid that we're holding on too hard to software right now. Remember that this move into more services emerged from the patterns we were seeing in customer requests in the first place. I feel like we have a sense of what we want to make possible, and we have a sense of our fears about what might happen if we fail. Isn't that enough to go on? Don't we all now have something of a sense of what to do next?"

"I'm not sure what to do next week," Jarred heard himself saying. "Now that we've been talking, I can see that I haven't been leaning hard enough into this space, but the truth is I'm not sure how to make a change in that or what to ask specifically of my people." He felt himself blushing furiously, wishing he could suck the words back into his mouth.

"To be honest, I'm not sure either," Murray admitted. The sound of vague agreement swept through the room.

Hannah smiled. "I don't think we're quite at the action point yet. Come on, we're a data company. Let's look at what we know so far!"

HARVESTING MULTIPLE PERSPECTIVES TO UNDERSTAND ATTRACTORS

There is another set of ideas from complexity theory that we find useful here as we build toward creating spaces for vision in organizations. This is the notion of *attractors*. If a boundary is something that creates a limit (something we don't want to cross), an attractor is something that pulls us toward itself. We both happen to live in New Zealand, and that's a land of great attractors and important boundaries. The mountains and the sea pull tourists and residents alike toward them, and the boundaries (of where you can swim or climb) help keep people from getting hurt in those majestic (and dangerous) spaces.

Organizations have attractors, too; these can be people or ideas or spaces: anything that others are drawn toward. Google is known for creating long tables in its cafeterias: attractors for conversations. Some leaders are known to attract the finest and most innovative people around them. Some ideas are (or can become) "sticky" and attract others. The tricky thing is that while many have tried to figure out the perfect recipe for an attractor, attractors don't get created and rolled out by an R&D team. Instead, they're often already in an organization, waiting to be discovered by people who are looking for them. Or they're created when some other initiative happens, without people meaning to create them at all. No matter how much gets written on how to make ideas (or products or CEOs) "stick," or how to create clusters of excellence, it is still more art than science, or perhaps more evolutionary possibility than grand, all-knowing design. Again, multiple and diverse perspectives help us all imagine and create possible new attractors. Because even though you can create the conditions for an attractor (by putting in those long lunch tables, tossing a baseball and bat to a bunch of kids gathered in an empty lot, and so on), you can't be sure it'll actually attract what you want it to attract (What if particular tables get permanently occupied by groups of staff? Or if the kids ignore the bat entirely—or start beating each other with it?).

Attractors, like boundaries, aren't inherently good or bad. A shared break room can attract creative collaboration or nasty gossip (or both). A powerful vision can attract excitement or dread (or both). In a complex system, leaders need to pay attention to both positive and negative attractors, and then encourage experiments (that are safe-to-fail rather than failsafe) that seek to minimize the negative aspects and increase the positive ones.

For example, social networking sites work only if they are strong attractors. No matter how brilliant the ideas and features, if you create a social networking site no one visits, you've got nothing. And once you've got members, you have to be careful not to weaken the way your site acts as an attractor. Yet you can't know for sure how your members will react to changes (nor can you tell how they'll react if nothing changes). Facebook takes some of its lessons from other social networking sites (sometimes you can learn where your boundaries should be by watching the mistakes of others who inadvertently created mistakes that are not safe to fail). Friendster, a precursor to Facebook, was wildly popular in its day, with more than 100 million users. Then it made a change to its user interface and the whole site collapsed; people left and took their friends with them. The site went from being a strong attractor to a weak one, and it experienced the sort of nonlinear change that characterizes complex systems. While that wasn't a safe-to-fail experiment for Friendster, it helped Facebook more carefully watch and shape its attractors. Now when Facebook wants to make a change, it'll tell users about it in advance, then roll out the change in waves to relatively small numbers of users and monitor the change carefully. This safe-to-fail approach means that if Facebook makes a change that pushes members away (or is clunky or buggy to use), it will affect only a small number of people, and Facebook can fix it before it creates exponential decline in use.[12] Keeping your eye on the changes in the main attractors—for better or for worse—will help you both pay close attention to the present conditions and shape the way the future emerges.

Right now Squint is finding that the idea of services is not yet attracting very much; at least it's not attracting anything that ends up in increasing percentage of revenue. And it's not that ideas can't be attractors; indeed, ideas, stories, and rumors can be the most powerful attractors of all (imagine the ways the stock market gyrates around on the abstract idea of consumer confidence). At Actualeyes, there could be many reasons the "service" idea isn't attracting new revenue. Maybe they don't have the people with the skills; maybe that 13% of revenue is all they're capable of right now. Maybe the customers don't see the company this way. Maybe those who are capable of this work are distracted with software concerns, as Jarred is now considering. Maybe there's a fear throughout the organization (that you'd see in the bottom half of a polarity map) that if it leans too far into service, people will end up getting fired. Maybe the reward systems and performance systems that have been built for a software organization undercut some of the more relational behaviors needed in a successful services firm (there is no charge code for creating trust in relationships). Some of these reasons might directly compete with others; there can be multiple true (and also contradictory) answers in a complex space. So there's no need to figure out what the "central reason" is; just design safe-to-fail experiments to both discover more about the system (and the multiple reasons the attractor isn't so attractive yet) and work to change the system in the desired ways.

Hannah sat on the floor in the big family room in front of the old coffee table that still bore the scars of Squint and Arlen's youthful misuse. "I found these on my closet shelf last night," she said, pouring handfuls of little metal pieces—balls and flat diamonds—onto the table.

"I loved those!" Squint said, the excitement in his voice drawing laughter from the group.

"It's going to be hellish to separate the shapes again," Arlen complained.

"I'm making a point," Hannah told him.

"You're making a mess," Arlen retorted.

"I am totally taking those back to my house in Proucheford," Squint muttered.

"I've been watching the work 4Sight is doing," Hannah said, smiling at Jarred. "One of its cool features is searching for attractors, those pieces of data that seem to have an unusual number of other pieces of data attached to them. I want us to look at the Actualeyes attractors. It'll be way less clear than the 4Sight report because we're people looking at people and not a computer program looking at data, but still, I think we can see patterns in our behavior—the way we see patterns of these metal pieces on this old table. What kinds of things do you notice here?" she asked the group as the balls settled and the pieces stopped moving.

"The round ones are more influenced by the scars in the table," someone noticed, pointing to the gathering of balls in the series of divots where Squint and Arlen had missed the nail in whatever invention they were constructing.

"Nice."

"There seems to be a dip in the middle where even the flat ones gather," someone else added, pointing to the area where Squint and Arlen had often landed as they leapt from couch to table to chair.

"Great! Now imagine this is us. Maybe the round ones are the people who are more easily influenced by the context—say the group of people who is really tuned in to what people are talking and thinking about. Maybe the flat pieces are like the people who like to find their own way and stay there. And you can think about the marks on the table as parts of our Actualeyes context. Perhaps the divots are like the software production shipping priorities that shape each team's behavior. Maybe they're like the way our desks are arranged in the office. Maybe the big dip in the middle is the current way we are doing our business planning or rewarding performance. Maybe it's the way we are having conversations in our teams. I'm not sure. What I'd like you to do is think about the big and little attractors that we have right now in our business that seem to be creating patterns of our behavior. And then . . ." She smiled and moved her hand under the table. The metal pieces started to clump together in new ways, balls rolling and the flat diamonds sliding across the table. "We want to talk about how we create new attractors—like these magnets I found on the closet shelf—that bring some new patterns that move us closer to our direction."

"Whoa, I thought you were holding a séance," cried Squint, feigning disappointment.

"I left my Ouija board at home," Hannah smiled. "But seriously, you've all been collecting data—from customers, from your people, from the market. Let's share what we know. Let's search for attractors. You're looking for patterns in the way people gather or ideas stick together or work gets done. Don't get lost in the individual stories right now, but see if you can pull far enough above the stories to see the patterns, like we did on the table. I know that's a little bit metaphorical, but is it clear enough what we're going to do?" There were murmurs of assent that sounded tentative to Jarred's ears, but maybe that's because he wasn't totally sure what to do himself.

"Give it a try," Hannah told them. "We're all just messing around in this space, so let's just go play with it."

USING MULTIPLE PERSPECTIVES TO BUILD SAFE-TO-FAIL EXPERIMENTS

In the predictable parts of our worlds, all of our efforts gathering data about the past and forecasting into the future might leave us with a clear path and a set of targets to help us know how to walk the path; we figure out what's most probable, and we plan for it. We focus on predicting what might work, prototyping and piloting solutions. The assumption is that there is a right answer within our grasp and it is a matter of narrowing down on it.

In the unpredictable portions of our worlds, there are too many possibilities to track, so it's agility and a thoughtful evolution that we want. Instead of predicting and piloting, our efforts are to create the conditions for a wide set of experiments that can be carried out at many levels throughout the organization to create the possibility for helpful attractors to form and negative ones to dissolve. At the same time, these practices create the conditions for people to learn while staying agile enough to handle the shocks that might come next. The experiments themselves need to be open to as much variety as the multiple perspectives can offer. If people, capabilities, or knowledge are distributed, then leaders have the even more difficult task of enabling experimentation across a decentralized organization or network. In both cases, the focus is on enabling experimentation and learning like mad from what happens next.

We have a set of ideas that will guide your thinking about safe-to-fail experiments, but it's important to also have a sense of the spirit with which these experiments should be created. There's a great TED Talk that embodies this idea. Tom Wujec talks about his "marshmallow challenge," in which teams are given spaghetti, string, tape, and a marshmallow and are instructed to build the tallest possible tower—with the marshmallow on top.[13] The very highest towers are built by architects who understand the design principles that make the towers stable (this is good news for all of us who live in buildings). The second most successful group of people are children, who build much taller towers than their untrained adult counterparts. Two key reasons the kids do better than us grownups are also important in the world of the safe-to-fail experiment. One is that kids prototype; they don't spend their time planning and debating and coming up with the one best idea. Instead, they try things and try other things and then try more, and in doing that, they learn while they're building rather than just thinking things through. This is key to the safe-to-fail approach. The second core reason that kids do better is that, well, they're kids. They have a childlike approach, a twinkle in their eye, a giggle about the wild and fun prospects they are creating. We have learned that that twinkle in the eye is also a key ingredient to creating really innovative and interesting safe-to-fail experiments. The most successful suite of experiments are created by groups that spend time laughing and trying out wild ideas, that bring in something they saw on reality TV or something they read about in a gossip magazine. When groups face the creation of safe-to-fail experiments as a serious and cognitive enterprise, they tend to come up with things that are, as they discover, just too safe (and often not particularly conducive to learning or to failure). Laughter and lightness fuel creativity.

With the mindsets of enabling experimentation and learning like curious kids, there are also a couple of principles to remember before starting on experiments: one is to develop and hold to an overarching direction; the other is to set clear safety boundaries for experimenting. Having developed an open-minded mindset and a direction, and set boundaries, we are ready to go. The first general safe-to-fail experiment guideline is that there must be several of these experiments running in parallel so that you can be gathering information about the system in several different ways simultaneously.[14] Remember, because the organization is changing as the experiments run, it doesn't work to learn from one experiment and then believe the organization will stay stable as you create a second experiment; this is why multiples are better. These experiments are not pilots to be rolled out across the whole organization eventually. They are small interventions that shift the system as people learn about it, so that you wouldn't anticipate that the same experiment in one place or time would have the same results as another place or time. If you were to ultimately see that one of the experiments works reliably across context and time, you might believe that really is in the probable world and roll it out more widely. That might be a happy and helpful discovery, but it is not the goal of these experiments.

More difficult than the idea that you have to run many experiments in parallel is that it helps to have some experiments that contradict one another, so that if one succeeds, another should fail. This idea emerges from the assumption that if all your experiments are headed in the same direction and with the same general assumptions, you are not testing and scanning the system widely enough. This is especially hard to get your head around because we so easily believe in the solutions we begin to develop. We had a financial services client who wanted to shift people's attention from short-term results toward longer-term thinking. A core set of experiments emerged that attempted to limit access information about short-term results, figuring that if people had less information about short-term results, they'd fixate less on them. Leaders designed one experiment around not distributing quarterly earnings reports, another about changing a meeting agenda in which monthly numbers were discussed, and so on. We noticed this pattern (all experiments moving in the same direction and controlled by the same basic set of assumptions about what would work), and we tried to move against this to create a new experiment. In this case, it was to overreport short-term financial results with daily or hourly information. We built a hypothesis that if people had a blizzard of short-term information, maybe it would become less interesting and their gaze would move to a longer time horizon. This idea might be totally misguided, but it was an experiment that could safely fail if only a small number of people were trying it out, and it looked like they'd learn a lot on the way. (Note that rolling this idea out across a whole organization or division would not make it safe to fail.)

The third condition for an experiment being safe to fail is that they are finely grained, pragmatic, short term, and cheap in the experimental phase. Remember that phrase "ambiguity is the enemy of change"? These experiments should be crisp and clear so that everyone knows exactly what new thing they're trying. It's not micromanaging to be so specific; it's about setting the rules of a short game meant to explore a new possibility. These are little experiments and shouldn't require lots of time, money, or organizational effort to try out.

Fourth, remember how important that neighborly idea was from Chapter 3? At least some of the experiments should be at the edges of the problem rather than at the center, perhaps not even focused on the particular issue you're trying to solve (but a neighbor of that issue). Again, this is about reaching out beyond where you think the solution is most likely to be found and widening your approach.

Fifth, as we will argue again and again, diversity matters. Snowden suggests that some experiments should use what he calls "naive capability." He means those people with deep expertise in a totally different field that might give new insight (like bringing in a scriptwriter to help solve a community engagement issue). The core idea here is to broaden even the way you're thinking about what makes up a diverse team. Think about the diversity you usually consider, and then think beyond that to other forms of diversity as well.

Finally, don't be afraid to experiment on multiple problems with cluster of experiments, and don't be afraid to take on a big issue with a small experiment. In a system, these problems are likely to clump together, so a single experiment might solve multiple related issues. Similarly, effort and results are unrelated, so a small effort can lead to a significant outcome (just as, disappointingly, a large effort can lead to little).

So the fundamentally different task of strategy in this volatile and uncertain context is to create the conditions to understand and move from the present into an emerging future. As sports coaches help athletes take a stance that allows them to move quickly in whatever direction a play takes them, leaders help keep an organization ready to move well in a changing context by choosing a direction and experimenting and learning into the future. As people understand how you want the inclinations in the system to shift over time, they'll be able to use that understanding to create a diversity of approaches—and learn from what works well and what fails (but safely). Leadership here is about shaping and ordering the field of play so that others will be able to innovate inside it.

Jarred looked around at the many flip charts covering the walls. They had moved inside to escape the threat of showers on the first night and stayed inside through the driving rain during the whole second day. He wondered about how to make sense of where this team had gotten to and how he would explain this to his mother when he got back to his place in Proucheford on Wednesday night. He wondered if she were as confused about her organizational issues as he was about these. She had so much more experience than he did, but it was also clear that her organization had many more levels of complexity than Actualeyes did.

Jarred understood the basics that they were working toward at Actualeyes. They had talked about a vision with a higher purpose: to enable more human connection through technology to create a more linked and richer world. There was a direction of moving more toward service but not a target of outputs, because they had talked about the dangers of targets. There was the question about what boundaries the vision and strategy might put in place because the boundaries would let them play in safe-to-fail ways, as Hannah kept reminding them.

And now there was this new question about attractors, which had been the topic of conversation this morning. They had pulled out data they had gathered to try to search for the patterns about what right now was attracting the kind of behavior they wanted (like engaging more in services) versus what was attracting the kind of behavior they didn't want (like spending all their time and resources dealing with building and selling software).

Some clear patterns had stood out. Their business model, teamwork model, and review system were all about creating faster programming cycles and getting new products to market. It was clear that these systems attracted the kind of behavior that built software at the expense of services. Jarred noticed in his team the way the rewards inside those models had created the incentives for him to break apart pieces of the programming tasks so that he could churn out faster and faster updates as feedback from customers came in. Following Murray's lead, he had automated the customer complaint system so that information could be quickly distributed to the relevant person. This created more distance between his people and the customers, and now Jarred realized that it had created the lack of engagement that Michelle had pointed to and others had reinforced.

"OK, we see this pattern across each of the product lines," Kelly, the head of people, summarized. "We see that our focus on launching products and rewarding programming work has attracted this same pattern of behavior, and that the folks who have been building the service work are the ones who were most interested in service work in the first place. I can think of a couple of HR systems we could fiddle with to see if they have any magnetic pull here."

"I think it's a good set of experiments there, actually," Squint said as he joined the group. He read the flip charts: "I like this one about patching through the customers to engineers once a week to talk through the bugs in the system. I bet we'll learn a lot from that one."

"Yeah, like how much our engineers hate to be interrupted when they're programming," Kelly joked.

"Maybe," Squint said smiling. "Remember that these don't need to work; they just need to help us learn new things." He turned to another flip chart. "This is confusing—what's this one about?"

Stephen, the new communications manager cleared his throat. "Um, that's my writing." Jarred had originally been surprised that Stephen had been invited after only one week on the job, but they were all surprised at how much his outsider perspective helped them build innovative ideas. "That was an idea that was just meant to pull in the opposite direction of that last one. In that last one we're putting customers and their needs first—as we should, I totally agree. But I'm wondering what would happen if we just left a couple of engineers to built whatever their fancy was for a week or so. Whatever product or feature they were most excited about. Some of them might lead to nothing, but some might get out in front of our customers and solve needs the customers haven't even noticed."

Squint smiled. "Very Steve Jobs of you," he said. "I'm game to try that one too—as long as we can contain the size of it and shut it off if it turns out engineers are infinitely happier when they never have to think of customers. But I've interrupted your process. What were you talking about before I arrived?"

"Um, we were just chatting, I think," Jarred admitted. "We were talking about how we did our interviews with folks in advance of this meeting and how easy it was to get people to sit down and talk with us."

"Yeah, I noticed that, too," Squint said. "People loved telling me about their jobs. I thought maybe it was because I was the CEO though. How'd you go in your first week, Stephen?"

"It was weird, really," Stephen said. "I happened to interview the guys outside smoking and I didn't know until later that those were the guys who are doing most of the software and services work. I didn't look for that set of people; I just caught them as they were hanging out on the front steps."

"I hate that cloud of smoke," Hannah muttered.

"All the marketing guys smoke, too," Jarred said. "It smells like an ashtray up there."

"Weird that the marketing guys and the software guys who are into service all smoke," Stephen joked. "Maybe if more of us picked up smoking, we'd increase our service offerings?"

"I don't think that counts as safe to fail," Hannah quipped, and the group laughed.

"Wait, though, isn't it?" Kelly asked. "Not the smoking, I mean, but the fact that those engineers were hanging out with the marketing guys every single day? Wouldn't that be a thing we could put in place?"

"Not with something carcinogenic," Squint said.

"Or hallucinogenic," added Hannah.

"No, but how about with something delicious and tempting. Food? Good coffee? Free office supplies? A 3-D printer? I don't know—but something that would keep the marketing guys and some different engineers in the same space."

"That is a great idea," Squint told her. "We could even figure out which foods are the most magnetic! I think these ideas are way better than the inspirational posters I was worried we'd be making."

"OK, this looks like a good set," Kelly said. "Squint, how will you choose which of these goes first?"

"Squint? Choosing? Fat chance!" snorted Hannah. "But, in reality, there shouldn't be much choosing to do."

Kelly looked confused. "But we have so many ideas alive right now, and we're just one group. There must be dozens of ideas across the whole set of us."

Hannah smiled and explained, "That's true, and we won't do them all, but we can do lots of them. When we get back together with the other groups, we'll drop out any experiments that fall outside the boundaries we decided on in terms of the direction, the safety zone, or the scale of the experiments. Everything left just has to pass one more test—we have to be sure that any experiment can be expanded if it goes well or dampened down if it goes badly. Then we just have to find people who are willing to lead the experiment. As long as we have that, we can run a bunch of these at once."

"I'm up for leading the experiment about the best food to attract marketing guys and engineers!" Jarred said, laughing.

"Yeah, and that one is easy to dampen. If it doesn't work, you can just take the food away," Stephen added.

"Now we can spot the newbie who is a tech virgin," Jarred teased. "You can't give free food to software engineers and then just take it away cold turkey! These things need to be withdrawn in carefully programmed stages. Otherwise there is flaming or dodgy code—or worse!"

"When do we run the experiment about how the strategy team that plays together comes to the best outcome?" Squint asked, eyeing the lake, now sunlit after the rain. "It's short term, finely grained, and very inexpensive to test out. We can look for whether we're more optimistic and creative after our swim than we were before it!"

Hannah laughed. "That sounds like an experiment we can't run in parallel, Squint. Who would run another one up against that?"

"Maybe we could have an experiment about swimming versus lounging in the sun?" Kelly suggested, smiling. "I'll lead the lounging portion."

"Would we have one about people staying inside and continuing to work, like a control group?" Jarred asked.

"No control groups in complexity," Hannah reminded him, but you could offer staying inside as a third experiment. That's pretty safe to fail."

"You're on!" Squint said. "Let's take 45 minutes and see what happens next." He called the parameters of the three experiments out to the rest of the room, and people burst into action and movement, heading back to the bunkhouse to change or heading out to the grass to just lie around.

"Looks like that last option was a real failure," Squint said to Jarred, as they stood in the empty room together. "But we lost nothing, and we're already learning."

"We should be already swimming," Jarred laughed, pulling off his T-shirt and grabbing a towel from the stack next to the door. "You're about to learn that I'm faster than you!" he said as he took off for the lake.

"No fair!" Squint called after him, pulling off his shirt. "You're not enabling learning at all! I already knew that!" But Jarred couldn't hear him over the rush of water in his ears.

5 MAKE RATIONAL USE OF HUMAN

IRRATIONALITY

Ramona was frustrated, and Yolanda could hardly blame her. The *Proucheford Chronicle* was calling for Ramona's resignation, and now her boss's boss was spending a week in her office. Even though Yolanda was clear she was only there to learn, she could see how this looked like a pretty odd thing for a CEO to be doing. Why wouldn't Ramona be defensive? Still, it was a pain to explain again, "I'm just trying to learn things, Ramona. It's kind of an experiment for me to be here, to see if I can see with new eyes and uncover a new pattern. As I've said, I don't have any particular agenda other than the one we share—to figure out how to create the best possible system to support and protect at-risk kids and families."

Ramona stopped pacing and looked at Yolanda warily. "Then you should let me do my job! I have talked with Margie about the two cases she's responsible for, and we've made significant changes. Even after the first incident I put new measures in place! I have been totally straight with you, with our people, with the press, with the community—with everyone."

"I want you to do your job, and I trust you to do it well. But I also need to learn more about what's going on here—not just for the families in your bureau but for all the families in our care across the state!"

"With respect," Ramona took a deep breath, "you have a whole organization to do the learning for you. You know we have reporting, oversight, auditors, and regularly scheduled reviews up the wazoo. Your idea about also now interviewing the caseworkers is disruptive. They are already overwhelmed, and you are likely to make them nervous and distracted. And they won't tell you anything I haven't already told you."

Yolanda could practically hear the voice of her younger self coming out of Ramona's mouth. She remembered well when she was so clear and passionate about what was true and not true and when she really believed there was one best way to go—and she knew which way that was. She felt an odd surge of affection for Ramona. In fact, there was a way she wished she could be as clear on this as Ramona was. Yolanda could not even be quite sure of what she was looking for on this trip to the Proucheford bureau office. She was just feeling her way. It was almost as if she knew more about her uncertainties than anything else. She knew this Proucheford experiment involved risks beyond ruffling Ramona and her staff. There was the risk of word racing through the FACS ranks that the boss was wandering uncertain and confused through local bureaus and avoiding the hard calls back at headquarters. There was also the risk that she would not find anything other than more clarity about what she did not know, or that she would grasp the first big insight that occurred to her and put it up in lights because a boss needs to be seen to know stuff. Still, all those risks were well inside the guardrails she had determined with Doug and Curtis. This was her stuff: she was torn by her desire to be open and comfortable about her uncertainties, and also to clearly be the leader people look to for a clear sense of direction.

"I think you're wrong that they won't tell me anything you haven't, Ramona," she said quietly. "My hunch is they're likely to know lots about the situation that you don't know—not because you're not knowledgeable about this, but because there's just so much to know. I bet they know lots that *they* don't even know they know. We just need to ask them some different questions to understand their many different perspectives."

Ramona sighed heavily. "You know how I feel about this, Yolanda. I have talked to Margie and she knows this is a big deal. We are working our way through to the most logical outcome here."

Yolanda smiled at her. "I have total confidence that you'll find the most appropriate and logical solution. But I'm looking for something a little less rational."

Ramona was perplexed. "Why would you be looking for something *less* rational?"

"We've been talking a lot lately about complexity, and I have a sense that it matches in some ways what I've studied about the quirks of human systems. I have a hunch that this stuff we're dealing with here isn't just about the way complex systems change but is also shaped by the way human beings are themselves complex and quirky. Just as systems don't behave in rational, linear ways, humans aren't wholly rational either. I'd just like to play around a little in that space."

"But this is not playtime, Yolanda," Ramona told her, surprising herself by her bluntness to her chief executive. "I have worked really hard to get the people here to really focus on what is most important. My people and I get absolutely that this is a deadly serious issue, and we're dedicated to finding a way through."

"I get that, Ramona—I really do. I don't think anyone could take this more seriously than I do." Yolanda was horrified to find her eyes welling up with tears. "I promise I'm not here to play. I am here to help. Not to help you to fix something that I find here in your office but to learn from what is happening here and to try to help across the whole organization. I know that what you most want is what's best for the at-risk families in Proucheford and the state—and you want what's best for the people here in the bureau. You have to know that that's what's most important to me, too. I just think we need to be working as many angles as we possibly can. You can see the logic of that, can't you?"

"Not exactly, boss, but I do know how totally committed you are to helping kids and families," Ramona said, with a rueful smile. "I know you don't just play at stuff. I'll keep pushing ahead with my rational plans, and you focus on the irrational ones."

"OK, so can we begin with what you found when you first got here?"

"Yolanda, we've been over this," Ramona said again.

"Humor me, OK? I have some new data and some new perspectives, and I think it will let me listen to your story in a new way. Tell me again about your assessment of this office when you took this job six months ago. I'm going to take the long walk from my perspective to yours and really try to see it the way you understand it."

Ramona took a sip of her black coffee, straightened her shoulders, and launched into a familiar story. "It was a mess, as you know. The caseworkers were working longer hours here than any other bureau in the state, and they were exhausted. No one was getting their paperwork in on time, and the files were in a terrible state. It took me the first couple of weeks to just be able to compile information about how many cases were open, under investigation, and so on. Each caseworker was more like a mother hen with a bunch of chicks, too busy to worry about the other mother hens, much less the whole farm. Everybody had their heads down and was working so hard they didn't notice what was going on with anyone else."

"That's really helpful. With all these people working so hard, were relations strained here at the office?"

"Actually, no. That's something my predecessor did particularly well—maybe even too well."

"What do you mean by 'too well'? Things were too friendly?" Yolanda looked up from her notes.

"Well, the office had crossed over the personal-professional boundary. I agree that workplaces should be happy places to be productive, but this was absurd. There were kids in the office all the time—and sometimes people had even begun bringing their dogs to work, saying that they were working so late into the night that they couldn't leave their dogs alone so long! It was more like going to a family barbecue than an office."

"Really? Geez! I hadn't heard that, though the engagement scores here always seemed oddly high in our yearly engagement survey, given how hard people seemed to be working and how short staffed they always seemed to be."

"It's that people weren't working efficiently. I came in and cleaned a lot of that up. Kids and dogs have to be at home because it's too distracting to have them here in the office—and dangerous, too, for the kids, the dogs, and the people around them. There was also a whole lot of working from home and I changed those rules so that only our top performers could take advantage of that—I'm not a big fan of letting people who can't focus well in the office work at home, where there might be more distractions. And to judge who was in that top-performer category, we started making some targets and posting some numbers about who was on target and who wasn't."

"Wow, that couldn't have been a popular move," Yolanda said, appreciating the logic of the decisions and remembering how hard she had wrestled with these kinds of issues in the past.

Ramona gave one of her rare smiles. "No, not a popular move. I'm not motivated by popularity, as you probably noticed. It's important to me that we do our jobs and that we do them with excellence. This is the sixth bureau I've seen in shambles across three different agencies, and I follow my regular approach—it's pretty simple work. You just have to maintain the dogged certainty that your way will take people to a better place—even as you get a whole lot of complaints."

"Tell me about that approach," Yolanda asked.

"First, you have to get the basics right—just get people coming to the office ready to work, and clean up the environment so that people can focus on their jobs. In the last department I worked in, they had music playing all the time, which was fine for the ones who were playing it, but really distracting or annoying to others. It didn't make me popular with the music players when I shut that down, but the others were grateful."

"OK, first the basics," Yolanda said, making notes. "In this office, instead of stopping the music players, it was getting people to leave their pets and kids at home, and getting them to work less from home themselves. Then what?"

"Next step is to understand the work itself and introduce efficiencies there. When are people doing redundant work? When are people not following proper procedure? When is proper procedure too vague?"

Yolanda was scribbling notes furiously. "OK, what'd you find here about that step?"

"Things were a mess from that perspective, too. People were following different procedures even for the same sorts of case. The checklists they were using to make decisions were vague and confusing and allowed for too much variety of response—not clear at all, which makes them not very helpful if you're using them to make judgments."

"Boy, that's a lot to institute in six months. How has it been going?"

"Well, I put in a new layer of supervisors to help make the changes. I found the most efficient caseworkers and reduced their caseloads so that they could support the others to take on some of these new procedures. I also cut some deadwood, letting five people go."

"I guess there's no surprise that your engagement scores have fallen so much over the past few months," Yolanda said, understanding this trend fully and feeling confused about it—much of what Ramona said sounded reasonable, and this had been the most disorganized and overworked bureau.

"I don't let emotion interfere with my work, Yolanda," Ramona told her with the quiet intensity she was known for. "In a job like this, you just have to use cool logic or else you'll get swept away."

We have in our collective imagination a vision of the logical leader who moves, Mr. Spock–like, through the world, unbothered by emotion or a physical body or other base concerns. And we can believe that people are (or should be) rational agents who act logically (except under specific, negative circumstances that we can try to fight). We have business systems set up to logically deliver rewards and punishments, we work to leave our emotions at the door, and we sometimes act as though our bodies were just the transport system that totes our brains from meeting to meeting.

It's true that one of the great things about humans is our capacity for rational thought and analysis. And it's also true, even though we don't often celebrate this, that our rationality is never unhooked from our emotional side, just as our brains are never unhooked from our bodies.[1] Even at our best, we are constantly influenced by our emotions, our preconceptions, our previous experiences. In fact, it *makes* us our best when we can make the most of these competing forces, knowing the ways our bodies and our intuitions guide us helpfully beyond our rationality—and when they're most likely to lead us into predictable errors. We don't want to get beyond or over our humanness; we want to become aware of the ways we are human and make the most of the things we are good at while reducing the impact of those ways that our reflexes lead us astray.

One of the most amusing (and, to be honest, very seriously dangerous) quirks researchers find about the way our minds work is that we do not recognize the various ways we are subject to the quirks of our minds. We tend to believe that we ourselves are nearly like those mysterious Spock-like creatures. We couldn't count up the number of people who have told us, when we introduce the framework in Chapter 3 (you remember, the one that asks you to state the data, the emotion, and the impact of something and then has you inquire about the other person's perspective) that they really *feel* nothing about things at work, that work is work and doesn't involve emotions. One of those leaders, who was explaining afterward why he never used an emotional word in the role-play he had just conducted, asked the group what they had seen in his video. "Looked to me like you wanted to bang the guy's head into the wall," one of his colleagues suggested. He laughed. "I guess that's true enough. You think that comes across?" The other participants burst into laughter. Yep. They thought so. This is not the absence of emotion; it's just the absence of talking about emotion (and sometimes the absence of noticing our own emotions). Just because we are taught in many ways to pretend that we don't have messy and unprofessional emotions at work, to pretend that we don't have bodies, to pretend that we're purely rational people—that doesn't make it so. It seems to us that it's better to acknowledge our wonderful messiness and take advantage of the many different ways it is glorious to be human instead of wishing we were more like machines.

There are books and books written on the various ways our bodies and minds work together to keep us safe in helpful ways (e.g., to keep us from being overwhelmed by too much data, to let us know when we are in danger) and in unhelpful ways (e.g., to keep us from knowing that we're wrong, to keep us from learning from our mistakes, to keep us from noticing the effects our emotions have on our decision making).[2] These forces—sometimes written about in psychology, sometimes in behavioral economics, sometimes in books on decision making or change or counseling—all add up to an almost unlimited set of quirks in the way we humans operate. In our work, we've tried to pick the particular quirks that are most salient to leaders, who are at least as quirky as folks who aren't leading things but who may need to think more carefully about not only their own foibles but also those of the other humans around them. It might be that we need to understand leaders as the most human humans of all, not the most Mr. Spockish ones. If you're leading a group of people who are from Vulcan, you can skip this chapter, but for those of you leading humans, you should probably read on.

See, the logical part of our brain, the frontal lobe, that place where we have our so-called executive functions, doesn't actually talk as well to the rest of the brain, or to our bodies, as we assume it might.[3] The idea of executive functions and the fact that they include the most recently evolved part of the brain might make you think they're kind of in charge of the rest of the brain, and also in charge of our bodies. Nope. It's not as fast as the rest of the brain, either, so it's often the last to know about what's going on (if it finds out at all). It gets to feel like it's in control because it tends to make up a story that helps us feel coherent and whole, and so we retain the illusion of control. Very often, though, those stories come *after* the event rather than *before* it. You know, like when you had a terrible day at work and you come home and yell at your kids. Your rational brain tells you that it was your kids' fault: they know you hate it when they leave their shoes in the middle of the hallway. But really, that's just a story you're telling yourself. You yelled at the kids because you had a bad day at work and you're grumpy. That was a much bigger factor than the shoes in the hallway. But unless you really think about it, you might never even know what most influenced your own behavior.

It's a bummer, but there is a way that this part of our brain (protected from much of the complexity of the real world by the body and the more emotional and impulsive parts of the brain) does actually sound a little bit like the old vision of executives in their private dining room, not quite sure about what's going on elsewhere but certain that they're very busy running the place just the same.

So the stories we have about our fantastic ability to notice, to reason, to weigh different pieces of data and come up with an objectively better solution—these are all little lies our brain tells us so that we won't spend too much of our time sweating the small stuff. Unfortunately, we don't get to tell our brains what the small stuff really is. All those decisions got made thousands of years ago as our brains evolved. And thousands of years ago the world was a really different place, and we needed to focus on really different things, like running away from a lion or sneaking up on lunch. But as we use our original wiring, we are oriented toward things that are ancient indeed: the straightforward search for the basics of food, shelter, safety, companionship. This leaves us with some quirks in our mental system that we mostly aren't even aware of.

We believe we consider all the data, but we're much more likely to see only data that support what we already believe or have already decided. We believe that we think carefully about the future, but we are actually fairly captured by thinking about the past (or superimposing the past on what we say the future will look like). We believe that we are seeing the world and our colleagues clearly, but really we are mostly judging by using our somewhat paranoid sense of the intentions we project on them. It's a wonder the whole thing works as well as it does! It takes work to build the habit of mind to at least notice the ways we lead ourselves astray.[4]

ASKING DIFFERENT QUESTIONS: HOW COULD I BE WRONG ABOUT THIS? HOW COULD I FIND OUT?

One of the great benefits of the Mr. Spock leader in our imagination is that he objectively analyzes the data he has collected. As we emulate him, we believe that we have done this, too—looked at the pertinent data and then made a decision based on those facts. One of us has a relative who is convinced that he lives his life objectively, that mere mortals look at the world through blurry emotions, but that he does not. This person fully believes that he is not subject to the pull of emotions or irrationality in the world. As he goes through the world, he is struck by the irrational ways other humans live, but he'll fight you to the death if you suggest some of these irrational ways affect him as well.

Just like his brain, our brains mislead us in a couple of ways here and always without informing us. First of all, our brains don't give us all the data available in any situation—we couldn't handle it. Whether it's what we see, what we hear, what we consider—we are always dealing with a miniscule subsection of the available data. This gets even worse when we're looking for something in particular. We think of this as the "too busy to notice" bias.[5] This is the very sensible idea that when you're paying hard attention to one thing, you miss other things. The surprise here is (1) you feel like you're not missing anything (remember, what you see is all there is) and (2) some of the things you miss really, really seem unmissable. To understand this, researchers put people in a variety of situations in which they search for things (like basketball players passing a ball back and forth or a suspect fleeing arrest) or are distracted by things (like talking on a cell phone) and then the researchers notice what those people miss. In these cases, people miss a person in a gorilla suit banging her chest, a mob beating and kicking a police officer, or a clown on a yellow unicycle. The biggest issue, of course, is our own lack of awareness of this lack of awareness—none of us would ever believe we were too busy to notice any of these events. We'd all say that no matter how busy we were, we would notice a criminal event, a clown, or a gorilla of any kind on a basketball court. But time after time, researchers find that if we are either distracted (by something like a cell phone) or focused on another task (like counting basketball bounces) we miss things right under our eyes.

Yolanda is seeking to overcome this bias by talking to a variety of people and working hard to ask questions even when she thinks she knows the answer. She tells Ramona she's trying to "listen in a new way," which involves slowing down a lot and making sense of the issue from a different perspective. Instead of leaping to judgment, Yolanda is trying to see through Ramona's eyes—at least temporarily—as she tries to set aside the patterns she normally sees in order to broadly scan the setting. She's trying not to be too busy to notice.[6]

There's also the "we search for what we want to find" bias.[7] We believe that we are objectively looking for data, and that it just so happens that the data that support our view are much more plentiful than the data that don't. Like when you're wanting to buy a house even though the housing market isn't so good, and suddenly there are articles everywhere about why buying a house right now is a good idea. We figure that those articles prove that we were objectively right in the first place. Silly us. In studies all over the world, researchers have found that our eyes seek out and linger on information that confirms our beliefs and that we skim over or skip information that might disconfirm our beliefs. Not only do we pick the newspaper or magazine or website that's aligned with our values in the first place, but even inside that medium we are drawn to things we agree with and repelled by things we disagree with. If a group of people, half on one side of an issue and half on the other, read two thoughtful articles—one supporting each side—everyone will use both articles as evidence that they're right. The evidence in the one that supports your belief will look fantastic to you, and the evidence in the other one will look hysterical or limited or whatever you need to discredit it. And the exact same case is made about exactly the same data in exactly the opposite way by the brains of those who believe what we don't. The idea that we're objectively reading and weighing evidence doesn't hold up to the, um, objective evidence. One of us, in the middle of a sentence where we condemned a colleague for watching only Fox News, realized to our dismay that we were guilty of exactly that same "crime" in reverse, having never ever watched Fox News. And to this day, we have not rectified that error. (And we might not ever—knowing about a bias doesn't make it go away, alas.) As economist John Kenneth Galbraith famously said, "Faced with the choice between changing one's mind and proving that there is no need to do so, almost everyone gets busy on the proof."

Ramona has probably fallen into this hole as she has created her process for straightening out the offices she is hired to fix. This idea of collecting data that lead only to a single (predetermined) conclusion would horrify her because she is working so hard to be logical. But going into six different complex situations in organizations and finding exactly the same thing in each might mean that she is looking for particular things and—because they're there—finding them. The mistake here is that just because the same issues are *present* in each office doesn't mean they are the *most important* pieces to deal with each time or that they should be dealt with in the ways that she's dealt with them before. In fact, Ramona is likely to be blind to the most important issues of this current office if they are different from what she's seen before. She might be watching the basketball game and totally missing the gorilla, and she'll never know that it's a problem because what she sees confirms her sense that what she's looking for is exactly right.

Related to this is the "if it reminds me of me, it must be good" bias.[8] Some of the studies on this bias are funny—like the ones about how if your name is Michael, you're statistically more likely to marry a Michelle than a Brenda, or if your name is Denise, you're statistically more likely to be a dentist than a lawyer. We look more favorably on those things that remind us most of ourselves.[9] Quirky! Unfortunately, this bias also leaves us with a chilling set of studies of good people, people who would consider themselves nondiscriminatory and objective, who make racist or sexist or other *-ist* decisions without noticing it, and sometimes even while thinking they were fighting against it. Imagine you were an HR director searching for talented new staff for your organization, and you knew that your company needed a more diverse employee base. You have a stack of résumés that you need to sift through to find people to interview. How often do you lean toward those with names that sound African American? The answer for the 1,250 companies in Chicago and Boston who were unwittingly part of an MIT and University of Chicago experiment was this: you don't. Researchers sent out four résumés to each organization: an average and a highly skilled version, one with a "white-sounding" name and one with a "black-sounding" name. The resumes with white-sounding names got 50% more callbacks, even from the organizations most actively seeking diverse candidates. Furthermore, "highly skilled candidates with white names got more calls than average white candidates, but lower-skilled candidates with white names got many more callbacks than even high skilled black applicants."[10] Here's the frightening flip side of this bias—if it doesn't remind me of me, I might automatically shy away from it, without even noticing.[11]

It might be that Yolanda approved the hiring of Ramona in part because she reminded Yolanda of her younger self, even though Ramona clearly has a somewhat abrupt style and a simplistic way of seeing a complex situation. The two women have much in common. Neither comes from a social work background, both have bumped around different agencies, both have a reputation as something of a department fixer—Yolanda at a larger scale, and later in her career. Yolanda recognizes her own drive and devotion in the younger woman, and perhaps forgives her fairly black-and-white thinking because she remembers so strongly the days when her own thinking was more black and white. It can be easy to overlook flaws in others that remind us of ourselves—they are all the more human because they are also me.[12]

Finally, there's the "if I can remember it, it must be important" bias.[13] This one is a quirk in which we emphasize events that were either really memorable (because the press made a meal of them) or really recent over things that are likely but not newsworthy. Jennifer lives at the beach, and recently someone asked whether there were stingrays in the waters. When Jennifer said yes, the person looked horrified. "Those are really dangerous!" the woman said. "Aren't you worried about your kids in the water?" Jennifer was puzzled, because stingrays are *not* particularly dangerous compared to the other risks in the sea. When she said as much, the woman countered, "But Steve Irwin [the Crocodile Hunter] died from one!" Now that's totally true: it was a front-page story in newspapers around the world. And it's also totally true that living near the sea is dangerous. But nearly everything about the sea is more dangerous than stingrays—most especially drowning, which according to the World Health Organization is the third leading cause of accidental-injury death worldwide and one of the leading causes of death in children. But Jennifer has never had anyone say to her, "Aren't you worried about your kids drowning?" although she gets lots of questions about sharks, jellyfish, and now stingrays.

The reason people ask about creatures and not about the deadly dangers of drowning is because stingrays and sharks are so vivid and unusual that they make the news. When they make the news, people pay attention to them and they stick in the mind. "If I can remember it, it must be important" means that we spend more of our time and attention focused on those things that happen to be memorable for some reason rather than on those things that happen to be important.

In Ramona's memory, for example, the idea of kids and dogs at work looms large. It's not clear how often those things really happened (was there a dog at the office twice in six months or puppies playing every day?), but they became strong symbols for her of a disorganized and unhealthy office—just as the music in her previous place was a symbol of what needed to be fixed. Similarly, Yolanda might be afraid that what is capturing the press's attention is the wrong area to look into altogether. Maybe instead of searching for the things that happened in the cases that went wrong, reporters should be looking for what happened in the cases that *almost* went wrong but didn't. In any case, each of us is so affected by this bias that it is hard for any of us to get out from under it. Instead, we need to notice what draws our attention, remember that it's likely to be pulled in ways that are sometimes unhelpful, and intentionally search for issues that might not be so memorable but may be more important.

Why do these quirks matter to you as a leader? Because each one of them might leave you feeling like you've considered something objectively and made clear and conscious decisions, and in each case your invisible bias might well have saved you all the trouble of worrying about it and just marched you carefully down a path of its choosing. The leaders we talk to, even (or maybe especially) those at the highest level of their organizations, talk about how much less control they have over their companies than they thought they would when they took the job. They spend some significant energy either trying to get more control over things or trying to come to terms with how little control senior leaders have.[14] We think maybe we should all spend more time marveling about how little control we have over *ourselves*. This is a discovery that helps us understand how to live with the stresses and complexities of life in a new way. It also helps us put new processes in place so we can take advantage of the quirks without falling prey to their shortcomings.

The leaders we work with have to go fast and make many decisions, and often with less immediate feedback from the system because people usually go along with the boss's vision (at least on the surface). If the leaders themselves aren't looking out for their own quirks of data collection and decision making, they may be seeing a very small, skewed piece of the world. If they aren't setting up systems and procedures to help others broaden their view, the entire organization can become myopic.

To avoid this, leaders can share the responsibility for working around these quirks. Some of these are process changes. Résumés and promotion material can first be viewed anonymously before we put names to them (as academic articles are). Some of them are team norms. People can work harder to search for discrepant evidence as they build their cases, so that they work specifically against some of the short cuts our brains provide for us. Some of these changes might be cultural. You might think about whether your meetings are set up for people to defend ideas from one another—a fast way to fall prey to our human tendency to narrow rather than expand and test our limits. We could all take a more tentative approach at meetings, seeking out the ways we are limited or wrong (because there will always be ways we are limited or wrong) and moving away from an attempt to argue or convince others. Leaders can, over time, put these new approaches and ways of being in place as they look for and reward certain behaviors and discourage others. (First, of course, the leader has to give herself permission to be wrong and to search for alternate perspectives.)

Yolanda looked at the notes that covered the walls around her. She had been in this conference room for the better part of three days now, furiously writing down what she was hearing on sticky notes and spreading them around the walls. On four large sticky notes at eye level in front of her seat were the four of the main biases she was trying so hard to avoid:

- Too busy to notice
- We search for what we want to find
- If it reminds me of me, it must be good
- If I can remember it, it must be important

She had learned so many things in the past three days that she thought her head might explode. She saw so many perspectives, had gotten so many different snippets of facts and opinions and certainties from so many people. She was trying to pay attention to those issues that drew people's attention, but she was also looking for the scrap of information that might not seem like a really big deal but was actually of key importance in designing the next set of safe-to-fail experiments to make this system work better.

Much of what Yolanda had found was a tangle of opinions, with some people coming down on one side and others as strongly planted on the other side.

There was lots of talk about the new systems Ramona had put in place, but polarized views about whether those were a good idea or not. Some folks were grateful that things were much clearer now. Before, there was a lot of personal judgment used to decide whether to recommend that a child be removed from a family, for example. Those decisions weighed very heavily on individuals and took up energy not only at work but also at home and on the weekends. Now there were clearer checklists and targets, and some people loved the security of being able to point to a number (if two-thirds of the issues are present, the child should be removed from the house) and not have to agonize so much about it on a case-by-case basis.

Others, however, hated the removing of the personal judgment and thought that a checklist would never be a tool that could actually create a decision. It was fine for supporting decisions, but it would never replace experience and judgment. If you had a gut feeling that something was really wrong in a house, you should remove the child, no matter what the checklist said.

The targets also were both appreciated and loathed. Some people pointed to the ways the targets had let them cut five staff members whose performance issues had gone unmanaged for years. Looking up at the target wall, everyone could see the number of cases each person had open. Those five had triple the number of open cases than the next-highest-ranking colleague. This had really made it clear that while they were nice people, they just weren't doing their jobs. Others found that the targets made people focus on the wrong issue, on closing cases quickly rather than keeping them open long enough to learn everything that needed to be learned. And in this case, too, it was obvious that both sides were right.

There was more consistency in people's unhappiness with Ramona, that was for sure. No matter how people felt about the changes, they seemed to blame Ramona for everything bad that had happened since she arrived. (Yolanda thought it was likely that people were even blaming Ramona for things that happened *before* she arrived.) Ramona was too controlling, or she had abandoned too much of her power to the new supervisors. She had come in and wrecked the family feel of the place, some people thought. People didn't warm to her, and, worse, they were finding that this was becoming more and more of a regular job and less of a calling—with more forms to manage and fewer celebrations, like the cakes the last manager had brought in for every little occasion. Yolanda noticed that Ramona was held personally responsible for things that were actually government-wide initiatives around reducing money for travel and for supplies and equipment in the office. She heard some of her own vision—to include families more fully in the decision-making process, for example—described back to her as a result of Ramona's personality ("She doesn't trust caseworkers, so she's trying to give away some of our responsibility"). Ramona had become an attractor for any complaint you might have about the system. This was dangerous for everyone, and even Yolanda felt herself pulled harder than she'd like toward a view that all of the ills of the Proucheford office were Ramona's fault. She stood up and wrote, "Someone must be at fault!" She added this as a fifth bias to her growing list of things she would try to avoid.

SEEING THE SYSTEM: HOW OUR PREFERENCE FOR INDIVIDUAL INTENT BLINDS US TO PATTERNS

Perhaps the one bias that is most visible throughout society is what psychologists call the fundamental attribution error. Yolanda thinks of this as the "someone must be at fault" bias. Yolanda is trying to resist the urge she has to point to Ramona (or someone close to her). This has been Ramona's nagging worry since she heard Yolanda was coming to Proucheford, because it fits how Ramona would be behaving if she were in the boss's classy pumps. It turns out that we are more likely to attribute an event to the traits or personalities or actions of a person rather than to circumstance. This means that we probably give people more credit—and more blame—than they deserve. We do not think about the circumstances that shape other people's actions, and so we tend to focus on what about those people themselves made that action most likely.

This happens with public figures all the time, and radio and television news shows just ramp up our natural inclination. They take a huge systemic issue (universal health care, say, or global warming) and turn it into a battle of two personalities rather than a huge bundle of systemic forces. It is so much easier for our brains to understand (or think we understand) individuals or groups and their motivations than it is for us to understand the way a system can create these divisions for us.

We do an exercise with our leadership program participants to give them a sense of this.[15] We take a long tent pole with rolls of tape at either end and lay it across the outstretched fingers of the folks who are lined up, pointing at each other. We tell them the objective is to move the stick to the ground without losing the "stakeholders" (the rolls of tape). And we tell them that they can't hook the stick with their pointer fingers and that they can't lose contact with the stick as it rests on the top of their pointer fingers. Then with these simple directions, we let them go. And the stick, which they are all wishing to bring carefully to the ground, sometimes stays utterly still or, more often, rises— sometimes so fast that it flies into the air. Early on in this exercise, you hear muttering about "those people" who are doing it wrong. They're lifting it too high and ignoring the rules. They're carelessly dipping too low and threaten- ing the stakeholders because they care more about their objective than about bringing people along. Or they're doing nothing because they lack courage. We were with a group recently in which one member asked if it was within the rules to take her hand off the stick to whack the person next to her! We ask them afterward how many of them felt the urge to blame others around them. Most hands go up. How about the urge to feel guilty for doing it wrong? Many hands go up again. How many of them thought about the inherent difficulty of the two simple instructions—lower the stick to the ground and don't lose contact with the stick on the top of your finger? Very few people have thought about the circumstances around them, how the system itself set them up to make even this most simple of tasks very difficult. Instead, they—and we— think mostly about individuals and their responsibility.

You see this in Yolanda's difficulty as well. No matter what the issue is, it seems to attach itself to Ramona and be considered part of her personality. Surely some of what's going on is because of Ramona and her quirks—a few of which we've discussed here. But Yolanda knows this isn't all true. Some of the most violent criticism of Ramona and her impossible, out-of-touch style comes from policy changes Yolanda and her team made in response to new government requirements. While the blame gets laid at Ramona's feet, Yolanda is learning a lot about the way her own policy (coming from what she hopes isn't too much of an out-of-touch style) has created more work for staff mem- bers rather than less. The expense policy particularly has spawned a number of creative work-arounds. At first these complaints and candid explanations of the gleeful ways people reported working around them left Yolanda wildly frustrated. It was a straightforward change designed to help make transparent the way the department spent public money. How could it end up in a web of competing demands and form filling? Then Yolanda—listening for patterns despite her frustration—realized that the work-arounds mainly came from committed caseworkers doing their best for clients, despite the new system. She heard a wide variety of examples, like finding a way to get bus money for a beneficiary when it was needed quickly rather than slowly trying to establish proof of entitlement. That made sense to her in a way she hadn't considered before.

Sitting in front of her wall of sticky notes (on bleak afternoons she thought of the arc of squares as her personal Bridge of Sighs), Yolanda could see how the clearer accountability measures were turning managers (in this case the new supervisor rank Ramona had created) into gatekeepers and compliance police on low-level financial issues. This not only led to bad feelings between the managers and the managed but also created bottlenecks, as staff had to ask permission for decisions they would previously have made on their own. Ramona, who had already raised the hackles of many staff members for the changes for which she was responsible, was also carrying the full brunt of blame for changes wrought by the system.

This isn't just a problem when it comes to blaming others. It's also a problem when it comes to fixing problems, because what seems like a people problem can often be a circumstance problem. What looks like a personality problem or interpersonal conflict between two people can actually be an overlapping roles or reward problem. What looks like a failure of two teams to communicate might be a systems problem. What looks like individual irresponsibility for someone who doesn't fill out her time sheets might be a process efficiency problem. Chip Heath and Dan Heath remind us to think about "shaping the path" when we're making a change.[16] This means that we have to make the new behaviors or interactions or mindsets easier because of the way we have set up systems or processes or even arranged the desks.[17]

TAKING MULTIPLE PERSPECTIVES ON
THE MEANING OF WORK

Finally, the last of these quirky bits we'd like to talk about isn't really a bias so much as a mindset or approach—we think of it as the "is this a relationship or just a job?" mindset. This one comes straight from the work of behavioral economists. We think it's so important for leaders because it's something we don't tend to think about, yet something that shapes people's experience of work and work relationships with organizations, and because leaders don't tend to know about this, they can make clumsy mistakes that are hard to recover, as Ramona unfortunately has. It is easy for leaders to have a perspective on this issue and not understand the perspectives of others in the organization. The big problem with this one is that the different perspectives can create different options for taking action, and an error by a leader here can have far-reaching consequences.

This mindset is about the difference between what economists think of as a "market relationship" versus a "social relationship." Here's why that matters. If we have a market relationship, we do things for money. It's a clear trade: my labor for your dollars. Your money should be a fair wage for my efforts. Logically, this sort of relationship makes sense to us, and we can imagine that all trading relationships feel this way. But surely they don't. You don't hand $40 to the friend who cooks you a fine dinner; you bring flowers or wine (maybe worth about $40). You don't give your parents $50 for watching your kids for an afternoon, even if that might be what a babysitter would charge for the same service. In some situations, we have an intuitive idea about what would be best, but in other situations it can be confusing.

When we have a social relationship, it's not based on money for effort. Instead it's about a relational good, something we do freely and without thought of a cash return. When we forget which side of the line we're on, we get in trouble. Think of a time you got an expensive gift out of the blue from a dear friend. What did you think about that? Now imagine you got an expensive gift out of the blue from a colleague with whom you have no social relationship at all. You think something very different, don't you? When a friend gives you a present, you don't usually wonder whether she wants something in return or is setting you up for something (well, depending on your friendship). When a colleague you hardly know does the same thing, you're much more likely to feel that there might be strings attached.

Now just knowing about this difference doesn't necessarily help you feel better about it. Jennifer had a few of these experiences as she was speaking at leadership events about her first book. At one conference, the organizers handed her a beautiful gift bag with a bottle of wine and a box of chocolates. At another, they handed her a "Karma Currency Card,"[18] which was a way for her to choose which philanthropic group got an undisclosed amount of money in her name. At a third, they gave her a $50 bill in an envelope. Even though she knows about these biases and can write these words on a page, she was still miffed about the $50. "Really, is that all they think I'm worth?" she wondered. She watched as these three gifts—probably each of them costing the hosting committee roughly the same amount of money—produced really different emotions in her. Here's the thing: if you're going to give cash, people are going to expect that you give them cash on a market value. Give me a bottle of wine worth $50 and it feels like a thank-you. Give me $50 for a half day's work and it feels like you're paying me less than minimum wage. This is why so many universities and schools talk about an "honorarium." That's code for "you deserve more but we don't have it," and because we mostly understand that code, we live with it. If Apple tried to make the same case, it wouldn't feel the same.

Why does this matter to you? Well, because when you convert a social relationship to a market relationship, you can get clarity, but you lose a lot, too. It can feel like a betrayal in some ways, the way it would if a date handed you $20 after your first real kiss ("Go buy yourself some flowers, sweetheart"). There is a rumor that circulates widely around Washington, DC, about the changes in the relationship that government workers have with their employer. The story is that thirty years ago, when you got your first job at a government agency, your boss's boss would take you out on your first day and help you buy a suit and then buy you lunch to celebrate (these rumors don't include women, or those whose positions aren't high enough on the organizational chart to need a suit). There would be a handshake after the transaction was finished, a clap of a hand on a shoulder, and the young employee would know that there was someone there who would take care of him and look out for him. It was a relationship, a commitment, a sign that you two were in this together for the long haul. Nowadays when people tell this story, they often tell it with dismay and talk about how working for the government can make you feel like a number. The sexism in this story might inspire other emotions, but if you pass over those for a minute, you can see the difference in the social versus the market relationships even at work.

Research shows that it's very hard to recover when a social relationship turns into a market relationship. What took years to build can take one or two events to dismantle. Ramona, with all the good intent in the world, may well be eroding the social relationship of the office. She has seen the way social relationships at work can be almost exploitative (with people working such long hours for the team), but she doesn't realize that there can also be also beauty in those relationships.

And so it is there for the thoughtful leader to wonder and ask questions about. As you think about rewarding people, as you think about the various forms of gratitude, celebration, and connection, you might wonder how you want to protect the social contract you have with your people rather than switching into a purely business mode. And to make this work, leaders need to allow themselves to also feel and get caught up in the social contract. In our work, we often see leaders shift from a social to a market perspective in a single sentence, as though the leader himself could choose how people make sense of things. But research shows that these are quite different perspectives in the mind of the employee, and it takes a long time to work toward a relationship perspective. This means that if a leader makes a change that transforms the relationship perspective people have developed at work, it might be a long way back. It might be less expensive in the long term to keep the coffee machines free in the office kitchen rather than having people leave the office for coffee a couple of times a day. It might be less expensive to keep on ten extra people— even during a difficult financial time—rather than have the sharp drop in productivity and loyalty that floods though an entire organization during times when people are afraid of losing their jobs. Or it might not make sense to do those things—but if you don't have your eye on the multiple perspectives about this issue, you may try to rely on straight logic (as though there were such a thing) and miss the other important pieces of the decision.

The point of this whole chapter is that when we think we are relying on our most precious human logic, we are often fooling ourselves. It's not our fault— we're drawn that way. But there is so much evidence about this, so many ways it's clear that our logic is often a story we tell ourselves, that it is unacceptable to keep telling this story with the confidence we might have once had. Our hope is that these ideas make you a little less sure, a little less confident, and a little more curious about your decisions—even when they feel so obviously logical. It is in this curiosity that we are most likely to get access to our whole selves—to the logic piece and the tightness in the chest that helps us understand our emotions are at play here, too. We're not suggesting that you ignore your intuition—nor are we suggesting you just find the whole thing impossible and head home for a nap! We're hoping you'll move away from building organizational procedures and processes that would work well for Mr. Spock and instead build organizations that are suitable for human beings. Notice your impulses and intuitions, but don't be a slave to them. Leadership is too hard to do wholly by impulse and intuition—those are designed for the savanna, not the multinational organization. Noticing your own quirks as you walk through the world will help you choose what to do about them (instead of closing your eyes and hoping they go away). And so being aware of the ways we are frustratingly and gloriously human gives us a great chance to try to take advantage of all we can do and all we are. And trust us, in a complex world, we need all that we can get.

Yolanda handed Ramona the tonic water with lime she had requested, and sat down with a sparkling water herself. She had picked the restaurant on purpose to relax the atmosphere, but clearly neither woman was going to relax with a glass of wine.

"So did you find your mysterious, illogical answer?" Ramona asked.

"I found many mysterious illogical questions." Yolanda smiled and then paused to get more serious and collect her thoughts. "It was really helpful to come here, and I have lots of ideas about what could happen next. How disruptive did it turn out in the end?"

Ramona smiled. "It was not too bad. People said you were clearly not on a witch hunt—they found you curious and asking good questions and listening well. But they will want to know what you found."

"I know. And I'm trying to figure out a way to tell that story. I want to be able to talk about the way people blame one another without actually blaming anyone for that. It's a system founded on blame and responsibility and on judging who is ultimately on the hook for which things. That sort of makes sense when we are working on the edge to protect at-risk kids. It is one of the ways our business has to work. We need to be clear about who is taking responsibility. Not surprisingly, we bring those pressures into the office, too. It means that when something goes wrong—even a little thing like the demise of Wednesday afternoon cake-and-coffee sessions—people are searching for someone to blame. Hell, I fall into it, too."

Ramona frowned deeply. "So have you found someone to blame?"

Yolanda sighed. "We're all to blame, really, Ramona. I have a piece of it, you have a piece of it, Margie has a piece of it. All of us have been involved in creating these patterns and all of us will need to change a little to fix them."

"That sounds like a cop-out," Ramona said. "Surely someone is more at fault than others."

"I'm sure that's true, and I'm also not convinced it matters," Yolanda answered. "I don't mean about the kids our system failed; it matters who had a hand in that. But in the larger question—the way the organization itself is failing to protect kids and families well enough—then I'm not sure that finding the single point of blame is most useful. We all need to look at the blame we each hold for not looking at all the right things, not supporting one another to do the best possible work. We need more open processes."

Ramona got out her pen and a notebook. "Go ahead, tell me what we need."

"I don't need you to write this all down, Ramona. I'd really like to talk about it together before the whole-staff meeting Monday. But my guess is that some of the innovations you brought in have been really helpful and some of them have been unhelpful. And before you get defensive about that," she began quickly, because she could see that Ramona was, in fact, getting defensive, "let me say that some of the innovations I brought in with my team have been helpful and others have been seriously unhelpful. We need to have much more honest conversations with one another to figure out the ways the system is broken and how that is shaping individual behavior. And we need to really think about individual behavior and see how that's shaping the system."

"I'm not hearing much I can actually take action on," Ramona said, putting her notebook away. "Did you learn anything actually useful at all?"

"I really think I did. I can make some recommendations that I think will be really helpful. I think your checklists are fantastic, for example, but they need to be used in a slightly different way. Your work for targets is on the right track, but targets are probably wrong for our business. My new budget controls have the right set of hopes, but they push down into way too much detail and the reporting mechanisms are unwieldy."

Ramona had pulled out her notebook again and was writing furiously.

"And I should say that not one of these is my idea. They are all from your people, who have some fantastic suggestions. And there's probably some noise there, and I can't tell the difference. But what I know is that we need to have a long conversation about how to experiment around with some of these things so that we can get them just right for Proucheford. And what works here might not work in the capital or Mountainview. And I need to figure out how to be OK with that as an executive director." Yolanda shrugged about that last point, not sure how she was going to be able to ensure compliance in the same way when she was beginning to think that different offices should move in such different directions.

"I'd like to talk to the staff about what I've heard, and I'd like to figure out together how to move forward. I'd like you to help me lead that meeting, but before we begin, I'd like to talk with you about some of what I've learned: not just about what's going on at the office but about more global issues around irrationality and emotion, and about complexity. And I'd like to introduce you to my son, whose software company is struggling with some of these same issues as well. I think if you take these ideas seriously, they'll rock your world and your management style as they've rocked mine, but I also think they'll help you grow into the leader I think you can become next."

Ramona put down her pen, and whether she was annoyed or just confused, Yolanda couldn't tell. "I know that you've been a really successful manager to date, Ramona," Yolanda said, trying to give some context to her thoughts. "And we're going to need you to be even better than you've ever been before if we're going to actually take this whole department into a new future. You'll need to be a different sort of leader, and I'll need to be different, too. And we'll have to give up on some things we believe are true, and stretch into believing things we can hardly imagine now."

"I'm not sure about believing new things, Yolanda. I'm as happy to learn new ideas as anyone, but I'm not going to become a different person. If you're look-ing for something so different, maybe this is the wrong place for me."

"I'm not wanting you to be a different person, Ramona. Believe me, I want all that you've learned so far in all of the work you've done. What I want is for you—and me and Doug and Margie and all the others—to begin to grow to understand our work in a new way. And I think we'll be able to figure that out together. Are you willing to give that a try?"

"I'm not quite sure what you're talking about," Ramona answered slowly. "But I know that you are genuinely committed to what we do and I'm willing to learn more about it before making up my mind about what's best."

"I don't think there's anything more I could ask," Yolanda told her. "Well, one more thing," she hesitated. "I know you have clear and firm boundaries be-tween work and play, but even though tomorrow is Saturday, I've asked for some folks to get together to begin to work through some of these ideas. It's just a casual conversation, an exploration. Would you be interested?"

"I guess I'm willing to give that a try too. Let me make a phone call or two to change some plans and tell me where to meet and when."

6 COMMUNICATE YOUR CERTAINTY ABOUT UNCERTAINTY

Jarred looked around with some surprise at the collection of people gathered in his living room. When his mother first wondered about having a couple of people over to talk about what she was learning at the Proucheford bureau office, he wasn't expecting it to turn into this. Doug was pouring coffee for Squint as Hannah tried to engage Ramona in conversation. Curtis was just coming in the front door with a box of doughnuts while Arlen and Yolanda carried healthier treats out from the kitchen—bowls of nuts and a fruit platter. Looked like people were settling in for a while.

The living room didn't look so shabby, even with this assortment of big wigs in it. Jarred had been fixing up this old Victorian house on weekends and holidays for the past three years, and at least this downstairs part looked pretty good. The furniture was newish, too—much newer than what he'd seen at Squint's lake house. With luck, no one would have to use the upstairs bathroom, which was still in its 1970s pink-porcelain splendor.

The group quieted and Jarred noticed that everyone was looking at his mom. She smiled and cleared her throat. "Thanks so much for giving up a sunny Saturday to think with me," she said. Jarred thought it was a measure of her importance either as an Actualeyes client or as a public servant leading a vital social agency that Squint didn't make a noise of distress when she pointed out the gleaming spring weather. "This is an eclectic assortment of people, and it might take a little introduction to both the players here and the work itself." She asked the folks in the room to introduce themselves and say a little about their work. When they had finished with the first round of introductions,

Yolanda stood again to give some background about the context of the meeting. "So everyone knows that Family and Children's Services has been in some trouble lately. We've not been protecting kids as well as we need to, and that needs to change."

Doug mumbled, "Amen, sister," under his breath and there were supportive murmurs of agreement from both Actualeyes and FACS folks.

Yolanda continued. "A disproportionate number of those cases have been here in Proucheford, which happens to be where our customer relationship management software company is located," here she smiled at Squint, "though I am not suggesting a correlation. And in the interest of full disclosure, let me say that my predecessor choose 4All several years ago when Jarred was a young programmer with the company. So while there's obviously a family connection here, that's not what drives this business partnership."

"It is what drives this meeting location, though," Squint said to the chuckles of those around him. "Neutral territory?"

"I thought it'd be nicer to spend our Saturday here than in either a bureau or an Actualeyes conference room," Yolanda explained.

"I totally agree," Squint affirmed. "I can't wait for a tour of the upstairs," he said quietly to Jarred.

"So here's the issue. After talking to Jarred about his retreat this week and after spending five interesting, if confusing, days at the local bureau office and talking with some of the community groups we partner with, I think I'd like to take a new approach to thinking about what happens next for us and how to talk about it. And I think this is the right set of people to help me think about it and get us ready to have a different kind of conversation. I've been more confused by this situation and about what to do with it than I can ever remember being. And I've been taking helpful counsel from Doug and Curtis about how to hold on to that confusion and use it to fuel our next steps as a department." Yolanda took a deep breath and continued.

"As I told Ramona last night, I think I'm going to have to be a different kind of leader to move us into our next phase as an organization. I'll need to be better able to deal with the complexity and uncertainty of this business without just wishing that away or trying to create structures to beat the uncertainty out. One of my findings this week is that nearly every thing Ramona or I have put in place to decrease the noise or increase the standardization of the work our people do has backfired in some obscure and unexpected way, often when some good things have also occurred along the way. We need to reduce the load on our folks and find ways to standardize our services, but we need to do that in ways that respect the complexity of our work rather than trying to override it." She held the group's attention tightly now.

Some were nodding; others looked puzzled, and Yolanda went with the puzzled ones. "Early on in the job it was very clear we had to cut through our processing loads and some of the duplicative checks and balances in our systems and free up time for staff at the frontline so I set up FIT Kids." Now all the Actualeyes folk were looking blank. "Oops. FIT Kids stood for 'Focus Is the Kids.' It was a project team studying our back-office functions, particularly how to simplify our core processes and systems and set clear service-delivery targets."

Hannah was nodding. "Been there and done that many times with different clients."

That caught Yolanda's interest. "Could you see any pattern in how your different projects played out?"

Hannah's normally open face furrowed. "That's a good question, and I wish I had done the thinking on it. First up, I'd say we always had some quick wins where we cleared away procedures, the ones no one could remember the logic for anymore, and there were some spectacular time savings, sometimes from quite small changes, and there was almost always something that bit back— some way that things interacted that was a complete surprise. When you got a couple of surprises together they could combine in ways that took you back to square one. My hunch is there are more of those in some of these projects, but the real effects do not emerge until the consultants are long gone."

"We could have used this conversation a year ago," Yolanda sighed. "I think we saw the quick wins from FIT Kids, and we moved quickly to implement the main recommendations and freed up some money for the roll out. There were steady declines in average processing times, and regional managers like Ramona really got behind it and pushed it along. It was 'all good,' as they say."

"I always worry when people say that," Doug grumbled. "I hear, 'We are just barely hanging on, apart from all the things that are going down the toilet.'"

Yolanda grinned with the rest of the room. "Yes, Doug, there were things going down the toilet. I have seen some of them this week in the way the staff were responding to the new procedures and the service targets by shifting folks from one waiting list to another to avoid exceeding the targeted waiting times." Yolanda watched Ramona turn scarlet. "No, Ramona, I'm not looking to blame you or your people. They are just being human, under pressure, and responding to the ways we have designed the system." Yolanda paused for breath. "So this takes me to my bigger challenge. I need people to design systems differently, but before that, I need them to observe the existing systems in more nuanced ways. It is not my job to design the systems or to even observe the existing systems, but I have to know enough about them and about the complexity and unpredictability of the world we are working in to be able to create the right context and set of directions to enable people to be successful. And I have to be able to communicate with staff, who of course want certainty. But I have to do it in a way that makes sense to our people and our communities and helps us all to learn and work more effectively in this strange and very uncertain place. Easy, eh? Just like reading *War and Peace* before breakfast—and tackling it in the original Russian!

"This is a whole new territory for me," Yolanda continued. "As I talked with Jarred about this challenge for me, he talked about the Actualeyes retreat this week. He seems to think he's going to have to make a similar set of changes as he supports the new direction at Actualeyes. Maybe, in fact, we're all going to have to change the way we show up as leaders—and the way we talk to our people about what's next. How's that for an introduction?" She sat down and looked around for comments from the others.

"Nobody dies in our business," Squint began, "so I'm a bit in awe of the responsibilities you and your people carry, but I am joined with you in thinking there has to be another way to lead into that space. I'm trying to learn how to lead Actualeyes through a whole lot of change as well, and I feel like I am making it up as I go along. So I wanted to come to this conversation—even though it's beautiful outside—not only to support a key client to make our community safer for children and families but also to learn and grow as a leader myself." Jarred was surprised to hear Squint talk so seriously and openly about what he had to learn. This was not the way most meetings went. It seemed Squint had chosen to leave his inner child out on the stoop.

"Thanks, Squint," Yolanda responded. "I knew this would be a helpful partnership for us for a variety of reasons. Let's get to some details. Curtis has talked with my team about complexity and change and how we need to make sense of things in a new way because we live in an unpredictable world. From Jarred I know that Hannah had a similar set of conversations with you at the Actualeyes retreat. And at the same time, my conversation with Ramona last night left me aware that I'm going to have to talk about this complexity stuff in careful ways. I mean, people are shaken up at bureaus throughout the state. The press is on our backs. They all want answers from me, and I'm getting more and more clear on the fact that I can't give them the sort of crisp answers they want." She smiled at Doug to signal that he could take it from there.

"But this doesn't mean we don't want to change," Doug carried on. "We know that there are some significant changes we need to make. We just don't know exactly what happens next or what the next set of changes will lead to. We don't have one of those helpful before-and-after drawings you get when you work with an architect—or one of those hair-regrowth places," he ran his fingers through his thinning hair unconsciously. "We know about *before*, and we think we know about *now*, and we know some things about what we want to be different in the future, but we don't want to narrow down exactly how that difference happens—we want to be sure we're allowing the fullest set of possibilities as we innovate our way forward."

"But we can't just tell people that!" Ramona exclaimed. "It's not enough to just say, 'We're going to innovate. Enjoy the fullest set of possibilities!' People need real direction so that they can feel good about getting on with their jobs. And if we just tell them we are going to innovate a third of them will think that is code for enjoying the fullest set of possibilities of being laid off and another third will think is an invitation to goof off! We have to get real here."

Doug nodded. "I agree, Ramona, we absolutely have to get real." He took a deep breath. "But we're learning that it's not very real to have a whole systems change like FIT Kids and pretend we are in control and can predict what will happen and end up with staff feeling they have to game the system to meet the targets. It might be more real to say, 'We cannot know what is going to happen but we are going to find safe ways to try things out and we are going to keep each other well informed on the journey and when you find things that work we will tell others and do more of that.' It may be more real and also feel like we have less control."

Doug went on: "That's why we're all here. I'd like to use our many different sets of perspectives and our experiences to think about how we want to move forward—and how we want to talk about these changes with our people. We need to find ways to communicate clearly without being certain about everything, and I feel like I am a wide-eyed learner in this place, and a bit uncertain about how to talk about that uncertainty!"

A core desire people have from their leaders is direction and a sense of safety that someone knows where they're all going. This is especially true in times of change. We are used to communications advice that tells leaders to be totally clear about the direction they're taking and communicate that in every message. Get on message and stay on message. You want something simple, that resonates with people's emotions, that they can remember and hold on to. You need to be consistent about your messaging, week in, week out.[1] We think the communication advice available on these issues is incredibly helpful—we use it and teach it ourselves.[2]

When leaders really understand that parts of their world really are complex and unpredictable, though, they have a different task. Instead of clarity about what the future will look like, the job for leaders in complex spaces is to get a diverse set of perspectives on the current conditions to make sense of what direction to take. They need to use that sense of direction to create the conditions for people to come up with a set of safe-to-fail experiments to learn from as they reshape the organization. This is a weird set of things to do, though, and doesn't look traditionally "leaderly." Leaders here need to have different sorts of conversations from the very beginning. Because this is an unusual approach, leaders need to model the way and support others to have a new mindset about the future. Perhaps most important, in times of complexity these leaders need to actually think and respond to their people in a different way. This is made more even more challenging because leaders are having to move back and forth between operating in the complicated domain (where a right answer might be within reach and repeating consistent stories will help get the message across) and the complex domain (where the best they can do is to probe and experiment and see what works, and where the story you communicate will have to change as you learn new things).

Instead of a linear process that helps you figure out *what* to communicate and then *how* to communicate it (sometimes using two different sets of experts from inside or outside your organization), a complexity approach offers a different rhythm of a process:

- Set the conditions for the initial direction and the initial boundaries (often by gathering lots of data about the current state).

- Hone and shape the language about those boundaries, communicating a mindset as well as a message.

- Use the best of the whole-of-person communication ideas: engaging emotions as well as logic, using stories and metaphors.

- Attach these ideas to experiments that have worked in the past so it doesn't seem like an out-of-the-blue direction.

- Watch for when the conditions are right to make a change in the message, not because you got it wrong the first time but because you are operating in a world of change and learning.

- Listen well to enable feedback and learning from all these experiments.

Table 6.1 shows that in the complicated domain there is much greater coherence in alignment between setting a direction, managing change, and communicating on these issues than there is in the complex domain. In the

TABLE 6.1 How direction setting, change management, and communications differ in complexity

	Complicated domain	Complex domain
Description	The relationships between cause and effect can be figured out and predicted for the future. Existing expertise and institutions can be used to analyze and solve problems. Implementation is manageable because goals are agreed and the needed capabilities are on hand.	There is so much variability and uncertainty that the relationship between cause and effect is visible only in retrospect and cannot be predicted. Issues are addressed by running safe-to-fail experiments across the system and amplifying or dampening the results. Implementation is less manageable because goals may be contentious and capabilities widely distributed.
Direction setting	Direction is set after research and analysis and is modified through measuring results against the specified goals.	Direction is set in broad terms and boundaries define the safe zone for trying things out. Direction may be modified in response to what works and what does not, and this may be done collaboratively. Small bets are amplified to drive bigger bets.
Adaptive change	Change management actions and group responses are predictable at the population or sector level based on past experience and analogous situations, but individual behaviors can vary significantly. Change actions can be designed as linear processes.	Group responses to change are emergent at local and larger scales and cannot be easily predicted in advance of trying things. Effects may be very localized. Change actions need to be designed as a series of iterative processes.
Communications	Communications experts figure out the key messages, to whom, by whom, and how these can best be communicated and clear and consistent messages are delivered in a disciplined way.	Clear and consistent messages are developed for the direction being followed, and these are then refined and changed as the change process and communications evolve and the details of the changes emerge from the process.

complex domain there is more of a tendency for the different elements to pull things into different ways of working and so it can be harder to achieve alignment. At the highest level, direction can be clear and crisp, but as it is applied at the individual level, there will necessarily be much greater variability. Communications people will tell you (using very clear and crisp language) that all this variability is just confusing babble unless it can be carefully segmented and targeted. Unless the message is crisp and clear and resonates with the audience, it will not land effectively. Variations and changes in messages may be what the complex world requires, but talking about it will just confuse people.

The communications challenge in the face of complexity is to manage this paradox: how do we speak clearly to different groups, listen to them, and deliver messages they experience as consistent and aligned with their ways of making sense of the world—and all while we are learning together, in the moment, about the nature of the situation and what might be helpful ways to make it better? The model we describe here for communicating in times of volatility, uncertainty, complexity, and ambiguity enables leaders and their organizations to thrive within this paradox.

You'll see parallels between this way of thinking about communicating and those in Chapter 4, which dealt with building the strategy in the first place. Those parallels are not only intentional; they're unavoidable. We don't know a way to keep communicating strategy and building strategy as different steps during complexity. In a simpler world, perhaps the leader or the senior team can set the strategy with such clear and compelling vision that, once the leader hums a few bars, the others can just sing along to the merry tune. In a complex world, the leaders couldn't possibly know enough to do this. So instead of tightening the reins and controlling what others do, leaders in this space need to loosen up and enable others to find a helpful path through the unknown. This means that not just the outcome of the strategy, but the process of building ideas together during complexity becomes a key shared resource.

For example, if Squint and his colleagues had decided in Chapter 4 that a target of 20% service offerings was the most important destination, they could have mandated that. They'd communicate it compellingly, cascade it through the organization, and align their reward system to this. (You can imagine the unanticipated consequences that might arise in response to such a target.)

They didn't do that, and instead they just described a move in the direction of more services and began exploring ways to experiment toward that direction in a safe way, and to learn like crazy from those experiments. But the leaders can't mandate curiosity or experimentation. Instead, they want all of the Jarreds and Michelles in the organization to hold as a goal that direction and the process by which the direction can emerge: the imagining and implementation of those experiments, and the conversation about what they learned from engaging in them.

So this is a different challenge than most communication books tackle. And while we said communication during complex and ambiguous times was nonlinear, we'll begin at the beginning, because the first time you intentionally communicate about complexity, it helps to be really clear about the boundaries you're setting.

SEE THE SYSTEM: GET CLEAR ABOUT DIRECTION AND BOUNDARIES

As we all surely see by now, in the complex space, you can't be crystal clear about the destination you want. Because you can't picture all the possibilities for the future, your limited imagination is a fragile basket to put your hopes in. If you're in a space of real complexity, there's no being sure of what will happen next. Things might unfold the way you think they will, and there might be a familiar pattern in how things play out even though the details probably vary each time. Or something will happen in your industry or the stock market or the government or the weather that makes your original plans seem absurd. That's a big deal, but maybe a bigger deal is that if you're pointed at a particular destination, your people are unlikely to be able to scan the horizon to take advantage of the changes that are unexpected. They will not be agile as they build toward this future, because they will be looking for evidence of what they believe (those biases we talked about in Chapter 5 are impossible to fully overcome). And as the whole organization points that way, the major threats on one side and the magnificent opportunities on the other may slip by unnoticed—until it is too late. Leaders have to watch out for the way they talk, or else their limited view of the future might well infect those with whom they work.

For example, there was a time when the mobile phone platform was a whole lot simpler, and most of us didn't have smart phones at all. Microsoft and BlackBerry were the reigning kings of the smart mobile technology that businesspeople used. They believed that what businesspeople wanted most was a keyboard and that any other technology would take people in the wrong direction. In January 2007, just before the iPhone was released, Microsoft's CEO Steve Ballmer looked at the design choices Apple had made and scorned them because they had broken away from the direction that looked most important to him. "That is the most expensive phone in the world," he said, "and it doesn't appeal to business customers because it doesn't have a keyboard, which makes it not a very good e-mail machine. . . . I kinda look at that and I say, well, I like our strategy. I like it a lot."[3] The focus on a single direction in a complex field may have contributed to Microsoft's current place at the bottom of the mobile market.[4]

We are not suggesting that leaders stop pointing to crisp and clear destinations. As long as you're dealing in a space that is relatively predictable, painting a clear picture of the future is still the most helpful and inspiring thing you can do. Having your people align their actions in the service of a crisp, clear destination greatly increases their chances of achieving that goal. If Yolanda had found that there was something relatively simple going on at FACS, perhaps she could have painted a picture of the change that was clear. If she had found out that they were suddenly at half the staffing levels they needed to be, and the money was readily available, she could have fixed that. If she had found out there were a couple of incompetent people in key positions and at the root of all the mistakes, she could have fixed that. What she found, though, was far more confusing than that, and the solution is unclear. She could make choices to declare a clear future anyway or narrow down to a single solution, but she has found—to her surprise—that some of her previous simple solutions are causing some of the present problems. Because of all this, she has been convinced that this situation is unpredictable and that the ideas about complexity she's been talking about with Curtis and Doug should fundamentally influence her work. So she needs a totally different approach.

In this case, Yolanda has been working to get a clear view of the current conditions by listening to many, many perspectives. She wants to send a message about overall direction and add to that a message about creating new experiments that gather around new possible attractors. She's seen some of what has been attracting conversation and attention so far, and it's not particularly healthy: complaints about regulations, anxiety about quality of care, gossip about pending changes. Instead, Yolanda wants to create new possibilities that move her people in the direction of being better able to care for at-risk children and families, without spending impossible amounts of taxpayer money and without ruining their lives in the process. But Ramona is right: Yolanda needs to help people feel that they are doing something, that they are moving in the right direction.

The message leaders need to give at a time like this is about what is safely inside and what is outside the boundaries, and what moves are considered the right direction. Without a clearly communicated and understood sense of the boundaries of play, people will not be able to have a sense of what experiments to build. But communicating these boundaries—as important as that is—isn't enough to get people to respond in new ways to the situation. You have to tap into some other habits of mind in order to support your people through the complexity.

ASK—AND ANSWER—DIFFERENT QUESTIONS: COMMUNICATE A MINDSET AND A MESSAGE

We've been talking for many pages now about how the questions you ask shape what's possible for you to learn—and what's possible for others to learn. In no space is this more important than when you are trying to communicate a new approach to dealing with complexity.

For example, we have a technology client that is trying to innovate but is well aware of its privileged position, always in the public eye. The leaders gave the message to innovate—"Be bold." They put the message inside backpacks and painted it on the wall so it would be top of mind. This wasn't just a slogan; these leaders really believed in the need for the organization to be bolder—or else be at risk of failure with too little innovation. The leaders also gave a clear direction to the "Be bold" action, made a clear boundary about what would count: make the user interface better. It seemed crisp enough, and there were metrics anyone could gather about how many users were on the site and what they were doing (gathering data about the current state wasn't a problem).

This boundary didn't seem to create innovation, though. While people knew the mandate, the stories most often told about innovation inside the organization were about initiatives that failed, publicly and badly. Or they were stories about times that leaders themselves stopped an innovation (or reshaped it to be a lot less bold). These stories grew like weeds, and they were the main way people got their information about whether innovation was safe or not. (The consensus: mostly not.)

To change this, the leaders needed to change the stories the people were telling. A first step toward that was for the leaders to make a decision about what kinds of innovation were actually safe to fail. At this tech organization, there was an unspoken rule: it is a big problem to mess with the website in ways that put it fundamentally at risk. Even among themselves, though, the leaders of the organization didn't know what it meant to put the website "fundamentally at risk." If they wanted people to really explore possibilities, they needed a clearer, more specific boundary. When pushed, the leadership group decided that the thing that was most dangerous was for the website to go down, even briefly. That was not safe to fail. But things that didn't make the website go down, even if they weren't guaranteed, felt safer (not always safe, but safer).

Now they had a boundary about direction and a boundary about safety— two pivotal things for creating new conditions for bold experimentation. But these are abstract ideas, and they don't change the minds, hearts, or actions of anyone (leaders included). Next, they needed some way to communicate these ideas to the organization. And here was the hardest part. The leaders found that while they could talk about a new and clear innovation boundary, it was hard for them to keep to that mindset in every meeting. When an idea came up in a meeting, someone was sure to say, "We tried that and the results showed that sort of thing won't work." We're guessing you've heard that sentence or one very like it in an organization near you (maybe you've even said it yourself—it's hard not to).

And it's not a terrible sentence. It's a form of learning from past experience, and it is designed to keep people safe and keep them from wasting energy chasing phantoms. Notice, though, that the idea that we can know "that sort of thing won't work because we've tried it before" comes straight from the complicated mindset. Collecting data, projecting forward from past experiences, these are all appropriate assumptions for a predictable world. They are inappropriate for the unpredictable world. The questions that guide our thinking about innovation boundaries need to be different. Not, "Did this work before?" Not even, "What are the odds this will work this time?" These are excellent questions, and we can and should learn from them, but they're not helpful in creating a boundary about what we should try next. Innovation requires edgy thinking, failure, missteps, and learning. This means the more helpful questions in complexity are, "How might this fail and how bad would that be?" and "What could we learn from this whether it is successful or not?" There may also be useful lessons from back when folks tried something and it did not work—is there anything they, or the organization, learned then that might help shape boundary setting and experimenting now?

Because these are new questions and they can make people nervous, it's even more important for the leaders to get their own minds—and orient their own mindsets—around them. In the complex space, leaders have to communicate more than a message: they have to communicate a mindset.

"OK," Yolanda said, gathering people's attention from the break they had taken after more than an hour of robust conversation. She absentmindedly picked the almonds from a bowl of mixed nuts in front of her. "From our conversations today and the conversations we've each had over the last weeks, I think we all agree that our job at FACS is a little different than we've seemed to think before. We have traditionally thought of ourselves as being able to *prevent* abuse and unnecessary deaths—if only we were good enough. Now, though, I think we can see a thing we've probably all always known inside—that abuse in families emerges from a wide variety of factors. We'll never be able to control all the factors, but we can glimpse the patterns to it. So instead, we are wanting to create the conditions for families and communities where abuse is way less likely to arise and having community support for intervening hard when we need to."[5]

"Well, that's not a particularly inspiring vision," Ramona muttered.

"Indeed," Yolanda admitted, fiddling with the almonds in her hand. "I'm not sure we want to announce that as the new mission statement to the press."

Doug took another doughnut from the plate and waved it at the scrawl-covered chart paper haphazardly covering the walls. Jarred had already got up to make sure the pens were not bleeding through onto his freshly painted walls. "I still think we should focus on the well-researched idea of a closer connection with families and communities," Doug said. "We knew the importance of family and community relationships before, but we haven't moved far enough in that direction. It seems like the idea that has the most possibility though from all we've talked about is this one. It moves us in the right direction to reduce those negative conditions—which are all about families and communities in the first place."

Curtis stood up and began straightening and rearranging the papers on the wall to make more space. As he tidied, he said, "It also makes sense as the right direction because the community is the place that knows what's going on way before we can find out—that's our most important network for keeping families safe."

Yolanda nodded to herself, "It's not like this is a brand new direction, either. We have known that more interaction with community members is vital—it's where the whole field is going these days. We've been moving in this direction, obviously, and I know there have been conversations about increasing this focus for the past several years or more from what I've been told. However, our talk seems to have been more aspiration than application. The trouble is how to get there—and how to retain all we do well, how to intervene really effectively, while also leaning more into the community space."

"The problem is also that the community often hates us," Ramona reminded them darkly. "My people get death threats for taking kids away from their families. Just last week, a huge flowerpot fell 'accidentally' from an upper story and landed just 18 inches away from where one of my caseworkers was standing waiting for someone to answer the door."

"Geez, in software development we only throw Koosh balls at each other," Arlen muttered to Hannah.

"Yes, we've got much more scope for safe to fail, don't we?" she whispered back.

Doug, listening to Arlen and Hannah, nodded his agreement. "It's a tough business for us all," he admitted. "So much responsibility, so little control, and we invest a lot of love without getting a lot of love back. It's tough love, and sometimes we get it too tough, and sometimes we err with too much love. Still, the story you're telling, Ramona, makes this direction even more important. If we could get the community even a little more united with us, we would probably reduce danger not only to our caseworkers but also to those in our care."

"Maybe the bigger end goal is to significantly reduce the number of people who need our care in the first place by really making communities stronger," Yolanda mused.

"I don't mean to sound critical," Ramona sighed. "I do like this direction, and none of us want any of this to be just platitudes, but where am I going to get the resources to apply it? My people are so busy already—how do they take on another thing? And where do we start? We deal with some really cruel and troubled people. Do we back away from that? How do we know which of our community initiatives is actually going to make a difference in protecting at-risk kids? We just don't know what really works." The room fell silent for a moment as they all sat with the challenging truths behind those questions.

Curtis broke the silence. "Look, no one can take on another thing! In a submarine it is always really clear—if something comes in, something else has to go out. We have to reduce the workload on our people."

"I totally agree with you, Curtis," Ramona surprised them by saying (she so rarely said that sentence), "but I happen to be running the bureau with a disproportionate number of visible failures and an absurdly long wait between referral and visitation. And I don't think my relationships with most of the community are particularly bad. How can we afford to do more in that space? My people can't keep up with the work they're doing, and they're not wasting any time now. I cannot see what I would put out to allow something more to come in."

"I'd have thought that, too, before my interviews this week," Yolanda told them. "But people are wasting tons of time, spinning their wheels, as they either wait for background checks to come back or follow procedures—often that I created—that make extra steps without adding any real value. I think there's time to be saved in this system."

"OK," Curtis said, writing on the fresh sheet of paper he'd just attached to the wall. "Sounds like we have a direction and a first place to make a difference: finding the value-sapping bureaucracy and duplication in the system."

Yolanda smiled. "OK, I like that." Murmurs of agreement spread throughout the room.

"So we want to innovate around decreasing bureaucracy and increasing the value of relationships without putting kids at risk," Curtis said while writing. "We want to be really clear about what a safe-to-fail experiment would include and what it wouldn't."

"I'm not comfortable experimenting with any of our crisis management systems," Yolanda said.

"Me neither!" Ramona agreed.

"OK, so no experiments right now in a crisis," Curtis wrote. "We might change these boundaries over time, but it's important to start with ones you can feel good about."

"Also I'm not ready at this time to mess with any procedures we have for the highly regulated parts of our business—removing kids from homes, approving foster families, and that sort of thing."

Jarred thought he saw Ramona take a deep breath before she asked, "Is it possible that these early experiments shouldn't really deal with kids at all at this point? I know I'm the most conservative here, but I am not ready to mess with any of our systems around keeping children safe."

Curtis smiled. "It's a real help to have diversity when you're trying to make sense of this stuff, Ramona. In the navy, we found that we were able to make real advances by creating boundaries that included even our core—and dangerous—work, but we sure didn't start with those. Remember the idea that we want to come at ideas from the side anyway. We might find ourselves improving key systems and even crisis management, but without even focusing on that at first."

"It would be OK to have any experiment that will increase connectivity to other agencies or to community—or even to other caseworkers—right?" Hannah wondered.

"Yes, good!"

"And if it eliminated paperwork or bureaucracy that didn't add value?" Hannah asked. The group murmured in agreement. "I think that's a set of boundaries for your innovation that overlaps with the innovation Actualeyes is trying to move toward," Hannah added. "So how about as a first possibility, we create a safe-to-fail experiment to see whether we can support any of the innovations your people come up with that require software modifications—at no charge to you because it'll help us understand our service line better, too?"

"I think we have our first safe-to-fail experiment!" Doug said, smiling. "And it meets the 'cheap' criteria for sure!"

TAKE MULTIPLE PERSPECTIVES:
ENGAGE EMOTIONS AND LOGIC

Once you've gotten really clear on the various boundaries of this new direction, you have to help other people get clear on them, too, so they can work and experiment inside those boundaries in this new way. Perhaps most important, you'll need to take multiple perspectives as you create and hone your language around the change in direction you're wanting to make. This involves a lot of listening and a lot of understanding what actually moves people to change the way they act or think. It involves remembering the various ways we are not logical (or anyway, not logical in the Mr. Spock way we think we are) from Chapter 5, plus all the good listening and clear data communication from Chapter 3.

You'll never get your people (or yourself, really) to make a change in the way they see the world unless you engage their emotions and get them excited about this new direction. This is hard, because complexity is confusing and overwhelming. You're wanting to let them understand that you're still leading the direction without trying to create the (false even though highly desired) belief that you know precisely what's going to happen next. This means you have to engage people's emotions in two different ways: (1) make complexity bearable, and (2) make your direction crisp and emotionally resonant. Let's look at what this might mean in practice.

MAKE COMPLEXITY BEARABLE

There are two ways to make complexity bearable, and we think you should do them both. One way is to help people learn to understand and thrive under complex conditions. This takes a long time and is in large measure what this whole book is about. The faster way is to remind people they are already dealing with complexity in many parts of their lives. It is an oddity of leadership that we often equate being a leader with having to predict, plan, and take control. This expectation is reinforced by the need to report that things *are* under control to the shareholders or the government or the board of a community group. We think of complexity as being the exception in our work lives, but when we expand our view (enlarge the boundary on our system) and look at our personal lives, we find that we are living with complexity as a part of our lives. We are raising families, caring for aging parents, living with pets. In our personal lives we are much less oriented to the long destination (which is, if we're honest, our death, our parents' deaths, and our pets' deaths—not destinations worth sprinting toward) and much more oriented to small markers along the journey that make the trip more fun.[6] And we cannot predict what paths these journeys might take. We care for our young children and aging parents to bring joy and peace into their lives and ours. We train our pets because we love their companionship along the way. Many of our daily choices are about how the journey of our lives is unfolding.

So we know how to be with the complexity of the journey and uncertainty about outcomes; we're just not used to thinking that way at work. At work we have the artifice of project plans and target outcomes. We're used to being hired and promoted on the basis of what we've accomplished rather than how we've gotten to our accomplishments. CEOs know this better than anyone else—they tend to be celebrated or reviled based on the current condition of their organizations, not on the journey they led to take people there. For some reason, our work metrics are mostly simple destination markers. (You know this is the case for every leader who gets promoted or celebrated for "good results" even when everyone knows she burns through her people. That is a destination celebration—and a short-term, simple destination celebration at that.)

Leading in this new way requires that you help people build bridges from their complex, journey-oriented home life to their workplace and link to the emotions that arise for them as they consider the new direction. Your raw materials are *journey* metaphors, symbols, and stories rather than *destination* ones as you describe what's next.

Because our lives are so full of journeys, there are a lot of metaphors to choose from, and many stories from your own life or from movies or literature. Are you setting out into the wilderness? Blazing a new path? Or just changing tack as the wind shifts? Do you want a sense of major force and change (burning the boats) or minor course correction (turning five degrees to starboard)? Is your core business mostly unchanged but you need a handful of scouts to see what's up over the next hill? Or are you fearing that the land you're on now is growing arid and you need the whole organization to move? Remember to ask yourself, "Are my stories and metaphors about a promised land (a destination) or about the joys of the journey, the benefits that will come from doing things better along the way?"

Another helpful thing about journeys is that they have rest areas and mile markers. You can play with these metaphors as you go along. What are the rest areas on your journey? Will you give an award in six weeks to the safe-to-fail idea that has failed both safely and spectacularly with lots of learning to harness? Will you take five months, review, and then hold a companywide conversation? Will you reach out to stakeholders in a year to see what they've noticed? Communicating interim steps that are about the journey and not about destination targets gives people something to reach for. Be careful not to communicate these in destination ideas, though ("Using these ideas, we'll come up with 7% savings in ten months"). Instead, talk about these interim destinations as a stop along the way, not an arrival ("The government wants a 7% cut in the next ten months, but what we're really trying to create is an ongoing quest to create value we hadn't thought about before. These safe-to-fail experiments should help us move regularly in that direction"). Another helpful question to carry with you: "Is this a destination (you've arrived) or a journey rest area (you're taking a breath and carrying on)?"

MAKE YOUR JOURNEY DIRECTION CRISP
AND EMOTIONALLY RESONANT

Clarity is a core communication goal, and you can be clear about your direction even if you can't be clear about your destination. Pay attention to what is clear to you and what you're wanting (or needing) to leave open, and then describe those two sets of things thoughtfully. In complexity, as in simplicity, it's useful to let people know what you don't know as well as what you do know, because often people experience silence as simply keeping secrets. Then they make stuff up to fill in the gaps. Being really straight with people ("I don't know exactly where we'll end up, but I know several things about our direction that are really key") is core to gaining their trust.

It doesn't actually matter if you're crisp about the journey if no one wants to come. Your appeal has to be emotionally relevant if you're going to lead people in this new direction. One of the most important ways to make something emotionally relevant is to actually talk about emotions—yours and others'. If an idea is exciting, say so. If it makes you anxious, say so. If it's both (most likely), you need to find a way to express both ideas. If you say it's exciting and leave out the anxiety part (usually for good reason, maybe because you fear it might make others anxious), there will be a little warning sign that goes off in the emotions of some of the people you're talking to, and they won't believe the "excited" part because it doesn't ring all the way true from the emotions they heard in your voice or message. They will wonder, "What's she holding back, and why?" Similarly, if there's an emotion that you pick up from those around you and you don't give a voice to that ("I can imagine that this new direction is both engaging and also threatening"), you'll risk their sense that you're out of touch.

It's not only the emotions you and others arrive with that create the tug toward the journey, though. Think about the emotions you wish to engender in others and how you might tell a story, use a metaphor, or give a tangible example that would help people come along. One of the teams we worked with wanted to move in the direction of creating a more civil workplace. They didn't want to come down heavily on their young and creative workforce, but they wanted people to know that they would be watching for "troll-like" behavior and giving people warning. They came up with the idea of Care Bear Patrol, which had a kind of light silliness they were going for, and they gave small stuffed bears to people who needed a little reminder of civility. They wanted their safe-to-fail experiment to make people smile, even as offenders were hearing the hard news that others had found their behavior distressing. They intentionally created a message that contained this subtle blend of emotions.

SEE THE SYSTEM: ATTACH THESE IDEAS TO EXPERIMENTS THAT HAVE WORKED IN THE PAST

Even people emotionally invested in your ideas and mindset about innovation might have a hard time beginning. If you step back from your current thinking and look across the organization or team, we're guessing you'll find lots of examples of people attempting little experiments. These are fantastic stories to tell. People probably haven't thought about these in the complexity space, but these are complexity moves people make automatically. The more you can show that this approach is not just some weird new management notion (and is a thoughtful expansion of a way people naturally have of being together), the better off you are as you lead this change. Connecting these past experiments with your new vision and strategy helps people do the following:

- See the scale and scope of these new experiments—even before anyone has come up with one in this new approach.
- Have a sense that they have already begun—which makes them more invested in continuing.
- Search for other examples from the past to bring into the present.

Each of these advantages makes the new direction and approach stickier and decreases the time and energy it takes to get them adopted.

See the Scale and Scope of the New Experiments

We find in our practice that it's really hard for people to get their head around what a leader means by "safe-to-fail experiments." The idea of "prototyping" isn't that much better. We've had experiences in which groups of people (like science advisers) begin to wonder about control groups and gathering data systematically and which peer-reviewed papers could be written afterward. It's really helpful for these folks to understand the scale and scope of what you're trying to encourage. Another colleague of ours observed that this approach was fine as long as the leaders chose the "right" experiments. We often find that this focus on "right" experiments (by which people often mean the ones that will succeed) takes much of the learning and innovation edge out of the safe-to-fail idea. But there are other worries, too.

We had a client who was interested in breaking down silos in his division and had decided that enforced job swaps were the right way to do this. He began to play with the idea of an "experiment" in which he randomly picked people to try out each other's jobs for a month or two. We noticed a couple of things about this. First of all, we thought that this might not feel safe-to-fail to those who were forced to swap jobs. Second, you might have noticed that this is also a destination goal: the goal is creating the job swaps. A journey goal is to become more connected as an organization, and job swaps are an idea that might help you along on that journey.

Some of his colleagues (in an action learning group—more on this later) pointed this out, helping him work back to thinking about this particular experiment in a more safe-to-fail way. "What job swaps have happened already, almost inadvertently?" someone asked. He told a handful of stories. "How could you look for and take advantage of those conditions again?" another person wondered. He pondered that question, too. He realized in his conversation that he didn't need to begin with an experiment that forced job swapping but with one that merely reduced the barriers that made it hard to job swap. He could go back to his team and communicate a message that was about the new direction of being more collaborative and tell them crisply about the experiment of sharply streamlining—for the next three months or so—the process by which everyone could swap jobs with one another. If that led to bedlam with everyone wanting to swap, he could shut it down. If it led to the sorts of results he was looking for, he could keep it going indefinitely. Looking at past experiments in this area helped him with the scale and scope and conditions of the plan.

Give People a Sense That They Have Already Begun

A second major advantage of sharing stories about experiments people have done in the past is that it reduces for them the scale of the change they need to make. Research shows that people are most likely to carry on with a change if they believe they have already begun to make it; the energy of starting a new thing is so much greater than the energy of just pushing a little harder on something you're already doing.[7] Connecting this new set of ideas to old behaviors builds that bridge—not just between home and work (as we've talked about already) but also between work and work. You want the complexity message to be something like, "This is a really new approach for us and we're going to be trying new things—but it should also feel really familiar to you because you've been doing this already."

One of the government agencies with whom we worked was accustomed to using lots of specific and measurable data and making iron-clad assurances to its customers. The idea of safe-to-fail came across to them as a 180-degree turn away from the quality control and certainty. The head of their internal audit division, surely predisposed to find safe-to-fail experiments worrisome, instead began to see the power of them for the work she was trying to do. One of the hardest elements of the culture she was trying to upend was the idea that her people were the police for the organization (which had the unfortunate effect of turning other members of the organization into metaphorical delinquents and ne'er-do-wells and, in this case, recidivists). Her people found the idea of experimenting with new relationships with their internal clients totally impossible, so she interviewed each member of her team and then interviewed the clients who had recently had internal audits. She collected examples of little "experiments" in new ways of handling customers on index cards, and she posted the cards haphazardly on the wall in the office. She didn't much care whether the experiment had had a good outcome or not (as long as it wasn't disastrous!), just that it was an attempt at a new thing. At a staff meeting, she had them explore the wall and add new cards right then about experiments that had been missed, and then continue to add them as new things came up. Her people came to quickly see that she wasn't suggesting a total turnaround but that they had been engaged in these practices for a while (some more than others, of course). They continued to add to the wall as they tried new approaches to treating their internal clients.

Search for Other Examples from the Past to Bring into the Present

As you can see in that last example, turning your attention—and the attention of others—toward experiments that have happened already can give people really good ideas about what to try next. As you tell the stories about all that you learned from past (and eventually present) experiments, whether they worked or not, you increase the odds that the learning from the experiments will spread around. It's key, though, to focus both on what was tried and also what was learned. If you just focus on successes, there will be less to learn (because people learn more from failure than from success), and there will be fewer ideas for others to borrow. Because complexity is so much about the context (e.g., a place, a set of people, a moment in time), an idea that failed in one place or at one time might be an idea that takes off somewhere else. Remember Friendster, the social networking site that began them all? It rose to fame (it was one of the world's most popular websites and it declined Google's offer of $30 million in 2003) and then fell from glory (by 2005 it was valued at one-twentieth of its 2003 value). If in 2004 Facebook (still www.thefacebook.com and not yet open to anyone outside college) had decided that the Friendster experiment had failed, the history of social networking might look very different.

"I think that was a really well-spent day," Squint told the group as he pulled on his bike helmet. "Thanks so much, Yolanda, for having us," he smiled at her, "and thanks to you, Jarred, for sharing that awesome 1970s monument upstairs. I can't remember the last time I saw a matching pink toilet, bathtub, and sink!"

Jarred laughed along with the others—so much for keeping his unrenovated upstairs bathroom a secret. The door closed behind Squint and Arlen—off to get ready to take a couple of their board members out to dinner.

Yolanda smiled at the group members who were left. "I think we've identified just about everything we need," she told them. "We have a direction, some safety boundaries—even some stories from past experiments to make the thing come to life for people. Now we just need to see what happens at the staff meeting on Monday."

"Do you want some help with the organizing and, dare I say it, scripting of what you want to say?" Hannah asked.

"Don't you have your board dinner?"

Hannah smiled and ran her fingers through her soft blonde curls. "Well, normally I might have cycled over as well, but with the dinner tonight, I'm afraid I was trying to protect the hair. It means I have an extra hour now though."

"OK, let's make the best of that, or do you want to work on your non–helmet hair?"

"Actually, this is much more fascinating than curl maintenance! I can do that with just my fingers. Thinking this through takes much more of me. I know it might seem odd, but I think it is quite energizing to puzzle through how we can talk with people about these things that are so not at all obvious to them. And frankly, it is way easier to think about what you might say, Yolanda, than if I were having to say it." Hannah smiled. "May I?" She picked up a marker pen and Curtis stacked the dozens of used chart papers neatly into a pile for easy reference. "Let's go over the most important pieces. Direction?"

Doug looked up from his laptop. "I've been fiddling around with the wording. How about: 'The Family and Child Services Division helps vulnerable families have successful relationships free of abuse, exploitation and harm. FACS works through relationships with community members to protect, educate, and heal.'"

"I think I'd like it better if you talked about 'we,' 'our,' and 'us,'" Jarred suggested.

"Can you really make it so that every family has successful relationships?" Curtis asked.

"Working with communities is important, but we also have to work with other agencies," Ramona reminded them.

"I'm not sure there's enough heart in that," Hannah said, looking at the page.

After a robust discussion, Hannah stepped away from a new piece of paper with: "We believe families are the most important building block of society. When they thrive, children and adults thrive with them. Our job is to make the hard work of families easier, by enabling people in all communities to create more nurturing family relationships, free of physical and emotional violence. We work through our deep relationships with communities and other government agencies to educate, protect, and heal."

Ramona smiled. "I really like that! I can imagine really using that as a guideline and asking ourselves the questions that arise from it—like, Are we really acting as if we believe families are the most important building blocks of society? Are our actions promoting educating, protecting, and healing?"

Doug glanced at Yolanda with a smile. This was as positive as they had ever seen Ramona.

"OK, great!" Hannah said. "Now, emotions?"

"Emotions?" Yolanda asked, confused.

"What are the emotions you are feeling about this change? You need to get a handle on them so that you can find the right words to describe your own sense of the change."

"Hmm. We'll, I guess I'm excited and happy about this new direction."

"Good. What else?"

"I'm upset about the events that led us here."

"Right. And?"

"Um, I guess I have a little trepidation about this whole package of ideas— and I'm also a little worried that I won't be able to deliver what it'll call for from me."

"OK, is that all?"

"Seems like a big mixed-up package to me!" Yolanda said with a smile.

"I don't think it's so mixed up. It's a bundle of emotions for a new change. So let's see, probably the key emotions are excited and happy—that's *delighted*, I think. You're delighted about the new possibilities." She wrote that down. "And upset and sad about the path that has brought us here. And anxious about what the change calls on all of you to do."

"Wow—I'm not sure about using words like *upset* or *sad* or *anxious*. What about *troubled* and *concerned*?"

Hannah laughed. "That sounds like management speak to me, Yolanda. If you're upset, go with it. If you're worried, go with it. If you are a little trepidatious, find another word for it! Let's start this thing off by saying how you really feel."

"Well, if we were going to be really honest, I was way more than upset about those kids—I was distressed."

"Devastated," Doug added.

"Heartbroken," Ramona murmured.

Yolanda nodded. "Yes, they're right. Devastated and heartbroken."

Hannah soberly wrote those words on the chart paper. "That feels very real now," she said.

"And the truth is, I'm not that anxious about this change. We need this. I'm eager for it!"

"I hope we're up to it," Ramona said, her eyes still downcast. "We can't have mistakes."

"Ah, but we can and will have mistakes," Curtis reminded them. "Just not the kind that break anyone's heart. Those are not safe to fail."

"Right, that failure part is hard for me to remember. I cannot imagine thinking it was OK for me to fail," Ramona admitted. "I have been fighting failure for as long as I can remember. It just seems so odd to set out to fail—just like it seemed weird to set out to understand the ways people aren't rational."

"I think that's a really important point to capture, Hannah," Doug said. "Lots of this stuff we're talking about does seem really counterintuitive, especially to people who have spent their careers in this very risk-averse bureaucracy."

"But our people are also trying new things all the time," Yolanda reminded him. "Remember those parenting classes for teenage fathers?"

Doug burst into laughter. "Those are legend! Oh, my, no one would come for the first several weeks and then a rumor spread that the homecoming queen was pregnant—which she wasn't, as far as we know—and then all those fellas came to the classes, preening and pretending that they were the mythic father of the imagined baby! We even had preteens coming along because they saw that our place was where the popular high school boys went after school on Wednesdays!"

"And remember the idea we had about an anger-management video game?" Curtis asked them. "Only playing the prototype we had developed made people more angry instead of less?"

"And there was the mix up at the Jewish Community Center meet and greet when instead of calling the kosher deli, the event manager called Kasher's Deli—fair enough mistake, but, oh, the platter with ham and cheese in neat little rolls." They were all laughing now as the stories tumbled out.

"See—we do make mistakes that we can laugh at, and none of those was fatal at all. The folks at the JCC were mad at first but they totally understood the mistake, and it led to really helpful conversations about Jewish families. The video-game people started that game that incorporated biofeedback—I'm not sure what ever happened there, but it certainly was a new direction. And a lot of those boys learned things about being a father that will come in handy when they're actually at that stage in their lives."

Ramona stifled a last chuckle. "OK, I get it. I can encourage that kind of failure I'm sure."

"And you can tell those stories," Hannah said, jotting notes, "to show what you mean."

"And actually, each of those is inside our direction and our boundary about staying away from anything about vulnerable children," Curtis noted.

"I'm not sure about the video game," Doug joked. "Who knows what that could have led to."

"Oh, geez, I'm going to be late!" Hannah said, looking at her watch.

"Thank you so much for staying," Yolanda said, scrambling to get Hannah's things together. "I'm really grateful for your perspective."

"Thank you for doing this job," Hannah said. "All of you. I am grateful to be a little part of this incredible work you do. And thanks, Jarred, for being such a great host." She took her things from Yolanda, and with one last glance behind her, she was gone.

ASK DIFFERENT QUESTIONS: WHAT ARE WE LEARNING?

The last piece of the communications package in this complex space will be familiar. While it's really important to think well about what you want to say in these complex times, it is probably at least as important to listen well and to learn from what you hear. It is vital to not get locked into a particular perspective or even a particular set of hopes about how things will go. Agility is the key stance in a complex and uncertain time, and listening and learning well are the keys to staying agile. What processes can you put in place to listen well to what is going on? How can you showcase the results of the safe-to-fail experiments—the ones that succeeded and the ones that failed?

Our human tendency to believe the current conditions will last forever needs to be fought against here by systematically looking for the ways you might be wrong and trying to keep scanning and learning from the horizon. These changes need to be a sign that the organization or team is thriving and growing—not that the leader has made a mistake and needs to try again to get it right. There is no getting it right. There are no maps here, no GPS. There are only new landscapes, new information, new opportunities and challenges, and the best leaders are those who are willing to listen well and make subtle changes to collectively recalculate the route again and again.

Yolanda put the last of the coffee cups in the dishwasher and turned it on. "Thanks so much, Jarred, for humoring your old mother today—and really all week."

Jarred smiled at his mom, who looked a lot better at the end of the day today than she had yesterday, or even back last Sunday night when she arrived. "It was great, Mom. I mean how many guys at my level get to spend a Saturday with the whole senior team? Besides, I think you really have given me this leadership bug. I really want to be better than I am, for the people I work with, and also for the people our products and services can help. I have a whole new sense of that after this week."

"I'm proud of you, Jarred. You really held your own today in a group where everyone was at least a decade older and much more experienced. And even when your mommy was in the room!"

Jarred's mocha skin turned rosy. "You know what, Mom? I'm proud of you, too. What a big job you have, and how many people—all over the state—are depending on you and your department to get it right. I'm really impressed."

"Well, don't be too impressed yet," she told her son, putting an arm around his shoulder and pulling him close to her. "I've only convinced the Saturday strategy group. Come Monday, I'll have to convince the rest of the organization."

"Mom, if you can get Ramona on board, you can get anyone!" Jarred reminded her. "This is an exciting new direction, and I think it might make a big difference in the lives of community members all across the state. And who knows? If this new approach works, maybe people in other departments or people protecting children in other places will learn from it, too, and the approach can spread. Someday this weekend will be famous for launching this new way of building and communicating strategy!"

Yolanda laughed. "You're still filled with big ideas, just like you used to be as a kid. But I think there is something new and important here, and while I hardly think this weekend is going to make it into the history books, it sure would be exciting if it made a change that we could look back at and feel good about."

"The thing I'm learning is that you can never know what's going to show up as important later," Jarred said. "But you have certainly created the conditions for a new set of possibilities to emerge, Mom."

Yolanda smiled at her son. "Well, I know one thing for sure. Complexity burns a lot of calories! Let's see if we can create the conditions for dinner to emerge!"

7 GROW YOUR PEOPLE TO BE BIGGER THAN YOUR PROBLEMS

Hannah tried one last time to smooth her unruly curls into a neat braid. She hadn't had time to change after leaving Jarred's house, so she was working with limited material to change her comfortable Saturday clothes into something that would work with Squint and Arlen and their three favorite board members. Luckily, she tended to be overprepared for most situations, and it was easy to trade her yoga pants for a long skirt that would match her sandals, and a silk scarf that would dress up her plain T-shirt. Her hair, however, was simply going to have to be tousled rather than controlled. She smiled to herself at the thought that she had spent the day talking about how to lead when you were not able to control things. All very well, but flyaway hair was in the chaotic domain!

Hannah felt her smile broaden as she approached the table where her partners and mentors were talking. While she had spent that day (and many others) with Squint and Arlen, she had had much less time with Nate, Jimmy, and Lela. The three used to make up the entire Actualeyes board back when they were all figuring out what a board did—and what Actualeyes did, too. Now there were seven other board members, but Nate, Jimmy, and Lela would always have a different relationship to the founders than the seven others.

Nate had been the professor who had brought Squint and Hannah together and then encouraged the business venture in the first place. Now retired, he brought the eager mind and deep theoretical appreciation of a professor along with something of Squint's boyish spirit. Together they had stumbled across Jimmy as they had looked for their initial funding. While Jimmy had made his fortune in farming equipment and still mostly dressed like a farmer in worn jeans and work boots, he had the mind of an engineer and loved the new (to him) world of computers. He was happy to invest half the money they needed in the beginning, but his questions and insights had become so useful that his perspective soon added more value than his cash. Lela, providing the other half of the cash, was a different sort of investor altogether. The only child of one of the oldest (and richest) Proucheford families, she had been educated to be a lady rather than a businesswoman. When she had discovered in her early 30s that many of her family's investment properties were crumbling houses rented to those with little other choice, Lela got serious about both business and home repair. The other women at her church suppers wouldn't have believed that Lela spent her days crawling under houses to get a sense of their foundations, that she spent her evenings trawling through accounts to get a sense of her crumbling financial foundations, and that she knew—and cared—more about the families of some of Proucheford's poorest families than the richest ones. Now well into her 70s, Lela had the straight bearing of her youth; even her perfectly neat white bun had been her companion for more than 40 years. These three had made Actualeyes possible, and their guidance had gotten more rather than less important as the business had grown.

Squint and Arlen were finishing up a summary of the day as the waiter brought their first round of drinks and took Hannah's order. "So I guess two things have come out of the day for me," Arlen was saying. "One is that we need to get a sense of the new ways of working and thinking that this increasing uncertainty seems to require, and the other is that we need to build software and services that help our clients understand this as well."

Lela put her hand on Arlen's arm and gave a throaty chuckle. "Darlin'," she began, "let's talk about the implications for the business planning at the meeting tomorrow. Tonight it might be more interesting to spend our time on how the senior team is doing in the face of all this uncertainty."

Arlen, who had been nearly ready to begin to outline some business changes, was momentarily taken aback, and it was Squint who responded first. "It's a great question, Lela," he answered thoughtfully. "I'm not sure we know yet what the implications might be for us personally. I know that I'm spending a lot more time feeling confused about what to do next than I have over the past few years, and I'm feeling a little more adrift than I'm used to. Generally the clear answer is obvious—or becomes obvious—and we can just pursue it. Now the answers don't seem obvious at all. It seems sort of like a mean joke to be thrown back into confusion about the business just as I felt like I was getting good at predicting what issues were going to come up and how to handle them when they did."

Jimmy barked out a laugh, "Life's full of surprises that way, isn't it? Who'd ever have guessed that I'd get out of tractors and begin messing with these strange coding languages." He turned on his best country drawl. "Some people might say I done never even learned English that good in the first place."

Nate gave Jimmy a playful nudge with his elbow. "I know you're kidding a bit, Jimmy—especially about the English—but there's a way our own experience of being thrown back into uncertainty ourselves, many years after we thought we'd figured things out, might help these younger people get a sense of what might be in store for them. They probably can't imagine how much learning about the world is still in front of them."

It's probably true that most of us don't have a sense of what learning is in front of us—and what that learning might feel like. When we ask adults about the changes in their lives, they tend to point to a mix of major turning points. Some of those changes have been ones people have seen coming, and even gone after: a big promotion, graduate school, a new baby. Some of the changes came from unexpected and unanticipated shifts—a mistake that led to a crisis of confidence, a change in the economy or industry or political climate that had bigger ramifications than expected, the end of a relationship that spins the world in a new way.

These learning spaces, like this moment right now for Squint, can be disorienting and unpleasant. We notice that we have lost a thing we used to have: certainty, comfort, a sense of competence in the world. Some of our most important values might be at risk. What was clear is now foggy, and we worry that it won't ever be clear again. In fact, because we tend not to have a way to think about these learning moments, we can worry that we're going backward instead of forward; we worry that we are simply losing what we once had rather than building something new.

A theory of adult growth and development offers us something of a guidebook to our potential growth, not to decide in advance what our journey might be, but to have a sense of the journey of others before us and some of the patterns of the discoveries people often make along the way. This sort of guide has been important through most of human history, as groups of people created rituals for what happens to us as we leave childhood, become adults, and eventually become older and (hopefully) wiser. In times of relative social stability, such guides have helped humans make sense of the changes in what it means to be a functioning human over time, changes that are shaped by the different (if mostly predictable) phases and stages of our lives. The modern Western world has lost most of these maps of our future—even as the maps of our current location have gotten more instant, more specific (a blinking blue dot on a street grid, a business card, a cell on an organizational chart). The more nuanced guides to our internal territory of change are often far less available than external markers of these phases. A "midlife crisis" is more marked in our minds by the accumulation of money that leads to the ritual of buying a sports car than to the accumulation of wisdom that leads to the ritual of others coming to us for guidance.

We have perhaps lost our connection to these earlier rituals because the world has become more complex and the phases of our lives are less predictable than they once were. When is the normal time to leave home these days? To get married? To have children? Even naming these as typical events feels odd—there are so many other choices available to us as we live our lives. At the same time, our lives increasingly demand that we take action and make sense of this complex and volatile world in which these choices exist. As the choices give us more freedom, they also challenge us with more uncertainty and ambiguity and thus increase our need for making sense of the complexity around us. Understanding how we might grow more capable of meeting those demands has never been more important. Organizations increasingly require leaders to think about the world, to set direction, to build cultures and make decisions fit for a complex world. These complex adaptive leaders are not created by a promotion, nor do they spring fully formed from their executive MBA programs. Just as a guidebook to another country helps us make key decisions, organize our experiences, and look out for avoidable peril (and be ready for the unavoidable), so, too, a kind of guidebook to our adult development possibilities supports us to make choices and see our lives in a new way. And, perhaps more important, this guidebook could help those who lead the organizations where we spend so much of our adult lives to create a more intentional and thoughtful developmental journey for us all.

ASKING DIFFERENT QUESTIONS: WHO HAVE I BEEN AND WHO AM I BECOMING?

The Stanford psychologist Carol Dweck discovered something unexpected as she researched the different ways people dealt with setbacks and failure.[1] Instead of finding out that some people are simply smart enough to turn failure into success, or that some people are wired for learning and others for freezing up, Dweck discovered that all of us seem to have a mindset about ourselves and about whether we are stable or fixed ("I have always been a stubborn person—that's just the way I am") or whether we are changing ("I have been too self-conscious, but I've been working on that"). This mindset—which itself is changeable—seems to make the difference between whether we take setbacks as a blow to our very core or identity (because we had thought we were smarter and shouldn't make mistakes like this) or whether we take those same setbacks as a piece of our evolving selves (because we knew we were needing to learn more and now we are certain we do!). People with a mindset that includes an orientation to their own growth are much better at learning from failure than their colleagues with a more fixed mindset.

Such a mindset also shapes the way leaders and organizations think and act. If a leader has a fixed mindset, he may be less likely to be focused on creating the conditions for growing his people and more focused on hiring and retaining the best people in the first place. If a senior team has a fixed mindset, the members may be less hopeful about the way their current staff is facing a change in business conditions (or more dismayed by the setbacks they and their people experience). Conversely, if leaders have what Dweck calls a "growth mindset," they are much more likely to talk about and support their own growth—and the growth of others. And they are much more likely to lead successful change initiatives.

Dweck has found that this difference shapes our relationships and our sense of our own possibilities across our lives. If we believe we are naturally talented, smart, or gifted at something, we are more likely to have a fixed mindset and try to protect this natural gift we were born with. It is almost as if the gift is bigger than us and we have to live up to it and not risk it too much. If we believe we are working at things, getting better, changing as we go (even if we happen to be talented, smart, or gifted), we are more likely to try to expand the natural gifts we were born with. We have a different relationship to our capabilities—we know they are fallible, and we know they could also be better. This makes a huge difference.

Many leaders focus on important questions like, "Who am I and what am I good at?" We'd like to expand those with different questions: "Who have I been and who is the leader I want to be next?" These different questions come from the growth mindset and point us to our own emerging possibilities.

This question and the growth mindset it encourages also make it more possible for each of us to learn from failure, which, as we've said again and again in this book, is key to living in complex, unpredictable spaces. If we can't learn from those things that didn't turn out as we'd hoped or expected, we'll never thrive in complexity. Without a growth mindset, we are much better suited to a more predictable, simpler world.

TAKING MULTIPLE PERSPECTIVES: DIFFERENT FORMS OF OUR DEVELOPING MINDS

Another key support to developing the growth mindset, and to helping yourself and others grow, is to have a sense of the patterns in the ways adults can grow and change over time. Here we understand really what the Talmud means when it says, "We do not see the world as it is. We see the world as we are." Theories of adult development help us understand what it means to "see the world as *we* are." We've seen in earlier chapters the way our brains shield us from too much information, making decisions for us that we don't have any conscious control over. Using adult development theories, though, we see the ways that shielding can change over time as we become better able to handle shades of gray, better able to handle volatility, uncertainty, complexity, and ambiguity. And we've seen the way mindsets—like the growth mindset and the people-as-sensemakers mindset—are important to creating the conditions for us all to learn from one another at work. There is a structure of our thinking that is deeper even than our mindsets, though. This is our developmental "form of mind," which is the shape of our whole meaning-making system. These forms of mind shape how we see the world, the choices we think we have, and the stories we tell about ourselves. Understanding the development path of these forms of mind is another chapter of the guidebook to our growing and changing adult lives.[2]

The pattern of this form of development has a common rhythm over the life span. At first we are subject to (or immersed within or unable to see) the rules or ideas that drive us. They are as invisible as the air we breathe, and just as necessary. Over time, as those rules or ideas become challenged by the complexity of the world around us, we are able to see them, think about them, have them as objects for our awareness and choice. As this happens, we are less unknowingly subject to these rules and ideas and more able to handle them as objects of our own intent. This, adult developmentalists say, is the pattern and hallmark of growth.

In practice, these phases of development look like this: When we're little kids, we tend to see the world as interconnected and magical. We believe in a world in which there aren't any clear laws of time and space, in which people actually are bigger or smaller depending on how far away they are from us. Eventually, as we grow into older kids, we come to see that there are stable rules to the way objects behave, and that they stay themselves no matter where we are in relationship to them. Those stable rules mean that the physical world becomes less magical, but they also mean that the interpersonal world becomes more mysterious. We make the discovery that each person has an internal and an external life—and that we have access only to their external lives. Jennifer's son, Aidan, was visibly upset as he was going through this transition, explaining: "Mom, do you know that all around the world, people are having thoughts right now—each person, everywhere—and I'll never know what those thoughts are unless I ask? And even then, they might be lying to me and I'll never know!" When we see the world through this, the self-sovereign form of mind, we can only interact with and make sense of our own internal lives, and so we become the monarch of our own tiny kingdom of one, working in a confusing world to get what we need. With this form of mind, interacting with the ideas of complexity and volatility is so unnatural that most complexity is just unseen, and the world appears quite simple. Ambiguity and volatility either are mysterious forces about which nothing can be done or—as is the case more often in the modern world—are taken as the fault or weakness of some other group (leaders in this corporation, or the government?) who should be able to solve this problem and make things clear if they were any

TABLE 7.1   Forms of mind as they interact with volatility, uncertainty, complexity, and ambiguity

Form of mind	Relationship to volatility, uncertainty, complexity, and ambiguity
Self-sovereign	The world is a volatile place and this is out of our control—nothing can be done. Ambiguity is the fault of the leaders, who should have the power or the good sense to make things clear. Complexity is mostly unseen. When people talk about interconnections or shades of gray, the self-sovereign mind may well reject those ideas as absurd (or intentionally misleading) ways to somehow make the situation come out to that person's advantage.
Socialized	Ideally, the world shouldn't be a volatile place, and with preparation and the right advice from the right experts, volatility can be fixed or at least minimized. Some volatility can be explained by the right experts. Uncertainty and ambiguity are to be solved with the appropriate processes, and complexity is to be broken down to its component parts to be well managed. In a very complex and uncertain time, additional experts need to be called in to provide research-based solutions.
Self-authored	We have enough perspective to recognize that the world is volatile and uncertain, and while we might not like it, we try to make use of it rather than wishing it away. Complexity, which we freely recognize, can be deployed to meet our self-authored goals. Ambiguity is a necessary evil and should be shifted toward clarity when possible and managed when not possible.
Self-transforming	Here we have the natural playground for uncertainty, complexity, and ambiguity. The world and its patterns appear to us as places we can influence but not control, and we are comfortable with that and agile enough to understand the predictable shifts that we might expect, as well as being prepared for that which is totally unpredictable. We understand the needs of others to eliminate as much ambiguity and volatility as possible, but we do not have that wish ourselves, knowing that ambiguity and volatility are the fabric of a complex world—eliminating them (if it were even possible) would leave us in a world less rich and wonderful than the one we inhabit.

good. (See Table 7.1 for a look at the different ways our form of mind shapes our relationship to volatility, uncertainty, complexity, and ambiguity.) While all children go through this self-sovereign stage, most begin to leave it in adolescence. Some of us, though, stay in this stage for years or even decades after our teenage years are behind us.

Most of us, though, begin to face the fact that the world is too complex for us to manage on our own. Our kingdom of one is just too perilous. We band together with some community or set of ideas that is larger than we are to help rescue us from that complexity, and we begin to put the needs of the collective above our own needs. For some people this looks like becoming immersed in a particular profession or organization. For others, the right answers come from a particular set of societal norms about what success looks like. As we begin to take on the views of these outside perspectives, we start to make sense through the *socialized* form of mind. We see that outside experts or perspectives offer us a safe guide to the confusing and complex world. This form of mind allows us to be full members of a collective of some kind—no longer ruler of our own tiny kingdom but fully functioning members of this larger society.[3]

You might be able to see even from this little description why this socialized form of mind, a developmental achievement that was probably all a person needed during most of human history, is probably not ideal for a leader during complex times. In a simpler world, there would be a place or a person we could visit to find out what the right answer was, what we should do when we were confused. In a complex world, though, it's much harder to find those guides, and harder still to believe in them over time (because in a complex world, they're likely to offer the wrong answer at least sometimes, disillusioning their followers). And when leaders do find such a guide, the leaders become limited by what the guide says (and their proximity to the guide) rather than being able to cope with the requirements of the context or of the people they are leading.

Complexity and ambiguity, mysterious and blame ridden in the self-sovereign form of mind, can now be simplified into problems to be taken apart and solved, spreadsheets and project plans to be developed and executed, or political change to enable or constrain governments or markets (depending on the particular ideology you are acting within). Volatility and change are to be managed and reduced. Appropriate experts are to be consulted to make these processes as neat as possible—and to work hard to ensure we don't fall into these dangerous places again.

It is when the socialized form of mind is too constraining to deal with the complexity around us that we push beyond it, beginning to see the ways we have been written by the opinions of some outside other and deciding instead to pick up the pen ourselves. This form of mind is known as *self-authoring*, because we are relying on inner guidance rather than an external set of ideas to write our own story. Instead of figuring out what the external guide would direct us to do, when we are making sense through the self-authoring form of mind, we run the ideas through our own internal set of values and principles, and thus see a wider set of options and a more nuanced set of decision criteria than we could have had before. In many ways, this is the form of mind of the stereotypical modern leader. She creates her own vision, makes decisions based on her inner compass, and can test out her ideas with others without losing her own center. Now complexity is visible, and leaders can begin to make use of it to create better systems and decisions to manage risk and to take advantage of opportunity—and simplify it for others. Ambiguity is an obvious part of what it means to be human, and it should be reduced when possible and lived with at other times. Change is to be deployed with care if it is self-generated, or responded to with speed if it comes from the outside world. These leaders still need new skills and support for interacting in the VUCA world, but their form of mind supports the growth of these new skills and perspectives. While this form of mind is really useful for leaders, it takes time and support to develop it, and it has been our experience that organizations encourage—and also often discourage—the development of this capacity.[4]

For a very small percentage of us, the complexity of the world becomes too much for even the sophisticated self-authoring form of mind to handle.[5] We discover the ways we have blindly devoted energy to perfecting our own internal self-authoring set of values and principles, continually tweaking and improving them to get a self-authored system that won't let us down. Eventually, we may discover that in a complex world, this is an impossible task, and the energy spent working toward that impossibility can be better spent in other ways. Here at the *self-transforming* form of mind, people begin to give up on their own self-authored system (just as in the earlier transformation people gave up on their more externally created system). Instead, they begin to see across systems, across the socialized system of some of their colleagues and the self-authored system of others. They can understand and hold the perspectives of multiple and opposing stakeholders at the same time, knowing that there is truth and importance even in starkly different perspectives. They begin to fully experience an idea of Niels Bohr: "The opposite of a correct statement is a false statement. The opposite of a profound truth may well be another profound truth."

The leadership literature is now full of guesses about what sort of capacities leaders of the future will need. The capacities of those with self-transforming forms of mind seem to be the ones that will be necessary to lead in this new millennium. It is these self-transforming leaders who handle complexity with the most grace, because their openness to learning and to questioning their most fundamental assumptions gives them the largest set of possibilities. Their perspective is so broad that others find them almost magical—seeing new options where others are hopeless, finding areas of commonality where others see only opposition. These leaders are comfortable with conflict, diversity, and ambiguity. They are also more likely to successfully lead an organizational change. According to theorist and researcher Bill Torbert, "In ten longitudinal organizational development efforts, the five CEOs measuring at the [post-self-authored] stage of development supported 15 progressive organizational transformations. By contrast, the five CEOs measuring at [self-authored or socialized] stages of development supported a total of [zero] progressive organizational transformations."[6]

These forms of mind are part of a developmental progression, and it can take years or decades to move between them—if we move at all. But the organization that figures out how to support people to grow, and to keep them interested and engaged once they've grown, will have a remarkable advantage in a complex world.

"You've been awfully quiet, Nate," Hannah noticed as the first course plates were cleared. "Where did we lose you?"

Nate smiled fondly at the three. "You didn't lose me, but I have been thinking about this whole situation from a different perspective. Remember when you talked about becoming more uncertain, Stephen?" (Nate had never been able to bring himself to call Squint by his nickname.) "And then you went on to talk about the ways you were more unsettled, and to compare that to ways you used to be more certain, and even to the ways you see certainty in some of your other managers like Murray and his colleagues."

"Yeah, *Stephen*, remember that?" Arlen teased, his inner 12-year-old never too far away.

Squint smiled. "Yes. I remember. Why? Are you noticing that I'm actually getting less competent rather than more competent? Are you thinking that things are working rather backward?"

"No, that's not it at all," Nate answered. "I'm noticing a phenomenon I've been wondering about for years, and I'm wondering about whether my esteemed colleagues might have noticed it, too. There's a way that I find I grow less certain over time, and that while that sounds like I'm losing something (and of course I am losing certainty), I've been amazed at how much I've gained in that loss."

The Actualeyes leaders looked a little puzzled, but Lela jumped right in. "I think I know what you mean, Nate. When I was younger, I knew just what to do, what was right and what was wrong. Oh my goodness, I told quite a lot of people what the right answer was! But things weren't quite as simple as I had thought they were, and the things that had seemed so obvious to me from the beginning started to get less obvious. I had to stop telling people what to do because I got less and less certain that I knew what they should do! I guess that must have been unsettling at first, but I have to say I really love it now. The whole world opens up in a way. I have to ask so many more questions because I see so many more possibilities."

"Yep, you younger folks will remember that when we started out together, I knew all the right things for you to do, even if I didn't know a darn thing about computers," Jimmy added. "Now, thanks to you, I know a whole lot more about computers and programming and high-tech business models. But I know less and less about what you should do next. I even wonder now about some of my certainties about tractors and the farm equipment industry, but that may be another story."

Arlen motioned to the waiter for another glass of wine. "It sounds to me like you people were more helpful to us a few years ago," he joked.

"I'm not sure that's right, Arlen," Hannah said, as usual more serious than her partners. "I mean, you look at how certain some of our team is about which way we should go, and actually that doesn't seem very helpful at all. It seems . . . simple somehow. Like they think there's only one right path and all we have to do is find it."

"True enough," Squint added. "I'm not sure I'd trust someone who had simple answers right now. We're trying to do something that no one has ever quite managed before, to create a set of products and services that join technology and human connection in a new and integrated way. We've seen organizations come closer to the sort of thing we're talking about, but we know that we've never seen anyone really nail it."

"I guess," Arlen said, grudgingly. "And even if they had nailed it ten years ago, the current tech environment is so different, and our clients and their needs are so different—it wouldn't be that helpful anyhow."

Hannah nodded. "Yeah, we see that in our own managers. Whenever they try to fix a problem and show us exactly what needs to be done, we all shy away from that, thinking that they're getting too narrow and simple too early— really moving against this bigger, more experimental frame we've been talking about at our meetings and at the FACS meeting today."

"OK, so we see that over time it might be more helpful to move to a perspective that has less certainty, and we can even begin to get a glimpse at what gains come from that, but how do you hire people who have something of that perspective? We tend to look for competence and particular skill sets in our new hires—not so much for this kind of uncertainty you describe. Because sometimes this facility with uncertainty is the bonus you're talking about and sometimes or in some people it's just a confusing mess. And even if we were able to tell the difference between the uncertainty that is unhelpful and this kind you're talking about, we might end up with a very small pool indeed. We can't just rely on you three to be like this, right? I think you folks would be rather outside our pay scale," Squint said, smiling.

Jimmy snorted. "Heck, you'd never have hired me in the first place! You only took a chance on putting me on your board because I had the money you needed, and Nate vouched for me. I don't have anything like the fancy pedigree you look for when you're hiring someone."

"This is an important point," Lela said. "I do believe the trick isn't to hire those people in—pedigree or no—but to grow them up. Turns out, I think Actualeyes needs to be in the people-growing business just as much as the software business. And I bet there are some things you are doing that not only aren't helpful to your people and their growth but also are downright stunting."

ASKING DIFFERENT QUESTIONS: HOW ARE SOME OF OUR VALUES GETTING IN THE WAY OF GROWTH?

We have a wide variety of clients who believe that the work their organizations need to do now is more complex than the people within them. This leads them to conclude that they need, as Lela suggests, to grow their people. And yet many of them are noticing that their organizations seem to be doing the opposite of growing people—they seem to be keeping people small. As we've talked with hundreds of people in organizations around the world, we've found some key ingredients that seem to lead to stifling growth. We're not talking here about the really bad things that everyone would know were bad: the nasty bosses, the corrupt systems, the unfair practices, the abuses of power. Instead, we're talking about reasonable and well-informed systems developed by well-intentioned people that seem to make people smaller, and the slight additions that might actually help people grow. Here are four examples of well-intentioned, fine-sounding approaches that are adopted for good reasons and that often constrain people in perverse ways:

- We hire the smartest people.
- We hold people accountable for results.

- Competition keeps people sharp.
- We treat people the same.

We Hire the Smartest People

For many of our clients, the brains of their employees are central. They care about how smart their people are and how deeply skilled they are in whatever their craft might be. They work to hire the very best "talent" either straight from university campuses, from their competitors, or from neighboring industries. Obviously, this is a key piece of their success, and it matters to keep doing this. And besides, it's much easier to measure current success than future potential. Past success is in the "known" bucket; future potential will always be in the complex space—we can never be certain about it.

However, there are some significant downsides to this approach, developmentally. First of all, there is the question of whether these smart and already successful people are as open to learning as others. Chris Argyris, in his classic *Harvard Business Review* article, "Teaching Smart People How to Learn," reports his finding that, "put simply, because many [highly paid, highly trained] professionals are almost always successful at what they do, they rarely experience failure. And because they have rarely failed, they have never learned how to learn from failure."[7] This is exactly aligned with Dweck's research that suggests that those who have always relied on their intelligence and their own success as core features of their personality are more likely to have a fixed rather than a growth mindset.

We are not arguing that organizations who are interested in growth should hire people who aren't smart. Rather, we believe that organizations need to hire people who are smart *and* also who have learned to—or are willing to learn how to—learn from their mistakes. This means not just checking for this experience with failure but also watching your own mindset as you listen. People who are used to hiring for intelligence and success might have a harder time tolerating people who can actually talk about their own flaws.

For example, one of us sat on an interview panel for a senior leadership position in an organization we knew well and loved, an organization that needed to grow and change and needed this new leader's support doing so. The job candidates were asked about their experience with failure, and they answered variously: one explained her minor failures away, one gently blamed others for his failures, and another told us why he had failed, learned from it, and now would never fail again. The last candidate threw her head back and laughed. "That's the easiest question you've asked yet! I fail at least once a day," she said. "What size failure shall we talk about?" This smart, capable leader took chances, and in those chances was not always successful. She explained the sorts of mistakes she was most likely to make, the ones that bothered her, and the sorts she was happy to make again and again because she learned so much from them. She was clear, too, about what was outside acceptable bounds for failure. To our ears, she had a fantastic relationship to learning from her own failure. To others on the panel, though, she had named a severe weakness. "We don't want someone who has such an easy relationship with failure," one of the other panelists said, troubled. "We want someone who takes failure really seriously, a safe pair of hands." We had all agreed as we created the interview protocol which issues were most important; innovation, boldness, and creativity were on the list, and safe pairs of hands were not. Boldness can be frightening, though, and safe pairs of hands tend not to be (though they might be frightening in the long run in an organization that needs to make change).

If you really want to hire people who have learned how to notice and learn from their mistakes, you'll have to tolerate conversation about failure without seeing it as a weakness. Or to put it another way, you'll have to be able to listen to conversations about failure and be able to judge more carefully when it really is a weakness. Someone who sounds careless is probably not a good idea. Someone with a string of failures and no real recovery system is also not a particularly impressive candidate. But someone who has a way of thinking about and recovering from the failures that come from taking risks and learning from those risks, well, that might be exactly the person you need in a complex world. Expanding from smart people who have no blemishes on their record (or who explain those blemishes away to circumstance) to people who are smart *and* have faced and overcome mistakes could help your organization develop a workforce more ready to grow over time.

We Hold People Accountable for Results

Organizations need to find ways to judge how well people are doing at work. They have to create and set budgets based on the successful management of projects, promote and reward people who have contributed in exceptional ways to the organizational mission, and find ways to uncover those areas (e.g., people, projects) that are not performing so that they can help them succeed or support them to move on. A focus on results seems like the most logical way to do this. It is fair, quantifiable, and really deals with the whole point of work: to accomplish the things you're supposed to accomplish. It seems hard to argue that this focus is misguided.

And we won't argue that this focus on results is misguided, just that it's partial and should be used with care. A simple focus on results—or even a complicated focus that looks only at results—is likely to stifle innovation and individual growth. We'll give two examples.

We work with an organization in the financial services industry that is struggling to support its people to be more self-authored. Its leaders have rolled out leadership programs in the effort to break out of what they think is a real sticking point in the socialized form of mind in their people. There is leadership coaching to support leaders to discover and grow their self-authored voices. The organization has added developmental conversations to their employee evaluation system. It is making significant investment in this idea, and the learning and development people are frustrated when the progress seems blocked in some way. But ask the leaders themselves, and they feel caught in what seems to them to be an organization that says one thing and does another. Yes, make up your own mind, set your own direction, pursue the areas of your passion to grow the organization and its products. But do that without slipping for a moment away from the results that you have reached before. Grow, by all means, but do it without faltering, without losing your focus on the results your evaluator thinks are most important, or else you'll be punished. The leaders—who have succeeded in part because they have been socialized into these collective goals and have some of their identity tied up in the ways they reach the goals—find it very hard to escape the gravitational pull of the organization to build their own center of gravity. One leader told us about his downward rating after taking a chance that hadn't worked (or perhaps hadn't yet worked). He explained that he had taken a very big hit to his self-esteem when his "excellent" rating slipped, and he was on his guard to never let it happen again. He was clear that he wouldn't take that kind of risk because he had found that it simply hurt too much. He would focus on the goals his organization had set out for him, and ignore the little voice inside him that was eager to try something else.

In a totally different industry, we watch the way a university has shaped and constrained the work—and perhaps the development—of its faculty. Most universities don't expect strong financial results (though some are very focused on grant funding), but even the multifaceted focus on results can push against people's development. Those things that produce results are most valued (like a publication in a major journal, or serving on an impressive blueribbon committee). Because people know they will be judged on the outcome of their work, they are more likely to make their choices with the university's preferred outcome in mind. There's a way this isn't a problem at all—of course a university wants faculty to select work that leads to outcomes that are important to the university! The problem is that faculty members who are concerned about promotion and tenure (which is most faculty members) often focus much more on what the university wants than on what they want, and they focus more on what is more certain to come to fruition rather than what they're passionate about creating that might be more innovative and risky.

Both of these cases create conditions in which people spend more of their time looking outside themselves to the opinion and views of others rather than searching inside themselves for what's most important to them. They also lean away from innovation. We worked with one senior academic who advised young faculty members away from following their own passion because building and following your passion takes too much time to deliver results. He hated this advice, but he gave it anyway because he had seen too many promising careers ruined by people discovering and following their own academic passions. This is obviously a perverse and unhealthy consequence of a focus on results.

We are not trying to suggest a solution that means that organizations no longer judge the results their people accomplish. Results matter very much.

But we are trying to show the ways that focusing only on outcomes limits the ability some (many) people may have to develop their own self-authored voice.

We believe a focus on results should be balanced with a focus on developing a personal passion, a focus on *attempts*. While we were working on our doctorates, both of us celebrated each time we or one of our friends submitted a major paper or proposal, because the submission was inside our control and the result was outside it. We believe organizations should be more like that too: celebrating the attempts as well as the successes. This doesn't just lead to a more safe-to-fail culture, but it also leads people to have to wonder for themselves what they care about and want to attempt. They have to decide what's important to them rather than just considering what's important to the organization. And there's even a hidden benefit to the organization's pushing for the development of a personal passion: sometimes it takes an external push to help someone begin to grow an internal self-authored voice. If the organization's focus is on developing self-authorship—or even on any kind of growth at all—the basis on which people are rewarded should include their interest in and success with growing themselves.

Competition Keeps People Sharp

Many things in organizations drive toward competition: forced rankings, distinguishing top talent, the constant need to decide who wins and loses in a budget during times of shrinking resources, citations and publication rankings for academics. There's plenty written about the ways these practices diminish collaboration, but there's less written about how these things can diminish individual (and thus eventually collective) growth. Competition drives particular behaviors that you'd probably find useful—drive, striving to be best, a focus on winning—but this focus on winning leads to a couple of behaviors that are likely to get in the way of our development.

The first issue is that competition always has people looking outside themselves for what's best. We've talked about that in the section above, and the lesson is nearly the same here. Focusing outside yourself to learn what to do and what is best is clearly not supportive of a growth to a more self-authoring form of mind, because people can learn to ignore (or never develop) their own self-evaluation system as they focus on what others see as important.

The second issue is that an emphasis on competition means that people are more likely to try hard to showcase the ways they are better than others. This has a diminishing return on their development of each of the habits of mind we're claiming are so helpful for development. A focus on competition and beating others narrows the questions people ask, urging them to be asking (and answering) the same question in the right way rather than risking different and potentially confusing questions without clear answers. This competitive spirit also severely limits people's capacity to take multiple perspectives in anything but the most utilitarian way because people are always trying to get ahead rather than really trying to understand. Finally, because we often need diverse views to be able to see more of the system, a competitive spirit that pits people against one another instead of supporting people to move toward one another is likely to limit our ability to see systems as well.

The competitive spirit we want to support might be the competition with self-designed goals. It might be this approach that supports people to become more self-authored over time, but even this focus on competition will limit people's growth beyond the self-authored form of mind. Instead, a more psychologically spacious approach to motivating people around their goals might take a more nuanced approach to setting and evaluating these comparative goals.

Obviously, competition has myriad benefits. Noticing who is achieving best (and worst) is clearly helpful data. Encouraging people to reach beyond themselves by giving them some external goal to get the blood moving is also obviously a help. The problem is that this is half of a solution, and organizations often use only this half. Unless the push for being the best is joined by a focus on noticing who is learning or changing most (and least), it may hinder rather than help you in the long run.

We Treat People the Same

In our travels, we get to spend time in all sorts of organizations, and we see the many ways people's beliefs about equity and fairness both are great gifts and paradoxically get in the way of real diversity. We work across many different sorts of organizations: public sector, private sector, education, and nongovernment. We work in industries where there are many more women than men, and we work in (more) industries where there are more men than women, especially at the top. We often find ourselves in organizations that lack racial diversity. We have been moved by the depth of caring we have seen in leaders about gender and racial imbalances, and about the commitment our clients— often privileged white men whom the system supports well—have to making real and lasting change.

It was one of those leaders, Fred, a middle-aged white man with a long history in the military and a relatively new interest in having women in leadership positions, who spoke most passionately to a group of colleagues about this issue. He was working to trial slightly different evaluation criteria for women after they returned from their parental leave. One of the other three (white, middle-aged) men had just asked him a question in his action learning group about whether the differential treatment he heard Fred talking about was really fair. Fred said something like:

> It's our desire to be fair that is the hardest part of this whole issue. I totally understand your point. I have asked that question plenty of times myself. But now I've talked to dozens of women across the business. And I've learned that what I think is fair comes straight out of my history and my experiences as a white guy. The things that feel fair to me aren't inherently fair—they're just a white guy's fair. An Asian woman's fair might be different. But one of the privileges of being a white guy in this firm is that most of us—mostly white guys—have the same idea about fair, so it's pretty easy to get that confused with some objective truth about fair. For us, fair is about treating everyone exactly the same, which, when you think about it, here is about treating everyone like a white man.

You might not agree with Fred about this issue; his own colleagues had lots to say about his perspective. As they talked about it, though, they began to unpack some of the assumptions they brought to their work: assumptions about gender, race, social class, and more. They found subtleties of agreement and disagreement they never knew existed between them. They began to question ideas that had just been invisible before.

Conversations about diversity do this. Diversity itself is quite likely to be developmental. People from different backgrounds often ask different kinds of questions. They have—and so can share with others—different perspectives. And since they come from different places in the system, they can help build a different way of seeing more of the system, seeing forces or connections that might be invisible to others. Yet far too many of the organizations we work with have senior ranks filled with people of the same gender, culture, and class background. Some of that inequity is, oddly, driven by the desire to treat people exactly equally.

We are not suggesting that the best approach would be to do away with the idea of fairness or equity. Instead, we are suggesting that taking multiple perspectives on this issue might open up entirely new definitions. For a long time in organizations in the West, we have treated the idea of fairness as a simple problem; if we treat everyone the same, give everyone the same opportunities, salaries, and the like, that will be simply fair.[8] Oddly, this leads to fewer women and people of color at the top of most organizations and to a significant pay differential as well. The simple rule has perverse consequences. If we treated fairness as a complex problem, where the causes and the effects are not clear and are not known until later, the simple answers about how to keep things equitable fly out the window.[9] Instead, people need more nuanced definitions and a set of safe-to-fail experiments.

While the dessert was on the table, there was only silence and small happy sounds, but once the plates had been cleaned fully, the group sat back in their chairs, full and content with the food and the conversation.

"OK, I think I'm convinced—or worn down by the excellence of this passion fruit tart," Arlen said with a sigh. "I can see how we need our people to actually think in new ways about their jobs and about the world. I can see that if we have programmers who just think of programming and marketing people who just think about marketing, we'll never get to be an integrated software and services company. Ironically, we need people who are less certain that they know the right answers, more flexible about the way they think about what they do, and more engaged with the larger enterprise of the business and where it's going. What I still don't get is how we're going to hire or grow these people."

"Well, we've got some excellent experience here," Lela said. "Arlen, what has helped you grow?"

"Passion fruit tart for one!" Arlen joked, patting his belly. Lela gave him one of her rare school-teacher looks and the smile died away from his face. "Er, um, OK, let's think. Well, you three, actually. Over the past decade, whenever I've felt I had something nailed, you three were sure to un-nail it. When we'd have meetings and talk through the next stage in the business, and I thought I was there to inform you and you thought you were there to really push the ideas around—those were a challenge for me. There were times when I didn't even like to tell you about my plans because I was sure you'd poke holes in them."

"The holes were there already, son, we just put the headlights on them so you could see them, too," Jimmy added helpfully.

"At the time it didn't always feel that way, but now I understand just what you mean, Jimmy. And all that experience with the holes—whether they were poked or highlighted—showed me that my ideas were just a little too small and simple for the task at hand. It got to the point where I could hear your different voices in my head, asking me questions about things, and I could see the holes myself. So that wasn't always enjoyable, but afterward the things we tried were always better from the conversation. How about you, Hannah? What has helped you change?"

"It's a really good question. And I agree about those meetings we had so often in the first few years as we were deciding what to do. I had a lot of holes poked in my ideas too—so many that I stopped coming in with ideas that I thought of as hole-free and started just bringing my questions and uncertainties to the table. That was huge for me and really hard to start with. I felt so vulnerable. My fear was that it seemed that I could not do my job anymore and I was exposing that to you by bringing you these half-formed problems to fix for me. But once I saw that you did not have answers either, just more questions, and that we could build things together, it made those meetings more fun and less painful. Another thing that was big for me were the performance conversations we used to have, Nate. I didn't find those conversations comfortable, because sometimes you gave me some really difficult feedback. As you know, I found the leadership stuff so difficult that I almost left Actualeyes once we tipped over from just a tiny company into a real enterprise. But I always felt that you listened to me and tried to really take my perspective, as well as representing what was best for the business."

Nate smiled softly. "Those conversations were awfully hard for me, too, Hannah. You can't begin to know how much I learned from you. Your struggle and your perspective made me rethink what I knew about leadership, about how to run an organization—even about having feedback conversations themselves. We have drifted away from having those conversations in part because I didn't think you needed me anymore. Shall we start up again?"

Hannah nodded. "I think this new phase for Actualeyes is going to test what we think about organizations and about leadership, Nate. It would be really good to have those conversations with you again."

"I'd like to put my hand up for those again, too," Squint said. "We have got to make room in our crazy busy schedules to keep on the edge of our own growing capabilities. And I have to figure out how to run meetings that are more productive as we try to build ideas together." He looked around the table. "I could probably use everyone's feedback on what I'm doing wrong there."

Arlen sat up straight in his chair and gave his watch a hard stare. "If we're going to tell you what you do wrong in meetings, this could take a while, Squint. How long is this place open, anyway?"

Squint laughed and motioned for the check. "I think it must be time to get going now before Arlen gets going on his list! But seriously, I do want to have a real conversation about it."

Arlen smiled. "I was just kidding, you know. I think you're surprisingly good with people, for a software geek who didn't even have his first date until he was 19. But I am totally serious that I think we could learn how to do this better, and that it might be the difference between achieving this next vision or being left by the side of the road as some other company achieves it while we watch."

SEEING THE SYSTEM: WORK AS A PLACE WHERE
PEOPLE GROW—OR DON'T

Organizations are always searching for what can make them distinctive in a marketplace that is ever more crowded and uncertain. They look for ways to have the competitive advantage by hiring the best people, creating the best products or services, having the leanest structures. We believe that if leaders made a shift to the growth mindset, organizationally, and if they specifically diminished the work practices that got in the way of development and created work practices that supported development, they'd not only have a competitive advantage for today but also be able to maintain one for the entire (long) life of the organization. Right now we separate our regular work from our professional development as though they were two different things. The organization that figures out that regular work and professional development are actually the same thing will have employees who rarely lose work time for professional development and who get professional development every single day. That's the most valuable synergy we know.

To take advantage of this synergy, though, you have to see the whole system of work in a new way. Now the goal isn't just to accomplish tasks but to accomplish tasks while stretching your capabilities. The goal isn't just to have meetings but to create collaborative spaces in which everyone learns something new while doing excellent work. Having this dual goal in mind is a shift that often looks at first as though it will be less productive. It's hard enough to just get things done with your incredibly busy schedule, and now you have to learn, too? It might look like a clunky and mismatched combination. We think, though, that the separation of work from learning is a bizarre and unhealthy divide. Perhaps in a simpler world where the work was repetitive and predictable, where a profession could be mastered, continual growth was less necessary to success. But now, when the growth of the capacities of your team could be the best competitive edge your organization has, weaving development into the warp and weft of your work really matters.

This is not just a theoretical idea. Bob Kegan, Lisa Lahey, and their colleagues researched what they call deliberately developmental organizations. They found that "deliberately developmental organizations may have found a way to steadily improve performance without simply improving what they're currently doing. That's because progress for their employees means becoming not only more capable and conventionally successful but also more flexible, creative, and resilient in the face of the challenges—for both personal and organizational growth—that these companies deliberately set before them."[10] This sounds like a new standard for the potential of organizations to both succeed and also help their people grow—as entwined and interdependent goals. Here we offer three initial suggestions to weave work and development together in the most effortless ways: performance conversations in which everyone grows, action learning groups for the hardest challenges, and meetings in which new ideas happen.

Build Performance Conversations Where Everyone Grows

We'll begin with this one because it's one of the things that happens at work that's already supposed to be about weaving the work and the learning together. We also think it's so important that we devoted an entire chapter to it earlier in this book. You might remember that the core questions we asked you to consider were the following: What if this person weren't a problem for you to solve but a key knowledge holder for you to understand? What is it that this person knows about the situation that would shift or change your mind, and how might you find out?

We talked about one really helpful way to enact this mindset: offer the other person your sense of the situation (clear data, feeling, and impact without extra judgment) and then take the long walk to understand what his or her experience was. Then, once you have all that on the table, you can tackle the most important issues together, both of you learning new approaches as you go. Getting practice giving and receiving feedback of all kinds—about what we do really well and should do more of and what we do less well and should improve on—might be the most important way to grow people at work. But it's not the only way.

Use Action Learning Groups to Tackle Some of Your Hardest Challenges

When Arlen talked about his most helpful learning experience, it wasn't in a workshop.[11] It was in a conversation about a piece of work, a setting where people he respected asked difficult questions about something he cared about. Action learning groups (ALGs) create the conditions for just that kind of conversation among people who are trying to progress complex challenges. This is a process designed both to significantly increase the odds that people will be able to gain traction on their most intractable issues and to help them grow along the way, a beautiful weaving of development and work. Their benefits have been widely researched and written about, and so we'll just touch on the process here briefly.[12]

ALGs are mostly formed to handle complex challenges. Like any group tackling something in the complex space, diversity is a gift, so we try to form groups to maximize whatever forms of diversity we have access to (e.g., age, gender, race, culture, work history, functional area). Then, in these relatively small groups (six to eight people works best), people take turns presenting an issue that stymies them: we borrow from Heifetz and his colleagues and call that the "adaptive challenge."[13] The others in the group then have 20 minutes or so to ask genuine and curious questions. They cannot make suggestions, tell stories of their own, or ask a question that is actually a suggestion in disguise (e.g., "Have you talked to Mary about that?"). The person presenting the challenge can answer the questions or not, because in this case it doesn't matter what the answer is so much as the thinking that opens new possibilities.

At first, groups struggle. Asking questions that are really questions turns out to be much harder than it sounds, and group members are astonished that they have so many suggestions and so little curiosity. But after a while, group members not only get better at asking questions but also find themselves actually becoming more curious. As they become more curious, they are also more helpful. (How ironic is it that it's often when we stop trying to solve problems for others that we help them more?)

After a few months in an action learning group, especially one connected to a program that also supports people in getting better at asking questions in the first place, leaders find that they are somehow more agile, more sophisticated, and better at dealing with conflict and complexity. Action learning has a kind of straightforward magic: by helping people spotlight the learning as much as the action, we put the possibility of learning and changing at work in people's minds in a new way. Declaring learning to be a part of action means that you're more likely to get both.

Hold Meetings Where New Ideas Happen

We regularly ask groups of people, all over the world, whether they waste too much time in meetings.[14] Regularly, nearly every hand goes up. In a world where we are so pressed for time, this seems like an extraordinary waste of time, and it doesn't have to be at all. By now you know our mantra on this: At every regularly held meeting, everyone in the room should learn something. At every regularly held meeting, something new should be created—a new idea, plan, product, or solution. At every regularly held meeting, most people should agree that their time wasn't wasted. If these things are already true for you—fantastic! If you're not quite there yet, here are some ways you can think about creating more value from your time together.

Prepare   Most meetings go wrong before they've even begun. Agenda setting and the work needed before a meeting are not glamorous, but an investment in getting things right makes the meeting infinitely more productive and leaves time both to get work done and to learn. This is basic stuff but rarely done. We all collect ideas for a meeting, but we rarely know what kind of idea it is. Is it an informational item for one person to inform the others? Is it a discussion item that some person or group wants to gain advice or perspectives about before making a decision themselves? Is it a matter that this whole collective needs to decide on? Tag every possible agenda item with its designation.

If you're going to make room for learning, informational items should almost always be handled outside of meetings. In common practice, when someone comes with an informational item, a couple of people ask questions in which the asker is at least vaguely interested, others might be totally disinterested, and no one can particularly change (or else it would have a different tag). So many senior teams use (waste) their collective time on informational agendas because the person who would have to type up the information doesn't have time to do that, and team members don't read memos from one another anyway. Commit as a group to do that prework, write the information down, ask questions offline. This creates better relationships, and if you're creating a culture of curious questioning, the whole enterprise will be self-reinforcing.

Select   Now that you've gotten the informational items off the agenda, you have to decide which remaining items make it on. A vital question that's rarely asked is: what is the group of people who would be most useful thinking partners about this issue? Is it the whole team or a subset? Or does it involve some people who do not normally attend? All the research on team effectiveness shows that a key to effectiveness is to have a team which forms intentionally and works together for some purpose. But most of the senior teams we work with meet more out of habit than intention (because they are the senior team and that's what senior teams do). When you're picking the agenda for a meeting, you want to pick things about which everyone in the room might have a useful perspective. You want to pick things from which everyone in the room might potentially learn. You want to pick things about which you might disagree. You might also want to pick the people you might most need to be there. Now you've got the ingredients for a helpful meeting. Give everything the time it needs and send out any prework that would save time when you're in person together.

Question Curiously   Now that you've got an agenda and you've done your prework, it's time to change how you show up with one another in the meeting room itself. This is a time to ask questions rather than making points, to open up to curiosity rather than defending perspectives, and to remember that everyone in room has a different and helpful viewpoint (or else they shouldn't have been invited). This means that the goal of the meeting, in part, would be to make some things visible for people rather than having the group be subject to their invisible assumptions. Often the assumptions are ones like: We've tried that before. That will never work because the senior vice president doesn't approve of those sorts of things. Customers aren't sophisticated enough to want that. And so on. If one of the goals of the meeting is learning and another is innovation, naming those things that are hidden is a key ingredient, which means that meetings need to be designed in such a way that there is space and time for people to declare and question assumptions, and that they have the structures and ideas in order to do that.

Two things will help in this regard. First, if everyone remembers that the larger goal (e.g., of solving an important team or organizational problem) is bigger than any individual person or the need to represent particular views or sections of the organization, you'll have people reduce their ego connection to the issue (as much as they can, developmentally) and their sense of obligation to speak up for others outside the room. There is a difference between ensuring the full diversity of views is explored and having an inevitably positional discussion between interest groups. Second, if people can make—and keep each other honest about—a commitment to ask questions that are really questions and not points they want to make, the questions won't create a battlefield and won't be as likely to raise defenses. And if you've got a space where people can ask curious questions, assumptions get put on the table, and the invisible becomes visible, people will find the meeting a good use of their time, the solution to whatever the problem is will be richer and more significant, and you've increased the chance that the people in the room will grow. Over time people will be more likely to state their main assumptions before being asked, thus making their thinking more explicit and enabling the discussion to go deeper more quickly.

Agree (This Is About Making Sure You're Doing the Work)   An oddly missed step in many meetings is to agree on whatever action plan came out of the meeting. This is something many people somehow collectively fear to make explicit. Who agreed to do which things? What exactly is it that person is supposed to do? By when? What are the conditions for the satisfactory completion of that item? Who judges? This step is the low-hanging fruit of meeting productivity. If everyone does this consistently, even if meetings don't become more about learning, they'll be more productive.

Review Learning (This Is About Making Sure You're Learning)   Just as groups should review the task assignment, it's really helpful to take a tiny amount of time (even just five minutes at the end of every meeting) to review the learning that the team has done together. Again, this helps bring learning and the growth mindset into view and solidifies the learning (as well as creating more of the culture that learning and growth are part of what goes on in your organization). If someone hasn't learned anything, the meeting was at least partially a failure—a safe-to-fail one for sure, that you can learn from on your way to creating better meetings in the future.

Increasing the possibility that people will grow at work means reshaping some old practices and habits and building new ones. But the payoff is both immediate (as people get quickly better at their work) and long term, as your organization takes full advantage of one of the most exciting parts of what it means to be human: our ability to learn, grow, and change over time and in connection with one another.

Squint, Hannah, and Arlen said good-bye to their mentors and walked to Hannah's car in the dark. They meant to simply say good night and just quickly go over the plan for the board meeting on Monday, but they found themselves musing about the questions their board members had asked and what they meant about their future together. What was it that was most important to them? How willing were they to make the growth of their people a core feature of their new strategy? As they stood in the warm spring night, they realized that this was a missing link in the way they had been thinking about the service and software connection. They knew they were wanting people to change so that there could be a better and more integrated look at service and software. The experiments they had created at the lake house were going to go part of the way toward moving people in this direction. But the conversation over dinner had reminded them that it wasn't just new ways of acting that they were wanting their people to take on; it was new ways of *being*, new ways of thinking about the world and their place in it. This was not a small ask for their collection of software engineers, sales and marketing folks, and call-center employees. They were going to have to put in a few experiments that were about changing the quality of the conversation about the growth of people as well.

"I wonder about how we can support our younger leaders, too, as we are asking folks to make that shift," Squint mused. "I was talking to Murray about Jarred a few weeks ago, and he was surprisingly negative about him. Murray said that Jarred was just too immature to lead the team and that maybe some-one like Michelle might be a better choice for that role."

"I followed up with Murray about this last week," Arlen added. "I think he has seen an improvement since his conversation with Jarred, which Murray relates to his own excellent feedback skills."

"Ha!" Hannah snorted. "Have we ever heard anyone say anything good about Murray's feedback skills? He may be an extraordinary engineer and he knows how to get the job done, but he is not my poster boy for excellent people skills."

"Indeed," Squint mused. "And we have made only halfhearted attempts to get him into a new place about this."

"Because each time we send him away on some training, it's just pour-ing good money after bad," Arlen reminded them. "A leopard can't change his spots."

"But that's just it, isn't it? A leopard can't change his spots, but a person can change the way he approaches the world," Squint said. "The whole point is I think we sort of give up on developing people. We give it a shot and then ei-ther give up, as we have with Murray, or replace the person with someone else, as Murray is hinting at with Jarred. There has to be another way."

"This might be one of the ways the FACS people can help us," Hannah pointed out. "They seem to know more about helping people grow than we do."

"Though that Ramona is the female twin of Murray," Arlen cracked.

"But I bet she won't be for all that long with Yolanda in the picture," Hannah reasoned. "I think they know something about people development that es-capes us and I think we could learn a lot from them."

Squint smiled. "Maybe we should try a more regular meeting with some of the FACS folks. There is a more pressing issue though. I think we need to come at the board meeting differently. I think we need to use it to explore uncer-tainty and unpredictability more, and I want to start that exploration when we meet with them on Monday. I think that means an early start to do some rede-sign before the meeting. How about seven Monday morning?"

"What? Seven?" Hannah sighed. She was not a morning person. "Give me a break, Squint. I worked all week on that board meeting design."

"But I bet you worked on it from a place of knowing and not a place of not knowing," Squint guessed. "You have worked so hard to make it right—to get the right materials and the right items and the right decisions. But I think we need to make the meeting more of a safe-to-fail space to discover stuff about how we are thinking about the business. That seems to be a critical part of governance when we do not know what will happen. Let's get into it."

"Come on, it'll be fun, in a masochistic sort of way. I'll pick up those weird crunchy seaweed things you love from that shop near me," Arlen promised, "to keep your brain functioning even at that outrageous hour."

Hannah smiled. "I love those. And you're right, I did design the meeting from a totally different mindset. OK. I'm in. I'll bring the coffee and my curiosity about the new way to do things, and I will try not to be too grouchy."

---

8 LEAD CHANGE AS THE NEW NORMAL

"He's here," Doug called into Yolanda's office. "Or, er, they're here. I'm getting the others now."

Yolanda nervously reapplied her lipstick and smoothed her hair back into a neat bun. She hoped this look—casual pants with a soft sweater—would be one he'd warm to. She slipped a little ball into her pocket and headed to the main conference room, her breath quickening with anticipation. The staff had done a beautiful job here, making what used to be a sterile government department room into a place where children and families could gather and feel safe and comfortable. One of their most successful safe-to-fail experiments over the past year had been about bringing the community into the offices—and bringing the offices into the community. This, their initial attempt, was imperfect, she now saw. The more successful rooms weren't quite so big as this one, and tended to be on the ground floor in the bureau offices and not a security check and elevator ride up, but today she was glad for the size of the room.

Then, over in the corner, she spied him and her eyes pricked with tears. He glanced up at her and smiled and she couldn't help but beam back at him. It had been a couple of months since she'd last seen him, and he looked even better than the last time. A little over a year ago she had thought of him as the ten-year-old in the Proucheford County Hospital. Today she knew him as Tobias Jones, "TJ" for short. His grandmother, talking to some of Yolanda's staff nearby, intercepted Yolanda on her way to TJ and enveloped her in a hug. Yolanda hugged her back, hard, grateful for everything they had learned from this family, and grateful to be able to have this meeting today to report on a year's worth of changes. Yolanda caught TJ's eye (not always easy to do with an Xbox in the room), and he reluctantly put down the controllers and joined her at the main table. She put her arm around him, noting again how much bigger he had grown and feeling grateful—as she always did when she saw him—that she was in a business where the TJs of the world came first. She asked him about his teacher this year ("Pretty nice, I guess") and about his friends, but his eyes didn't really sparkle until he started to talk about his new kitten. Yolanda, who had known the kitten was coming, reached into her pocket and pulled out a catnip ball. TJ held it, vibrating with excitement about the kitten's evening of chasing it around the house. Yolanda pulled herself away and motioned for the room to get quiet.

"Thank you so much for coming," Yolanda said to the families and community leaders who were gathered at the far table, helping themselves to tea and cookies. "This, as you know, is a celebration of our collaboration, because as we all know, it takes all of us working together to make our communities and families good places for our most precious members, our children. A year ago we came to a decision here at Family and Children's Services about redoubling our efforts to connect with those who cared as much about vulnerable kids and families as we did. That turns out to be a lot of people; if I had invited them all, we'd have needed to rent out the convention center! But you were all with us, in one way or another, in those first difficult months as we tried to make this pivot, and so this is our celebration of you and of what we can all do for the folks who need us. Reverend Welcher, will you open our meeting with a prayer?"

As they bowed their heads Yolanda heard a few more guests trickle in. Hannah, Squint, and Arlen slipped into the room and smiled at Jarred who had come over earlier to help Yolanda's staff set up for this party. Yolanda smiled. The reverend was mindful of the need to not be explicitly Christian in his prayer—just as Yolanda was mindful of the need for the reverend's presence in the first place, even though he was opening a meeting in a government bureau. Each of them had flexed a little to come toward one another, which was true for everyone in the room, really. That was one of the first things she had learned about this entire change process: you have to do a lot of listening to one another to build solutions you could all live with. The answer that was in her head was rarely the one they ended up with, in part because it was so hard to predict which solutions would attract real change. She hadn't imagined last year the probability that she might be standing in this bright green room with low tables and beanbags in the corners, bending some of the separation of church and state laws, but suddenly she was delighted it had all been possible in the first place.

Throughout this book, we've explored the new ways leaders need to act, think, and be during times of volatility, uncertainty, complexity, and ambiguity. We've pointed to a whole different set of ways leaders need to strategize, give and receive feedback, and communicate about a new way of acting into the future. Each of these ideas or ways of thinking or acting is enhanced and developed by the habits of mind: asking different questions, taking multiple perspectives, and seeing systems, which also support us in our helpfully irrational and ever-growing humanity.

These habits help individual leaders grow, and they support leaders to grow their people and their organizations during uncertain times. But they all, together, also form a framework for supporting what Harvard leadership theorist Ron Heifetz and colleagues call "adaptive change": any change that requires people to alter their behavior, thinking, or values.[1] Using these habits of mind while facing adaptive change is a lovely loop: these ways leaders are required to be different during times of uncertainty are the same ways leaders can intentionally use to create a change in their organization (which is, of course, a time of uncertainty). So, whether you're a leader wanting to create change or a leader who is having change created all around you, here are some core responses:

- Determine what's predictable and what's not, and lean in to leading in unpredictable settings.
- Create a feedback-rich organization in which you and others can constantly learn about what needs to change.

- Choose a direction and build guardrails.
- Examine the present, and look for attractors.
- Experiment and learn.
- Communicate clearly in uncertain times.
- All the while, develop a growth mindset in yourself and others.

These things don't create a linear change model, but when leaders enact these ideas over time, they create the conditions for successful change in their organizations.

DETERMINE WHAT'S PREDICTABLE AND WHAT'S NOT, AND LEAN IN TO LEADING IN UNPREDICTABLE SETTINGS

It pays to remember that our brains and bodies are searching for the predictable patterns of the probable rather than seeking out the novel byways of the possible. This has served humans well for thousands of years, and those whose brains and bodies took shortcuts to avoid the predictable forms of death ("Yikes! A lion! Run!") passed on their DNA while those whose brains were more captivated by a range of possibilities ("Wow! a lion! I wonder what might be attracting the lion to this area? Maybe there's a drought up north, or maybe . . .") were probably lunch. This serves us well in times of simple cause and effect that were probably the norm for most of human history (lions equal danger).

Now our problems are incredibly gray. Wiretapping our allies equals danger? Safety? Illegality? Government initiative? Leaking information about that wiretapping equals an abuse of the law? A public service? Tagging your friends on Facebook equals a sense of warmth and connection? An opening to data mining for abuse? Most of the lions we get to see now are safely in zoos, and it's the people around us who are creating the complexity and unpredictability of the world most of us have to navigate.

Our internal systems didn't get that memo though. Perhaps most of the genes for those humans who could see wider possibilities ended up as lion lunch. Our brains and bodies are still working on the ancient agreement they have not to distract us while they keep us safe from the threats they understand—while not noticing the complexity of the threats right in front of us. People are much more afraid in their guts of shark attacks (which kill between five and fifteen people a year worldwide)[2] than about global warming (which could wipe out entire cities and create widespread flooding and famine). That's just a misfiring system if we're looking at an objective understanding of risk. It's easy to understand the misfire when we remember that for most of our evolutionary history, the threats that were tangible, immediate, and recurring were most important, rather than the incredibly complex and intangible ones that might be most important today.

This means that unless we are vigilant, our brains will solve the easier (fictional) problem rather than the more complex (actual) problem that's in front of us. And you'll probably remember that our brains do this without alerting us to that short cut unless we can tune into some of the clues we can find that are signals from the background workings of our bodies (like the tightening of your chest that you might not even notice just before you decide you shouldn't give that feedback to your boss as you had planned). We carry with us at all times a great simplifier who is just trying to make our lives easier (while often ignoring the rather significant problems that we're about to get into).

But this combination of your nonconscious reactions and your mind's impulse to oversimplify means that most of your habits in conditions of change—and most of the habits of the people with whom you work—are to not notice the biggest most wicked problems, not notice that we are solving for the probable rather than the possible, and not to notice that our solutions are founded on what is known from the past rather than built on what is emerging from the present and creating a new set of possibilities in the future.

Now this does not mean we should reshape all of our habits and instincts in this regard. If people are questioning whether it's possible that one day we won't have gravity holding us to the earth, it might be hard for them to create that community engagement strategy. Throughout organizational history, some of the most important gains have been made in treating complicated, predictable problems with thought and care. No matter how complex the world becomes, there will still be problems that will be helpfully solved in the predictable space, and getting these right is very important.

But bringing the different questions about what is complex and lives in the land of the possible (and thus needs to be explored in a new way) and what is relatively predictable and lives in the land of the probable (and thus needs to be explored in familiar ways by the right experts) means that you can tease apart these issues instead of having your old habits in the driver's seat. And you have to keep remembering to ask these questions, again and again, because the pull of our habits (and the lazy force of our brains) is so strong. Leaders need to create systems and rituals that enable these different questions to be asked.

One way we've seen leaders do this is just to slow down the group and forbid the jump to problem solving that most of us are prone to. Creating spaces in which people talk more about the problem and the present inclinations of the system, in the absence of jumping to (and then getting attached to and trying to convince others of the worth of) the best solutions, allows this possibility to come to light. Action learning (which we discussed in Chapter 7) has a set of these rituals inside it with its forced inquiry rather than simple solution building. Some leaders will explain, "For this meeting, we want to spend the first 30 minutes just exploring the problem and the workings of the system. If you have a solution, by all means write it down, but hold onto it lightly, because the solution itself might get in the way of your full understanding."

Combining this kind of ritualized solution avoidance with some of the different questions that fill this book (and the others that have probably arisen for you as you've read), leaves the space for people to really be able to pull apart what is complex from what is complicated without allowing the preferences they have to shape their understanding of the issue. We nearly always draw the Cynefin squiggles on the board as a symbol for our clients to remember that there are domains outside their area of preference that may well offer better ways to describe the issue and to explore solutions.[3] Remembering that there are different ways to act during times of unpredictability (some of which we've highlighted in this book) means that people are less likely to solve these emerging problems the way they have approached more standard, complicated problems in the past. Understanding that it's complex is the first part of the battle.

"I admit that at first I thought Yolanda was crazy," Ramona admitted to the chuckles of the group.

"You ain't the only one!" TJ's grandmother called from the back of the room.

Ramona smiled broadly. "This whole idea that we would release some of our precious—and limited—control at exactly the minute it seemed that things were most out of control: that seemed insane to me. But as you know, this new direction was about sharing control with all of you, and as I grew to know you, I saw what an incredibly smart thing that was to do. I needed to understand that there were some things, like our criminal investigations and our statutory requirements, that we needed to control and hold onto tightly. Holding tight is one of my big strengths as a manager!" She smiled as some of the Proucheford community members laughed. "Other pieces, like our intervention programs and some of our systems for finding the best placements for our kids, were more mysterious and evolving. That meant that we could experiment with and release control of some of those. That was a huge step for me. And I guess that step never would have come if I hadn't been totally convinced that we could not manage this on our own. There was a way I was lost and I was also found. No matter how good our systems were, no matter how good our people were, protecting vulnerable family members is just too big for any single department. The causes of family violence are just too woven through our communities and our histories, and we can't predict where violence will erupt. But we can get better at seeing the patterns, especially in the highest-risk settings, and with our new partnership with all of you, we can work on many levels and in many different places, and our different forms of expertise add to each other rather than competing."

"If you hadn't let go of some of that control, sugar, I wouldn't have gotten my TJ," his grandma said, her arm resting protectively around the boy. "Heck, I'm not even sure I would have known he existed. My good-for-nothin' son wasn't much for sharing with his momma."

"See, that's what I mean," Ramona said, excitedly. "When we asked in the community about what would be a good placement for TJ, it was ultimately the reverend who suggested following up with the family in Mountainview, where TJ's mom used to live. He knew some pastors over there, and they followed some leads and eventually found you. We'd never have found you otherwise, and TJ might still be bouncing around different foster families."

"The Lord brought my TJ home," his grandma said. "He was the answer to my prayers." TJ squirmed at the attention, but his eyes were bright, and Yolanda noticed he didn't try wrestle out of his grandmother's arms.

"Well," Doug continued, "we now have dozens of stories like that—maybe hundreds. Thanks to you folks and to your counterparts across the state, we've been able to follow through with our new community-centered direction and do better at protecting our most vulnerable community members. You've come to us with wacky ideas—like creating links between delinquent kids and the vulnerable elderly—and you've helped us implement them in ways that kept people safe. Even the ones that failed miserably were safe enough with the guardrails we put in place and with Yolanda's support to not insist on a success every time. We have learned so much about what it takes to really connect with communities to strengthen vulnerable families. Now we have projects connecting kids at risk with elderly at risk in different ways across the state, and other states are coming in to follow our direction. The hardest part has been convincing the others that the relationships in the community have to come first and that this is not just a solution that can be airlifted from one place to the next. The Proucheford partnership looks really different from the one here in the capital because those are really different places with different kinds of relationships. But the idea of building tight relationships is now driving us at FACS in every bureau across the state. We've had to learn that listening is more important than just about anything else—more important than the perfect solution or the best roll out or anything. We've had to really get that you can't learn if you don't listen."

CREATE A FEEDBACK-RICH ORGANIZATION IN WHICH YOU AND OTHERS CAN LEARN ABOUT WHAT NEEDS TO CHANGE

A core difference between teams that thrive and those that falter is the quality and amount of feedback that is available to everyone. As we've talked about feedback with leaders, researchers, and consultants around the world, we've found that most of us spend most of our time in relatively feedback-poor organizations, where people are often hungry for knowing more about how they're doing. People also tend to be not so good at receiving feedback—especially as they head up the food chain in organizations. The more power a leader has, the more people are inclined to insulate the leader from hearing things that might make her unhappy. This feels better in the short term (because we don't hear things we don't want to hear!) but is corrosive and dangerous in the long term. We think that learning to give and listen to feedback is so vital that it was one of the first core skills we introduced in this book (back in Chapter 3), and it's almost always the first thing we teach the leaders with whom we work. So this is a foundational building block, and we could probably all stand to do a better job here.

This shows up in a chapter about change because of the great importance of understanding the present and getting out of your own head when you're engaged in a change project. Feedback is the lifeblood of change in a complex world, whether it's the kind we give one another or the kind that is available inside a system if you go and look for it. Without a constant diet of data (and perspectives) from those around them, people are trapped inside their own perspective and the quirks of their own, beautifully human brains. The ability to give and receive feedback, and to organize work and conversations so that feedback is richly available, is not only a basic necessity in an organization (although it is that); it is also a core change capability.

The thing is, feedback happens in systems whether we like it or not; feedback is the information force that creates the shape of the system. But many leaders and organizations end up creating perverse sorts of feedback flows which in turn create perverse shapes to organizations. For example, we know of an organization where one division head acted as a blocker of information and feedback from his division to the rest of the organization to protect his people from the annoyances of the larger organization so they might better focus on their own priorities. This may have enabled concentration but it also meant over time that people inside his division had a skewed notion about what was going on in the organization overall, and those outside the division had a twisted notion of what was happening there. This created a lot of churn that, perversely, ended up being quite a distraction, the way a rock in a river creates frothy and dangerous currents and undertows as the water rushes around it. A new leader with a new orientation (toward sharing rather than protecting) brought each group amazing insights about the other. The organization, which had found itself churned up in trying to avoid this particular division, suddenly had smooth and easy access to information. The rock moved and the river took its more consistent, less dangerous shape again.

What we are suggesting here is that leaders more explicitly create organizations where individuals have as much access to clear and helpful feedback as possible, both about what isn't working and what is working beautifully. There are at least three ways leaders can build a feedback culture: (1) do it well and often, (2) talk about the ways feedback is shaping the organization (which makes a feedback loop about feedback loops), and (3) change systems to support feedback.

We've talked about giving feedback well. Most feedback models offered to leaders and managers are *message out*; often people are counseled to diagnose the situation and the solution at the same time and offer that on a plate. And indeed, in a simpler world, that would be a kind of a gift. But remember that it's not actually a feedback loop—it's a one-way street, and it dead-ends when the other person receives (and hopefully acts on) your sage advice. Offering and using the simple but sometimes frightening "when I feel because" feedback model, and then listening clearly for the intent or meaning of the other person means that the feedback loop carries on, that both people learn from each other, and that the problem and the possible solutions are looked at by multiple perspectives. That's much better from a complexity perspective.

Leaders don't just need to create systems and cultures where feedback about what's *not* going well gets shared. Leaders also need to create systems and cultures in which feedback about what *is* working really well gets shared. No longer can we assume that if it's going well, we don't need to single it out because it's already there. In a fast-moving system, you have to work to hold on to what is good just as much as you have to work to try to change what isn't so good. In fact, it is a source of constant frustration that we hear people talking about "constructive" feedback and "positive" feedback as though they are different. *Positive* feedback tends to be something like: "I'll tell you something I think you're doing well in the hopes that you keep doing it." *Constructive* tends to mean, "I'll tell you something you're doing wrong but I'll tell it to you nicely so you don't feel hurt by it." We'd like to think of all feedback as constructive, because it all is done in a way that constructs a set of new possibilities as it assumes that it is not the whole truth.

This idea is reinforced as leaders talk about what feedback contributes to their thinking and work. Telling and soliciting stories about the contributions of feedback to the work can normalize feedback and make it a core part of the culture. Meetings can begin with a very short look at what someone learned from a piece of feedback (either about something that was working well or something that wasn't) and the organizational benefit that he created because of that piece of feedback. In this way, thoughtful feedback becomes a part of the culture itself.

Finally, we urge leaders to make feedback a structural and regular part of their workday, to just build in systems and procedures for giving and receiving feedback as a matter of course. There are performance reviews, obviously, but there are also systems like monthly operating reviews and other formal interactions that organizations can build into their regular patterns. Meetings, too, can be spaces in which there are formal areas for feedback. One of the easiest to initiate comes from Kegan and Lahey and their practice of "ongoing regard."[4] This is when people make space at the end of every meeting to be clear about what it was that someone else did that made a difference for you. This is the same basic thread of the "When/I feel/because" conversation we've talked about earlier, but it focuses on something someone did that really worked for you. It can be a tiny thing or a major thing, but the format is the same.[5]

Because we humans tend to be good at avoiding clear and direct feedback of any variety (whether about something we want you to keep doing or something we want you to stop), leaders need to design pathways and rituals to make this more possible. This creates the conditions for healthy organizations, but even more important, it creates the conditions for organizations to be more prepared for and more responsive when changes in the context require changes in people's actions or thoughts.

CHOOSE A DIRECTION AND BUILD GUARDRAILS

The pervasive quest for alignment that we hear in organizations around the world is a call for a common direction so that people will be moving in some kind of synch. We think this is a swing to one side of a polarity (alignment versus diversification) that arises from organizations that are so large and diverse, or whose mission or work is so riddled with complexity that it has been easy to slip into going in many different directions. Even in organizations that haven't intentionally changed to diversify, the complexity in the work and the changes in the marketplace have led to difficulty with getting different divisions or teams to work in the same basic direction.

When change and complexity are zooming toward you, it's important to create boundaries that make some things in bounds and some things out of bounds. When you're trying to create a change yourself (which we guess is sort of like zooming toward change and complexity), this step is just as important because you know that you need alignment, but you also know that you need diversity (of experimentation). Offering a clear direction and building guardrails around the safe zone allows you to stay on top of the polarity instead of falling to one side or the other.

We've seen Yolanda and her team wrestling with this issue, because everything a Family and Children's Services department does is pretty high stakes. Their particular safety zone—don't mess with anything regulatory or with anything where there is an immediate risk to a child—leaves lots of room inside the guardrails, even though some of that roomy space still feels pretty dangerous to the staff. Leaders often have to work to loosen the bounds on people rather than tighten them; people are often risk averse themselves and quick to pick up on anything that sounds like a danger sign. You just want them to be oriented to the right sort of risk (important losses) rather than the wrong kind (personal fiefdoms or reputational vibrations). There is too much evidence of people, left to their own devices, focusing on the personal and immediate idea about what's dangerous (that I'll lose my bonus) rather than on something that would be in the best interests of a bigger group of people (e.g., we need to stop making such dangerous, short term wins at the expense of our longer term financial health). This makes sense in a species that is oriented for threat as well as connection. A leader who is silent about the direction and guardrails (or who herself moves them around capriciously depending on the weather or what she ate for lunch) leaves a space for others to create their own boundaries with only the guidance of rumor, self-interest, and personal preference.

This is not to say that the guardrails can't change as the conditions change. For example, we work with Jessica, a leader in one government department who is leading a new team with a relatively unclear remit. Some might have worried that her people might not have enough to do, but Jessica determined a direction and then created a culture in her team that was about jumping in and helping out without concerns about status. "If it's inside the three issues we care most about, just find a way to help them, regardless of organizational politics or clear reporting lines or accountabilities"—that was Jessica's internal direction and guardrail. Rather than having too little to do, in short measure her team had far too much to do, and team members were burning out. Now Jessica had to change some of the put-your-hand-up-to-help culture she had initially created, and make a wider space for her people to say no and celebrate that. Jessica kept the same vision and direction, but she moved some of the guardrails to create a different safe field of play. She experimented with keeping a "We Said No" board of the requests they had said no to that week and how much time was saved. Leaders need to be constantly monitoring the current condition and being explicit about subtle changes in the direction or the guardrails.

EXAMINE THE PRESENT, AND LOOK FOR ATTRACTORS

For years, leaders have been told that their job is to look toward the future: have a long time horizon, think ten years out or more, do the vision thing. We have wanted our leaders to be in the prediction business, looking at what was most probable and orienting themselves to take full advantage of their long view. In a complex and unpredictable world, where the past might mislead us about what's possible in the future, leaders need to add another capacity to their work: paying deeper attention to the present.

This is not about getting caught in the weeds of the work, editing the emails of people two layers below you, searching for solutions or approaches others have missed, or startling like a hypervigilant deer at every criticism appearing on social media. Yolanda had to fight this impulse when she went to visit the FACS Proucheford bureau office. There were small suggestions she wanted to make that would make things so much better, thoughts she had about the ways Ramona wasn't doing the right job. But she was able to resist those impulses to solve the problems she could see so that she could get some detail about the patterns in the present to learn from so that they could experiment into the future.

Hannah at Actualeyes had the same difficulty as she had teams report back about what they had discovered from their variety of investigations. Each time the group wanted to focus on what needed to be fixed, she brought their attention back to the idea of attractors. She was looking not for a single solution but for a whole constellation of possibilities. She led them away from wondering about what was most important and instead clumped together things that all had the potential to be important.

These attractors—which we generally can't see until we step back and try to get a bigger picture of the system—are involved in keeping the current system acting in the ways it acts. Change in complex systems isn't logical or linear. If we want to create change, instead of looking for the very best way or the central root cause or any of the most logical approaches, we may need to change something about the way the attractors are attracting.

For example, in one of the organizations we work with, there was a sense of competition and mistrust in the various managers of the different engineering functions. They tried a variety of team building exercises, all ending up in different shades of failure (ranging from a waste of time to disastrous). Looking at some of what was attracting this behavior gave them a new set of questions, a new thing to examine. They began to look beyond just the interactions they had with one another and pay attention to the interactions they had with their boss, the chief information officer. This was a new place of examination, because none of them had previously thought those meetings needed any improvement. Each engineer had weekly meetings one-on-one with the CIO and forged excellent relationships with him. As they looked across their experiences, though, they noticed that there was a way of relating to the CIO that the engineers didn't even know they were engaged in until they saw the pattern. They saw, in fact, that perhaps they were all competing in one way or another for the CIO's attention and they had a guess that the competition was fueled in part by their one-on-one meetings. They asked to change that attractor by simply shifting to weekly meetings of the whole group with the CIO and all the engineers and de-emphasizing their one-on-one meetings by having them monthly. Suddenly, the interactions among the engineers changed. They began to see the overlaps in their work. They reduced their sense of competition and increased their sense of cooperation. Rather than trying to make their own projects work, even at the expense of the others, they began to try to make the whole engineering department work. This switch in their meetings was not a change any of them would have ever suggested, because they all enjoyed their meetings with the CIO and wouldn't have wanted to put them at risk; those meetings enabled the feelings of appreciation and admiration that they all enjoyed. But seeing the ways those meetings attracted some of the miseries in their work as well as good feelings in the moment, they were willing to exchange a thing that felt good for the larger good of more cooperative, more civil work lives.

So it is a particular kind of watching and listening to the present that we're after, and it has a very different quality than the collect-just-enough-information-to-put-out-the-fire approach that so many of us have been rewarded for in our work. The point isn't to be the hero and solve things; the point of the leader in a complex world is to enable and unleash as many heroes and as many solutions as possible. The core work isn't to find the one best or root cause of anything or to predict which change is going to make the biggest difference. It's to experiment thoughtfully and learn like mad.

EXPERIMENT AND LEARN

Often leaders are promoted into their positions because they've done an admirable job predicting the most important problems to solve and then investigating and implementing the most likely solutions. Many of the leaders with whom we work have a laser focus on problem solving and do it well. We believe firmly that those are important and helpful traits inside organizations around the world. In a space of true uncertainty and unpredictability, though, the work shifts. The best a leader can do is widen the range (rather than narrowing), enable multiple experiments (rather than choosing the best one), and encourage and insist upon learning (rather than driving for immediate success).

This marks a fairly radical distinction from the way we often see change projects undertaken. We understand that this approach might feel unsettling and out of control to leaders, as it did to Ramona at FACS. Leaders often go in exactly the opposite direction, first diagnosing what's wrong, figuring out what in the structure gets in the way, and then reorganizing to create a structure that is more conducive to the changes they have envisioned.

We are not suggesting that reorganizations are always a bad idea when a leader wants to make a significant change. There is ample evidence, though, that these reorganizations (and most mergers and acquisitions) don't actually deliver the results that those who envisioned them most wanted.[6] But as far as direct control goes, for many leaders, a reorganization is the hammer and most organizational change challenges look like nails.

The experiment-and-iterate approach to major organizational change requires that leaders release some of their sense of control. But since much of that control is illusory anyway, we think we could stand to give some of it up. Take these two approaches to organizational change we've seen recently.

Organization 1: Because of changes in stakeholders and market, this organization needed to create a totally new way of working—both across the organization and with stakeholders in a wider variety of places than they had ever faced. The senior team created a new vision and direction and socialized that across the organization so that everyone could name (and most people believed in) this new approach. Then, to make the behavioral changes happen, the leaders took a structured and logical approach to the change. They created a structure that they thought made the most sense for this new direction. They wrote new job descriptions, investigated the most important capacities needed by people in those new jobs, determined who had those capacities with a series of interviews and psychometric tests, and then created a new organizational structure with people in the right roles with the right capacities. The organization, understandably, fell into confusion and the stakeholders were confused and unsettled. Many people were emotionally bruised as their friends were fired and long-time relationships severed by lay-offs and location or position changes; others were enthusiastic about the changes and the spaces created to work differently, although often confused about how it was going to work and how good features of the old order might be retained. Work slowed as people began haltingly to figure out what they were supposed to do next, and work sped up the most in those areas where the change could be most easily ignored.

Organization 2: Because of changes in the marketplace and in the economy generally and because of the rise of technology, this organization needed to create a whole new way of working—both across the organization and with clients. Senior leaders needed to support people to do a new thing, interact with new and different people, and raise the level of their work. This was especially difficult because these were people who had often done their jobs the same way for 15 years or more. In part because a reorganization was so difficult because of their current structure, they took a complexity approach to this change and began to experiment with different sorts of changes: a newly configured building with new sorts of work spaces, a new leadership program with a focus on experimentation, a new way of making decisions at the highest level that cascaded authority through the organization. They enabled more of their leaders to try more experiments and lifted some of the penalties for failure. Work was mostly undisrupted because there was no great shock to the organization, but change rippled through unevenly, spreading and becoming contagious in some areas and dying off in some others.

Neither of these scenarios has a fairy-tale ending. This is because neither one is a fairy tale and neither has ended. But one of these organizations was able to create small but expanding waves of change through the organization while work continued, and the other fell into a time of costly disorganization as relationships and work were disrupted. In Organization 1, trust went down as people felt that the changes were happening to them. In Organization 2, trust went up as people felt empowered to make more of their own decisions as they moved to make the vision come alive. Maybe in five years we'll make a fuller assessment about which organization was more successful, but what we can see now is that Organization 1 has put all of its bets on a single solution, which is always a risky move. Organization 2 has a wide variety of much smaller bets out, and some resources are going to the creation of even more bets. In a world where people orient to the possible rather than the probable, Organization 2 is clearly in better shape for an uncertain future. The leaders in Organization 1 would probably disagree with this. They have argued their existing organizational culture was so strong and resistant to change that a major shock was essential; they believe they couldn't go down an experimental route because it wasn't clear how any small bets could achieve the large change required. Of course, this exactly the issue with being in a complex space and making small bets to try things out. We cannot forecast what will work or not.

"And so I'd like to raise a glass to you all," Yolanda said, her sparkling cider raised high in the air, "who have contributed ideas, preached about family violence from the pulpit and the basketball court, handed out the admittedly ugly T-shirts." People laughed as Yolanda waved in the direction of a box of "FACS and me" T-shirts, a $1,246 failed experiment. "Feel free to take one—or even many—with you as you go," she urged, smiling. "We can't know how many of our vulnerable community members your actions saved," Yolanda said, more serious now, "because we can't count the tragedies that *didn't* occur because of your actions. But we know there has been only one foster kid hospitalized in the past six months, and she had appendicitis, and the hospitalization was as a result of the care and attention of her foster parents and not because of their negligence. They saved her life." She met the eyes of those foster parents across the room and raised her glass a little higher. "We will never completely solve the family violence issue. There will always be vulnerable people who are at risk. But because of you, we have reduced the risk, and we are on a path to reducing the numbers of the vulnerable.

"It is not all sweetness and light on this journey. You are all aware of the many risks families face—you live in communities where those risks are close at hand. And it is not just the T-shirts where we have learnt about what may not be working well. We still struggle with caseworkers who have too many clients and too little time. We still struggle with disconnections between the various agencies that are seeking to protect the vulnerable. I sometimes feel frustrated and even disheartened about this. We are not yet innovative enough or experimental enough to really dismantle some of the systemic problems that keep us from genuinely putting kids at the center of our thinking and our egos and prejudices and judgments off to one side.

"With you, we went back and looked hard at how we think about family violence. We discovered we had been too focused on incidents of physical abuse and not enough on patterns that might highlight future dangers—like when abusers combine controlling behaviors with physical violence and threats of violence. As we have had to change our assumptions, so have you as community leaders. We need to be looking for different signs from the ones we have been looking out for in the past. Changing our assumptions and being alert to different signs is an evolutionary process. So today is a celebration, but it is also a call to arms—not in the sense of taking up arms to fight but of linking our arms to form a unified protective embrace around our communities and our most vulnerable citizens.

"There is still a long way to travel. But in our journey to do a little better each day, and to try to make life a little easier for the most vulnerable among us, I can think of no better companions than you and our other partners in communities and agencies across the state. Today I raise my glass to you, not for the arrival at our final destination, but from a higher vantage point than we've had before, and from a place more welcoming of our many different ways of knowing about and caring about our communities. I have never been so proud of a collection of people and efforts as I am of this past year, never been so moved by what I see around me. Let's admire the view from here for this afternoon, and then head back to work trying to come ever closer to a day when family violence is something that used to happen around here."

There was applause across the room and then the scattering of small conversations as the guests sensed that the speeches were over. Through the increasing din, Reverend Welcher's resonant voice cut through. "I'd like to offer up my gratitude to you, Yolanda. I have always been in the business of protecting the vulnerable—that tradition goes back two thousand years in my profession. But I have not had the pleasure and honor of being connected to so many others who care as deeply, in their own different ways, as I do. In our community, FACS has been too often been seen on the far side of the moral line, breaking up families and frightening children who are already at risk. Having a partner who listens to us and builds solutions alongside us instead of telling us what to do—that is a gift from God during this difficult time. Now let us pray."

Yolanda's eyes met Squint's across the room just as her head was bowing, and he raised his glass to her. She beamed at him and mouthed "thank you," before closing her eyes to listen to the reverend. She was not a churchgoing woman herself, but she had come to understand the great blessings the reverend and his colleagues had brought to her and to the people FACS protected. That was surely a gift that emerged from somewhere.

COMMUNICATE CLEARLY IN UNCERTAIN TIMES

This more emergent, distributed change process we describe, especially when guided by thoughtful leaders, is probably easier on individuals than the typical top-down reorganization. But it's not what people are used to, and because of that, it needs to be communicated clearly at several different levels. If you're going to try to shape a change that takes advantage of the quirks of complexity, you'll have to get others to understand and make sense of those quirks. Remember that this is about communicating a mindset about change as well as a reason for the change in the first place. That is a big story and you'll have to get clear about a variety of things. Obviously, the direction and the guardrails need to be communicated again and again. Similarly, the process of safe-to-fail experiments and the importance of learning needs to be at the center of the change initiative. But we all know that having the right content won't in itself convince anyone to change anything. It's also the way you communicate that matters so much.

People need to understand the big story about the change and they need to see why it matters to them. They need to peer into your thinking about it a little. They also need to be convinced in their nonrational selves too, and sense into your feeling about it. And they also need to know how it connects to what matters most to them, to their values, to why they come to work in the first place. This requires a careful blend of the logic of the argument and also the emotion of the argument.

You can see that one of the key elements Yolanda and her team needed to change was the way community members made sense of the department. People's assumptions shape what evidence they notice and tend to be very self-reinforcing. This meant that Yolanda's work was about creating a different kind of emotional connection with people—from the pulpits to the basketball courts. And this wasn't the sort of change Yolanda could mandate. She needed to help Ramona understand it so Ramona could connect with her people, and so on. You don't do this armed only with a really good set of PowerPoint slides, or by just giving out free T-shirts (much to the chagrin of the person who thought that was a great way to win hearts and minds).

Instead, you have to tell stories. You have to appeal to the back of people's brains as well as the front. This is where all that thought about the direction and guardrails and all that attention to the present comes in handy. And you'll have to listen, probably harder than you've ever listened before. You'll have to listen not in the usual way to confirm what you think but in a new way to really learn new things. All that listening will pay off because then you'll have a wealth of examples and metaphors that come from the present to ground your conversations. Each example, clearly honed and delivered, is a connection that gets made not only to the logic center of the mind but to the emotional center. The stories we tell carry the culture we have, and so as we try to influence culture, it matters to use stories well. In complex and ambiguous times of change, leaders can't communicate a clear story about a destination or the map of the way forward. They can communicate the big picture story about the vision, though, help people feel safe by telling stories about the careful use of guardrails, and support the telling of stories about safe-to-fail experiments that worked and that failed—and about the helpful learning that emerged from them.

PLAN FOR THE LONG ROAD: DEVELOP A GROWTH MINDSET IN YOURSELF AND OTHERS

If there is a single overarching message we would like you to retain after all that you've read and thought about with us, it's this: the world is making a new set of demands upon us, and we can grow ourselves and others to be ready for the challenge. We don't know exactly what it will take to get you and your team or your family or your organization ready to face all the uncertainty and change that will swirl around you and threaten to destabilize you, but we know that if you use these habits of mind, you'll be in better shape to face what the world brings to you.

We think, too, that if we use these habits of mind, we'll be in better shape to bring our best selves to the world. To see one another with more compassion, to hold a bigger view of our place faced with seemingly intractable problems, to experiment and play our way to a better tomorrow, even—or especially— when we can't predict what tomorrow will be like.

There is no skipping to the end of the book in our lives, no carefully reading the clues about how we turn out. Like any complex event—which is what all of our lives surely are—we know how it goes only when we can look back on it. This is why these habits of mind are a comfort and a reminder to us even as they are a good guide to our practice, at home and at work. The fabric of our lives is woven from volatility, uncertainty, complexity, and ambiguity. When we believe that things are clear and straightforward, when we believe we know how the next chapter will go, we are just telling ourselves a myth to bring us comfort around the campfire, as our ancestors have for thousands of years before us. Humans have always tried to make sense of those things that we can't tell straight cause-and-effect stories about; we have tried to find order in disorder, clarity in ambiguity, and the simple cause-and-effect inside a complex situation. The tools in this book are not meant to solve those fundamental needs for order and clarity. Instead, they are intended to offer us new ways to live with joy in a world that often can't supply what we most wish. Perhaps, though, they will also help us wish for new things, for the startling beauty of a new perspective, for the sense of power when we see some piece of the system that was hidden to us before, and for the key of a different question that unlocks a door we didn't know existed before. The complex world will not get more simple to make us more comfortable. Now is our chance to grow as big as the world requires us to be.

"Try one of these. It is hardly the beet, goat cheese, and arugula salad at La Prouche, but it hits a spot." Squint grinned as he passed Yolanda a ham and cheese sandwich. "But I am famous for my sandwiches, and my peach chutney." He offered her coffee from his thermos while the boat rocked gently at anchor. It was a mild spring day, but with a gentle breeze it was still chilly on the lake.

"I hate beets," Yolanda said, smiling. "And I love peach chutney."

Squint had invited Yolanda to lunch in Proucheford after her community celebration, and he'd been speechless when she had suggested a fishing trip on the lake instead. The thought of his surprise still made Yolanda smile. She realized that while Doug sometimes reminded her of her older brother, Squint made her think of her little brother. Squint was younger than Willy but he had something of the same mischievous glint in his eye. Yolanda and her brothers used to get in trouble when their dad took them fishing as kids; they were always too loud and impatient to wait out the fish. As she grew older, though, she came to love the quiet slowness on the lake, and it became a place where she had spent time with her dad as he got sick, and with her brothers after he was gone. She was glad Jarred had told her about Squint's love for fishing, and she relaxed into the warmth of the sun on her face. The sandwich wasn't half bad either.

As they cast their lines off the stern they looped around the conversation Squint had been itching to have. "You run a much bigger and more complex organization than I do," he began. "And you've been through a massive change in the last year or so. And I could tell at the event last week that your change has taken off like wildfire. I am so impressed. I have also been leading a change at Actualeyes, and that has taken hold some in the last months as well, after getting off to a surprisingly slow start."

"That's one of the lessons we should both take away from the last year," Yolanda interrupted. "Change moves at an unpredictable pace. I thought we were off to an extremely slow start, and then suddenly things started to happen quite quickly. I was surprised by both the sluggishness and the speed in turn."

Squint smiled. "Me too, now that you mention it. And yet, we're not half as far along in our change process as you seem to be in yours, and yours is so much more complex than ours is, with so many more stakeholders involved. I mean, we've made progress this year and I can see the way things are beginning to change, but it still seems really slow compared to the way FACS has turned around. And you're supposed to be a government-run turtle and we're the IT hare. I guess I just want to know how you did it."

"Hmm. I don't really know. Maybe it's kind of like fishing in a way. You can increase the odds that you'll catch a fish—by going fishing in the first place, by choosing the right kind of line, the right kind of bait, the right time of day. But you can't force the fish to bite. I think every other time I've ever tried to make a major change happen, I've tried to force the fish to bite. This time, I just worked on the quality of the bait and the number of lines. That worked better."

"I think you're selling yourself short," Squint told her. "I keep trying to make those same moves, to communicate the change I want to see, to build coalitions and set people experimenting, and I think that maybe I just keep turning people in different directions. I catch myself telling people to experiment but then urging them not to fail. I know this is a mixed message and it gets in the way. I'm guessing that the quality of the leadership you offer is somehow different from the quality I offer." Squint looked into the water thoughtfully. "Actualeyes and the people who work there really matter to me. I'm surprised at how much. Really I'm just a software engineer who took a wrong turn and became a CEO. I know I have a lot to learn about this leadership thing and I think I can learn some of that from you."

Yolanda smiled. "I wonder if leadership is often a kind of accident. I was a social activist trying to change the world and I stumbled into government work. When I became a leader I was all over the place, uncomfortable with my own power and then frustrated with how little power it felt like I had. Leadership requires quite a lot of practice and thought, as it turns out. I am a very different leader today than I was when I was your age."

"Are you going to give me one of those way-back-in-the-olden-days talks?" Squint teased.

"I'll try to resist," Yolanda said, laughing. "But listen up, sonny boy, I guess I believe in change in a whole different way than I did once. I think I used to say that I believed that people could change, that organizations could change, that society could change. And I did believe it, to a point. But I also believed that things were basically the way they were and I needed to just tinker a little at the edges. That belief has been shifting for me in the past decade or so, but never has it been more alive than this year. And I think the way I believe about change and what is possible really matters. It might sound sort of magical, but I think that what I believe—really, deeply, truly believe about myself and others and how we all can change—well, I think that creates the conditions for the change to happen. I know that's not the only thing that *makes* change happen, of course. There is a lot of power and politics and resistance and falling back and all that in change as well—we've both seen that this year. But one of the things I've been struck by is that my own thinking about whether a person or bureau could change (or not) seems to have a strong impact on whether, in fact, that person or bureau changes."

"Wait a second, doesn't that just prove you're doing it right and that you can pick the ones who will change and the ones who can't?" Squint asked.

"I thought that, too, of course. But then I tried collecting a little data about my own actions, and I found out that most of my staff could tell who I was backing and who I thought wouldn't make it. And whenever I had the thought, 'This isn't worth the time,' I knew I would be working—without meaning to of course—to undermine the change process for that person."

"So does that mean you have to believe everyone can change to become everything all the time? Doesn't that feel just a little Pollyannaish to you?" Squint wondered.

"Maybe a little. And of course I don't really believe that everyone *will* change, but I believe that everyone *can* make a change. Does that make more sense?"

"Yes, I guess so. It does strike me as a little weird to think that what you believe about another person's ability to change would have such a powerful influence on whether they changed, but I can sort of get what you say." Squint paused and looked out toward the shore. "I am just noticing that so much about what I need to change is about me and how I am and what I believe in the world. That sounds pretty daunting to me."

"Who we are as leaders really does matter, I think," Yolanda said seriously. "And I guess the good news is that for me anyway, these changes have become more natural over time. I don't have to push myself as much to believe in people and their ability to change. I'm more comfortable than I used to be with this messy stuff. The stakes for my organization are very high, but I am less nervous than I was when I was younger, even as I'm less certain."

"Argh, now you sound like my board members," Squint sighed. "I love the feeling of certainty, of knowing where things have gone wrong and nailing the programming to make it work just the way I wanted. Why would I move toward more uncertainty?"

"I know it's pretty counterintuitive, and I'm not sure I would have chosen it myself," Yolanda answered. "All I know is that I'm able to hold my nerve better, to listen better, and to see more possibilities for solutions when the voice of certainty is quieter. And I think that has helped in this transition to spending more time listening to the community and less time trying to fix them.

"It is also the case that none of this has been straightforward," she continued. "It was really only halfway through the past year that we realized that many of our assumptions about family violence needed to change. Boy, was that a radical shift! It still is. And there is a way I have to thank Actualeyes for that."

"Uh-oh! Where is this one going?" said Squint, not actually intending to say his thought out loud.

Yolanda grinned. "No, I am genuinely grateful to Hannah. She took Curtis aside during the meeting at Jarred's house and pointed out that our hopes to engage much more with the community and also strengthen some of our tougher interventions in high-risk cases sounded to her like a polarity. She drew it out for Curtis and off he went. And it turned out that we did have to manage this as a polarity, and that meant that some of the assumptions at the core of our work needed to change. Curtis trawled back through all the cases over the past two years, including a host of near misses, and looked at the most recent writing in the field. It was all new to him, and there was a way that was really frustrating to Doug, who had been slogging his way along the same path for so long. But Curtis started to point to things that none of the rest of us had seen."

Yolanda continued: "The work he has done has had us thinking really deeply inside FACS and with community leaders about the patterns of family violence and the assumptions we have been holding. I think I was too new to the field and too consumed by being an ED to see it, and Doug would say he was too attached to an earlier paradigm about empowering the victims to take action, and Ramona would say she was too stuck in fixing her bureau. We had all gotten stuck." Yolanda paused before continuing.

"Years ago making a shift in thinking like this would have been too much of a wrench for me. I would have been ashamed and felt a fool for getting things wrong, and I would have kept pretending things were fine for far too long. Being less certain and listening more has really helped me take a bigger view."

"Wow, I so admire that you can point to that in yourself," Squint said. "I feel like I am miles away from where you are now—but I'm hopeful that if I work hard, I'll be able to reach toward what you've achieved." Yolanda suddenly got very focused on her fishing line, and Squint thought perhaps he'd change the subject. "You know, it's funny now that you say that you're easier with uncertainty. I've noticed that Jarred is moving into that space as well. Can I tell you about that, or is it too weird since you're his mom?" Yolanda motioned for Squint to continue. "I happened to see Jarred running a tough meeting last week. There was a big group of us, and we were dealing with some tricky variations in the 4Sight project. There were so many people in the room, I don't think he particularly noticed me, but I was noticing him and how skilled and easy he has become at dealing with conflict over the issue as well as his own uncertainty about what the best course of action is. I would have had no idea of how to balance all those things when I was his age. I'm not sure I do it so well now. It was a real wake up call for me about how much people can grow, and fast."

Yolanda smiled with a mother's pride, although she also thought it funny that Squint, all of eight years older than Jarred, could speak of him as belonging to another age. "Actually, Jarred told me that you came up to him after the meeting and congratulated him on the way he was managing the process. Good for you. It meant a lot to him and I think it is especially important for Jarred and others to see us confused and be OK with that. He has seen plenty of it from me in the past year."

"Yes, and I'll try to make it so people see more of that from me, more reliably. Any other tips on what to do?"

Yolanda paused, unsure of what to say. Then she launched in: "Can I tell you something that might sound really New Agey to a computer engineer?"

"Hey, I'm an engineer of a new age!" Squint protested. "Don't hold back."

"I find that the best way to move into this space is to pay better attention to the signals my body is giving me, and then make decisions about what to do about them. It's like I have to get on the balcony of myself and look out over my actions and feelings. I noticed last year that when I was in an uncertain place, I started using big words and cutting people off. I traced that to what it felt like in my body, and there was a tightness in my chest that felt constricting. It was almost like I talked louder to avoid that feeling."

"OK, that is a little weird. What did you do about it?"

"I noticed it and then tried not to let it run me. Now I think of that tightness in my chest as a kind of signal that I have to think carefully about what I say, because my body is anxious and might derail me."

"Woman conquering her bodily impulses," Squint proclaimed. "Very evolved of you."

"Oh, no, that's not what I meant at all. I wasn't trying to conquer them at all but to *learn* from them. It turns out there are times when my body is giving me signals about something I should move toward, too. A kind of tingle of excitement when a new possibility emerges, like champagne in my blood. I know to listen carefully then and pay close attention. I guess I'm just trying to use my body as a kind of barometer and then make decisions from that more informed place."

Squint groaned. "I think of my body as a transportation device, not a barometer. There's another thing for me to learn."

"I suspect it is both a barometer and a transportation device. I figure there will never be a time when there isn't something to learn. I guess that's one of the beauties and miseries of our job as leaders in the first place. I think we need a kind of compassion for ourselves as well as our people if we're going to go well in this space."

"I think we also need companions," Squint told her. "I was wondering whether you might join me in a little lunch group I'm forming. I'm trying to not have any clear goals for this group but just have a set of CEOs from a variety of different organizations meet together once a month to share stories and ask each other questions. We've started running some action learning groups at Actualeyes and they're making a big difference. I know you're really busy, but I wonder whether you'd be interested in joining me for something like that."

Yolanda smiled. "I would so love to join you for that," she said. "I think we've got a lot to learn from one another and our organizations have a lot to contribute to the world. We could meet at La Prouche and call it 'On the Beets'? We could learn heaps from our successes and more from our failures."

"Thanks, Yolanda. It's not that likely that you and I would have met, but I'm sure glad it turned out to be possible."

"It's those improbable things that turn out to be possible that are the most wonderful sometimes," Yolanda said, thinking about TJ and his grandma.

"And the most horrible," Squint said, thinking about one of his young programmers who was recently diagnosed with a rare and deadly cancer. They sat in silence for a few minutes, the water lapping at the boat. "I guess it's leading through whatever is possible that we have to do these days."

"I guess it is," Yolanda answered. "And we need all the help we can get with that task." She pointed to the fishing pole propped on the side of the boat, its line twitching more and more sharply. "Looks like we'll have a little more fuel for the journey," she said, smiling as Squint tugged and reeled the fish to the surface. As it broke through the water they both laughed.

"I guess it's possible to use this for fuel," Squint said staring doubtfully at the huge waterlogged boot dangling from the end of his line, "but it's not probable that I'll find a way." They both laughed, their voices echoing across the empty lake, the probable and the possible coming together for one moment in the present, as they always do.

NOTES

CHAPTER ONE

1. When we talk about "leaders," we are casting a wide net. We mean people in formal and informal leadership roles, people who intend to become formal or informal leaders, or anyone who leads thought or action of any kind.

2. The rules have changed for all of us but for those who have responsibility for leading, the increases in complexity are more stark and the penalty for not thinking in this way more severe.

3. When we talk about "minds" we are not talking about just what happens in your logical brain. We think of the mind as the entire integrated system of your brain and your body— the whole entity that makes up your thinking and feeling self. Knowing and making use of your whole mind (and not just the logical part you have the easiest access to) is a key component of the work of this book.

4. Literally. More on this in Chapter 5.

5. There will be a lot more on this later. In particular see Chapter 7 and Berger, J. G., 2012, *Changing on the job: Developing leaders for a complex world*, Stanford, CA, Stanford Business Books.

6. Gladwell, M., 2005, *Blink: The power of thinking without thinking*, Boston, MA, Back Bay Books.

7. You'll notice that we tend to alternate between the singular pronouns *he* and *she* when we are referring to an indeterminate-gendered person. We find this the least clumsy of a set of bad choices: the universal (and sexist) *he*, the nongendered (and grammatically incorrect) *they*, and the correct but awkward *she or he*.

8. *Obstaculizar* is a Spanish verb that might do a better job of describing how this person affects you than anything we can find in English.

9. This is commonly attributed to Paul Batalden.

10. For discussion of analyzing the power in issues, situations, and institutions and how to work constructively with power issues, see Gaventa, J., 2006, "Finding the spaces for change: A power analysis," *IDS Bulletin*, *37*(6), 23–33; Green, D., 2008, *From poverty to power: How active citizens and effective states can change the world*, Oxford, UK, Oxfam International; Kahane, A., 2010, *Power and love: A theory and practice of social change*, San Francisco, CA,

Berrett-Koehler; Mulgan, G., 2006, *Good and bad power: The ideals and betrayals of government*, London, UK, Penguin.

11. Torbert, W. R., *Brief definitions*, Boston, MA, Action Inquiry Associates.

CHAPTER TWO

1. Kurtz, C. F., and Snowden, D. J., 2003, "The new dynamics of strategy: Sense-making in a complex and complicated world," *IBM Systems Journal*, 42(3), 462–83. See also Snowden, D. J., and Boone, M. E., 2007, "A leader's framework for decision making," *Harvard Business Review*, 85(11, November), 69–76.

2. There are a number of similar constructs that have been developed to deal with the contrast between complicated and complex problems and the different responses needed to deal with these issues. The different categorizations make different distinctions, particularly about the extent to which complex issues might be resolved and the extent to which the situation might be knowable, but they also have much in common. Four others that are among the most helpful are Heifetz and colleagues' contrast between technical problems versus adaptive challenges; the line of thinkers starting with Rittel who have described tame versus wicked problems and/or "messes"; Stacey's complex responsive processes, and Eoyang and Holladay's framework for adaptive action. On adaptive challenges, see Heifetz, R., Grashow, A., and Linsky, M., 2009, *The practice of adaptive leadership: Tools and tactics for changing your organization and the world*, Boston, MA, Harvard Business Press. On wicked problems and messes, see Rittel, Horst W. J., and Webber, Melvin M., 1973, "Dilemmas in a general theory of planning," *Policy Sciences* 4, 155–69; Conklin, Jeffrey, 2006, *Dialogue mapping: Building shared understanding of wicked problems*, Chichester, UK, Wiley; Australian Public Service Commission, 2007, *Tackling wicked problems: A public policy perspective*, http://www.apsc.gov.au/publications-and-media/archive/publications-archive/tackling-wicked-problems; Ackoff, R., 1974, "Systems, messes, and interactive planning," in *Redesigning the future*, New York, NY, Wiley; Horn, R. E., and Weber, R. P., 2007, *New tools for resolving wicked problems: Mess mapping and resolution mapping processes*, Watertown, MA, Strategy Kinetics. On complex responsive processes, see Stacey, R., 2012, *Tools and techniques of leadership and management: Meeting the challenge of complexity*, Abingdon, UK, Routledge. On adaptive action, see Eoyang, G. H., and Holladay, R. J., 2013, *Adaptive action: Leveraging uncertainty in your organization*, Stanford, CA, Stanford University Press.

3. Albert Michotte, a psychologist in the mid-twentieth century, did research to show that seeing causality is as natural a function of our brains as seeing color. About Michotte's work, Kahneman writes, "We are evidently ready from birth to have impressions of causality, which do not depend on reasoning about patterns of causation." Kahneman, D., 2011, *Thinking fast and slow*, New York, NY, Farrar, Straus & Giroux, 76.

4. Ibid., 75.

5. *Cynefin* is commonly translated into English as *habitat* or *place* but is used by David Snowden in its fuller Welsh meaning to convey the sense that we all have multiple pasts and connections of which we can be only partly aware: cultural, religious, geographic, tribal, and so on. "The word is sometimes used to describe an environment where a person feels they belong or knowledge and sense of place that is passed down the generations." It can also refer to fleeting moments in time where we might feel most connected (see "Cyne-

fin," Wikipedia, http://en.wikipedia.org/wiki/Cynefin, accessed October 1, 2014). As New Zealanders, we are struck by the strong similarities between *Cynefin* and the Maori word *turangawaewae*. This is literally translated as "a place to stand," but in addition to describing the place one is connected to through *whakapapa* (geneaology), *turangawaewae* also signifies a place where a person belongs and feels empowered or connected.

6. For more on these questions, see Hummelbrunner, R., and Jones, H., 2013, *A guide to managing in the face of complexity*, background note, London, UK, Overseas Development Institute.

7. In 2014 Snowden changed the name of the simple domain to *obvious*, because the relationship between cause and effect is obvious to all. We have used the term *simple* throughout the writing of this book and in our teaching, and we have found, for the moment at least, that it is simpler to stick with *simple*.

8. For an unexpectedly interesting look at the unexpectedly vital work of creating checklists, see Gawande, A., 2009, *The checklist manifesto: How to get things right*, New York, Metropolitan Books.

9. These patterns have been described as coercive control, where coercive tactics such as violence and intimidation are combined with controlling actions such as isolation and deprivation. Stark, E., 2007, *Coercive control: How men entrap women in personal life*, New York, NY, Oxford University Press; Johnson, M., 2008, *A typology of domestic violence: Intimate terrorism, violent resistance, and situational couple violence*, Boston, MA, Northeastern University Press.

10. Family Violence Death Review Committee, 2014, *Fourth annual report: January 2013 to December 2013*, Wellington, New Zealand, Family Violence Death Review Committee, http://www.hqsc.govt.nz/assets/FVDRC/Publications/FVDRC-4th-report-June-2014.pdf.

11. Readers with any background in complexity may bristle at the term *chaos* being used to describe such a state. Here, Snowden uses that word in its commonplace understanding and not in the more scientific way chaos is understood—which is much more like his complexity domain. We'd have chosen different words, but we offer Snowden's model because it's so helpful in so many ways. If you'd like him to alter his words, we encourage you to write to him on his very active blog at the Cognitive Edge Network (http://cognitive-edge.com/blog/).

12. Though of course this book seeks to help you remember to do just that.

13. Kay, J., 2010, *Obliquity: Why our goals are best achieved indirectly*, London, UK, Profile Books.

14. There are links between this approach and recent developments in design thinking, although safe-to-fail experimentation puts more emphasis on trying many things at the same time. For design thinking, see Brown, T., 2009, *Change by design: How design thinking transforms organizations and inspires innovation*, New York, NY, HarperCollins; Kelley, T., 2001, *The art of innovation: Lessons in creativity from IDEO, America's leading design firm*, New York, NY, Currency/Doubleday. For more on the social and conversational aspects of leading in complexity, see Stacey, R., 2012, *Tools and techniques of leadership and management: Meeting the challenge of complexity*, Abingdon, UK, Routledge.

15. Duhigg, C., 2012, *The power of habit: Why we do what we do in life and business*, New York, NY, Random House.

16. Ibid., xviii.

CHAPTER THREE

1. Patterson, K., Grenny, J., McMillan, R., and Switzler, L., 2002, *Crucial conversations: Tools for talking when stakes are high*, New York, NY, McGraw-Hill.

2. Torbert, W., personal communication, Growth Edge Network call, 2013.

3. We are indebted in this work to our mentors Joan Wofford and Barry Jentz, who taught us over many years the power of feedback and the joys of teaching it to others.

4. Jentz, B., 2007, *Talk sense: Communicating to lead and learn*, Acton, MA, Research for Better Teaching; Kegan, R., and Lahey, L., 2001, *How the way we talk can change the way we work: Seven languages for transformation*, San Francisco, CA, Jossey-Bass.

5. Kahneman, D., 2011, *Thinking fast and slow*, New York, NY, Farrar, Straus & Giroux, 85.

6. We sometimes call this the shit sandwich, which isn't so appetizing but does get the point across that the quality of the bread isn't a real issue here.

7. Losada, M., 1999, "The complex dynamics of high performance teams," *Mathematical and Computer Modelling*, 30(9–10), 179–92.

8. Patterson et al., *Crucial conversations*, 21.

9. One of the perverse consequences of the view that it is "unprofessional" to talk about one's feelings might be the fact that people find it very difficult to separate their feelings from the data. If we do not practice talking about our feelings, we might find it hard to actually identify them. Instead, we get lost in our feelings without even noticing.

10. Stone, D., Patton, B., and Heen, S., 2000, *Difficult conversations: How to discuss what matters most*, New York, NY, Penguin, 13.

11. Johnson, S. K., 2008, "I second that emotion: Effects of emotional contagion and affect at work on leader and follower outcomes," *Leadership Quarterly*, 19(1), 1–19, http://www.sciencedirect.com/science/article/pii/S1048984307001464.

CHAPTER FOUR

1. Heath, C., and Heath, D., 2010, *Switch: How to change things when change is hard*, New York, NY, Broadway, 53.

2. Boal, K., and Schultz, P., 2007. "Storytelling, time, and evolution: The role of strategic leadership in complex adaptive systems," *Leadership Quarterly*, 18, 411–28.

3. Sustaining businesses over the medium to long term has gotten much harder. The average time in 1958 that a corporation spent in the S&P 500 index was 61 years. By 2011 this had dropped to 18 years. Foster, R. N., 2012, "Creative destruction whips through corporate America," *Innosight Executive Briefing*, Winter, Lexington, MA, http://www.innosight.com/innovation-resources/strategy-innovation/upload/creative-destruction-whips-through-corporate-america_final2012.pdf.

4. Evolution didn't set out to create a giraffe. Evolution insisted that the creature be good enough at eating to survive and to find ways to beat its competition during times of scarcity. It just happened that the long neck was most useful under the circumstances.

5. They could ask questions like, What seems to be happening right now to others who face the question of volume versus quality? What seems to create the conditions for one of those choices to thrive over another in insurance and other industries?

6. Many leading systems thinkers, such as Gerald Midgley, see critiquing and setting boundaries as being at the core of systems thinking and making interventions in systems. See Midgley, G., 2000, *Systemic intervention: Philosophy, methodology, and practice*, New York, NY, Kluwer Academic and Plenum.

7. Most complexity and systems-thinking writers are scathing about targets for this reason. For some of the most scathing, see the work of John Seddon. Because the consequences are so backward from their intended results, the stories would be funny except that so many of them feature disadvantaged people—or people in critical care conditions—and so they are not funny at all. Seddon, J., 2008, *Systems thinking in the public sector: The failure of the reform regime . . . and a manifesto for a better way*, Axminster, UK, Triarchy Press.

8. Note, however, that a safe-to-fail experiment can in fact have a kind of target feel— briefly and for the purposes of learning instead of the purposes of solving the issue once and for all. It would be a bad idea to roll out a policy to have each person in the organiza- tion contact a client every week. But it might be a good safe-to-fail experiment to have each person in the bounded small experiment group give it a try and see what he learns.

9. Barry Johnson has a great website with lots of helpful material on his technique, at http://www.polaritypartnerships.com. Johnson, B., 1996, *Polarity management: Identifying and managing unsolvable problems*, Amherst, MA, HRD Press.

10. There is a polarity for consultants—using two-by-two matrices, not using two-by-two matrices.

11. Barry Johnson and his colleagues suggest going even deeper—noting at the top the greatest hopes that emerge from the top half of the map and noting at the bottom the worst fears that seem to be lurking in both halves of the bottom.

12. We first heard about this strategy on NPR, "The life cycle of a social network: Keeping friends in times of change," *all tech considered* (blog), March 8, 2013, http://www.npr.org/ blogs/alltechconsidered/2013/03/08/173772488/the-life-cycle-of-a-social-network-keep ing-friends-in-times-of-change.

13. Tom Wujec, "Build a tower, build a team," TED, filmed February 2010, http://www.ted .com/talks/tom_wujec_build_a_tower.

14. Many of these ideas are adapted from Dave Snowden's musings on his blog at the Cog- nitive Edge Network, "And so to SCRUM/KANBAN," April 17, 2013, http://cognitive-edge .com/blog/entry/5990/complex-domain-applied-to-scrum-kanban/.

CHAPTER FIVE

1. It might be said, though, that most of literature and all of poetry is there to celebrate our inability to leave our emotions behind. Just imagine how boring we'd be without this quirk!

2. Kahneman, D., 2011, *Thinking fast and slow*, New York, NY, Farrar, Straus & Giroux; Duhigg, C., 2012, *The power of habit: Why we do what we do in life and business*, New York, NY, Random House; Ariely, D., 2009, *Predictably irrational: The hidden forces that shape our decisions*, New York, NY, Hardcover; Schulz, K., 2011, *Being wrong: Adventures in the margin of error*, New York, NY, HarperCollins; Wilson, T. D., 2002, *Strangers to ourselves: Discover- ing the adaptive unconscious*, Cambridge, MA, Belknap Press of Harvard University Press.

3. *Executive functions* is an umbrella term for the management (regulation, control) of cognitive processes, including working memory, reasoning, task flexibility, and problem solving, as well as planning and execution. Historically these functions have been seen as regulated by the prefrontal regions of the frontal lobes although other structures of the brain may also be involved.

4. A pragmatic application of these ideas to child protection work, and also some of the systemic weaknesses that arise in practice as a result of our biases and perceptions, is provided in Broadhurst, K., White, S., Fish, S., Munro, E., Fletcher, K., and Lincoln, H., 2010, *Ten pitfalls and how to avoid them: What research tells us*, London, UK, National Society for the Prevention of Cruelty to Children, http://www.nspcc.org.uk/inform/publications/downloads/tenpitfalls_wdf48122.pdf.

5. This and all the other biases have official names. We're going to use the names Yolanda—and other leaders with whom we've worked—find easier to remember. In this case, the official name is *inattentional blindness*.

6. Interestingly, Ramona is frustrated that Yolanda wants to try and see things through her eyes because she has already told Yolanda how she sees the situation. She cannot imagine that Yolanda does not just get it the way Ramona has described it. It's hard for us to really embrace the idea that others may see the world so differently that they might need to hear something that is totally clear (to us) again to make sense of it.

7. This one is officially known as *confirmation bias*.

8. More formally known as *implicit egotism* or *implicit self-esteem*.

9. Pelham, B. W., Mirenberg, M. C., and Jones, J. T., 2002, "Why Susie sells seashells by the seashore: Implicit egotism and major life decisions," *Journal of Personality and Social Psychology*, 82(4), 469–87.

10. Vedantam, S., 2005, "See no bias," *Washington Post*, January 23, W12.

11. There is a huge literature about our racial, gender, and cultural biases, and there are a variety of ways to uncover your own biases. One good place to start is with the Harvard Implicit Association Test (https://implicit.harvard.edu), a well-researched—and sobering—look at the biases that might be running at the back of your brain. For another, see Gladwell, M., 2005, *Blink: The power of thinking without thinking*, Boston, MA, Back Bay Books.

12. This also works in reverse sometimes. In these cases we might hate in others a flaw we hate in ourselves. Same principle, but working the opposite way—also unconsciously.

13. This one is also known as *availability bias*.

14. One public service CEO we know captures this surprising sense of not having control with a clucky metaphor. He says his direct reports, and the second-tier managers of other chief executives in his sector, treat their bosses as if they were "feeding the chooks." By that he means these chief executives are like backyard hens, tossed chicken feed each day by their managers to keep them contented and laying.

15. Sweeney, L. B., and Meadows, D., 1995, *The systems thinking playbook: Exercises to stretch and build learning and systems thinking capabilities*, 95–106, Durham, NH, University of New Hampshire.

16. Heath, C., and Heath, D., 2010, *Switch: How to change things when change is hard*, New York, NY, Broadway.

17. Of course, we also want to avoid believing that a change in systems or structures or furniture will do all the work to create the change we want. Change is hard. We want to use all the possibilities at hand.

18. Karma Currency is a cool Australian philanthropic group (http://www.karmacurrency .com.au). There are others like it around the world.

CHAPTER SIX

1. Collins and Hansen argue that the companies who most successfully moved through periods of great uncertainty were those with leaders who were specific, methodical, and consistent about the messages they were giving. Those leaders were also open to making rare but major changes in the direction and messaging if experimentation and small bets suggested big bets would be worth making and/or their deep understanding of the external environment required a shift in direction. This was also observed, in a much smaller way, in Keith's doctoral thesis, where the most effective regional environmental management organizations were lead not by people who profiled as the most complex thinkers but by those who were extremely good clarifiers who could distill a complex situation into a clear organizational direction and message and who were prepared to review, learn, and adjust approaches and messaging when practical experiences showed that things were not working and changes were required. See Collins, J., and Hansen, M. T., 2011, *Great by choice: Uncertainty, chaos, and luck—why some thrive despite them all,* New York, NY, Harper, 128; Johnston, K., 2008, "Complexity of thinking and levels of self-complexity required to sustainably manage the environment," PhD diss., Australian National University, Canberra.

2. Heath, C., and Heath, D., 2007, *Made to stick: Why some ideas survive and others die,* New York, NY, Random House; Duarte, N., 2010, *Resonate: Present visual stories that transform audiences,* New York, NY, Wiley; Crossland, R., 2012, *Voice lessons: Applying science to the art of leadership communication,* CreateSpace.

3. "Microsoft CEO Ballmer laughs at Apple iPhone," *MacDailyNews,* January 17, 2007, http://macdailynews.com/2007/01/17/microsoft_ceo_ballmer_laughs_at_apple_iphone/.

4. Perhaps ironically, given Microsoft's more recent experience, Bill Gates's pursuit of a portfolio of strategic experiments in the late 1980s, many of them in competition with one another, is cited as a powerful contribution to Microsoft's success. See Beinhocker, E. D., 2006, *The origin of wealth: Evolution, complexity, and the radical remaking of economics,* Cambridge, MA, Harvard Business School Press, 335–37.

5. We are grateful for our conversations with social workers in the field and to these authors for pointing some of the way for our FACS strategy: Stevens, I., and Cox, P., 2008, "Complexity theory: Developing new understandings of child protection in field settings and in residential child care," *British Journal of Social Work,* 38(7), 1320–36; Warren-Adamson, C., 2010, *The usefulness of the complexity paradigm to child and family practice,* presentation paper, School of Applied Social Science, University of Brighton, Brighton, UK, http://about .brighton.ac.uk/sass/complex-systems/resources/AdaptedComplexitypaper.pdf; Family Violence Death Review Committee, 2014, *Fourth Annual Report: January 2013 to December 2013,* Wellington, New Zealand, Family Violence Death Review Committee.

6. In our families we also focus on outcomes, but we cannot predict how things will turn out, such as how the lives of our children will unfold. The observation "raising children is not rocket science" emphasizes that most people get to do it and that raising children does not take highly specialized expertise. Applying a complexity lens, rocket science is a complicated technical task within the reach of existing expertise and largely predictable in its results. Raising a family, however, is complex. It is within the reach of most of us but is

highly unpredictable in terms of short-term details and longer-term outcomes. See Licata A., 2009, *It's not rocket science: Down-to-earth advice on raising stellar kids*, http://www.lulu .com/shop/alice-licata-phd/its-not-rocket-science-down-to-earth-advice-on-raising-stel lar-kids/paperback/product-5565389.html.

7. Heath, C., and Heath, D., 2010, *Switch: How to change things when change is hard*, New York, NY, Broadway.

CHAPTER SEVEN

1. Dweck, C., 2006, *Mindset: The new psychology of success*, New York, NY, Ballantine.

2. Theorists call this sort of theory of adult growth a constructive-developmental theory because it is both about the way we see the world—the way we construct it—and about the change in that construction over time. Berger, J. G., 2012, *Changing on the job: Developing leaders for a complex world*, Stanford, CA, Stanford University Press; Kegan, R., 1994, *In over our heads: The mental demands of modern life*, Cambridge, MA, Harvard University Press.

3. Notice here that this doesn't have to be a functioning or beneficial society. A person can be socialized into a neo-Nazi society or even an anarchist society (as long as the rules of anarchy are clear enough). What matters is that at the socialized form of mind, we get our ideas about right and wrong from the groups to which we belong.

4. We have found that many of the organizations with which we work seem to wish that their leaders would be more self-authored, to think outside the box, but only in particular, organization-sanctioned ways. A kind of socialized version of self-authorship.

5. Research shows that between 5% and 10% of adults make this move.

6. Fisher, D., Rooke, D., and Torbert, W., 2003, *Personal and organisational transformations: Through action inquiry*, Edge\Work Press.

7. Argyris, C. 1991, "Teaching smart people how to learn," *Harvard Business Review*, 69(3), 99–109.

8. Of course, this presupposed a fair and equitable starting place for each individual. A little time spent seeing the systemic privileges unravels that assumption.

9. Take, for example, the disparity between men's and women's pay in many organizations. People often look at the cause and effect relationship as though it were simple: women are more likely to take time out of the workforce to raise a family, they are more likely to work part-time, and they are more likely to avoid working the crazy hours some leadership positions demand. Each of these is associated with a simple drop in salary that adds up over time and across numbers of women who make these choices. But here the idea of fair is to have women be as much like men and to dock their salary for the times when they are less like men. If we had a different perspective on this issue, we might be able to see the benefits women bring to organizations because of their potentially different approaches and perspectives. That might be a real added value to the organization. A complex view would look at the current situation and ask about the ways men and women are collectively and individually adding value in their different ways, and then support them to add value even more than they have before. Then there could be safe-to-fail experiments that spring from that hope. Norming women against the way men work is a simple answer to a complex issue.

10. Kegan, R., Lahey, L., Fleming, A., and Miller, M., 2014, "Making business personal" *Harvard Business Review*, 92(4), 3–10.

11. Don't get us wrong: we believe lots of important things happen in workshops. But we've come to believe that perhaps the most wonderful outcome of a workshop is a new way to learn from your colleagues and your work. It sounds like it should be automatic, but actually it can be tricky to learn how to learn from our experiences in ways that really help us grow.

12. Marquardt, M. J., 1999, *Action learning in action: Transforming problems and people for world-class organizational learning*, San Francisco, CA, Davies-Black; Fisher, Rooke, and Torbert, *Personal and organisational transformations.*

13. Heifetz, R., Grashow, A., and Linsky, M., 2009, *The practice of adaptive leadership: Tools and tactics for changing your organization and the world*, Boston, MA, Harvard Business Press.

14. Adapted from exhibit 8.3, "Thinking and creating together: Cultivating developmental meetings," in *Changing on the job: Developing leaders for a complex world*, Stanford, CA, Stanford University Press, 175–77. © 2012 Jennifer Garvey Berger. By permission of the publisher.

CHAPTER EIGHT

1. Heifetz, R, 1998, *Leadership without easy answers*, Cambridge, MA, Harvard University Press; Heifetz, R., & Linskey, M., 2002, *Leadership on the line: Staying alive through the dangers of leading*, Cambridge, MA, Harvard Business Review Press.

2. In the United States there is, on average, one death about every two years from a shark attack, and lightning strikes kill about 40 people per year. Handwerk, B., 2005, "Shark facts: Attack stats, record swims, more," *National Geographic News*, June 13, http://news.national-geographic.com/news/2005/06/0613_050613_sharkfacts.html.

3. See Chapter 2 for a full exploration of these squiggles.

4. Kegan, R., and Lahey, L., 2001, *How the way we talk can change the way we work: Seven languages for transformation*, San Francisco, CA, Jossey-Bass, 94–102.

5. *When* means be specific about which event you're talking about, and speak directly to the person and not about the person, even in front of others: "Stephen, yesterday, when we talked through that tech problem I was having trying to get the video to show in my presentation . . ." "I feel" means use a feeling and make it personal. Invite the human back into the workplace and let someone know what it meant to you: "I felt relieved and grateful . . ." "Because" means showing the impact on you of the other person's assistance: "because of two things, I guess—that you helped me solve my problem and didn't make me feel stupid for not finding the solution myself."

6. Keller, S., and Aiken, C., 2009, *The inconvenient truth about change management*, McKinsey and Company, http://www.mckinsey.com/App_Media/Reports/Financial _Services/The_Inconvenient_Truth_About_Change_Management; Beer, M., Eisenstat, R. A., and Spencer, B., 1990, "Why change programs don't produce change," *Harvard Business Review*, 68(6), 158–66; Kotter, J. P., 1995, "Leading change: Why transformation efforts fail," *Harvard Business Review*, 73(2), 59–67.

BIBLIOGRAPHY

Ackoff, R. 1974, "Systems, messes, and interactive planning," In *Redesigning the future*. New York, NY, Wiley.

Argyris, C. 1991, "Teaching smart people how to learn," *Harvard Business Review*, 69(3), 99–109.

Ariely, D. 2008, *Predictably irrational: The hidden forces that shape our decisions*, New York, NY, Harper.

Australian Public Service Commission. 2007, *Tackling wicked problems: A public policy perspective*. Policy paper of the Australian Public Service Commission, Canberra, http://www.apsc.gov.au/publications-and-media/archive/publications-archive/tackling-wicked-problems.

Beer, M., Eisenstat, R. A., & Spencer, B. 1990, "Why change programs don't produce change," *Harvard Business Review*, 68(6), 158–66.

Beinhocker, E. D. 2006, *The origin of wealth: Evolution, complexity, and the radical remaking of economics*, Cambridge, MA, Harvard Business School Press.

Berger, J. G. 2012, *Changing on the job: Developing leaders for a complex world*, Stanford, CA, Stanford Business Books.

Boal, K., & Schultz, P. 2007, "Storytelling, time, and evolution: The role of strategic leadership in complex adaptive systems," *Leadership Quarterly*, 18, 411–28.

Broadhurst, K., White, S., Fish, S., Munro, E., Fletcher, K., & Lincoln, H. 2010, *Ten pitfalls and how to avoid them: What research tells us*, London, UK, National Society for the Prevention of Cruelty to Children, http://www.nspcc.org.uk/inform/publications/downloads/tenpitfalls_wdf48122.pdf.

Brown, T. 2009, *Change by design: How design thinking transforms organizations and inspires innovation*, New York, NY, HarperCollins.

Collins, J., & Hansen, M. T. 2011, *Great by choice: Uncertainty, chaos, and luck—why some thrive despite them all*, New York, NY, Harper.

Conklin, J. 2006, *Dialogue mapping: Building shared understanding of wicked problems*, Chichester, UK, Wiley.

Crossland, R. 2012, *Voice lessons: Applying science to the art of leadership communication*, CreateSpace.

Duarte, N. 2010, *Resonate: Present visual stories that transform audiences*, New York, NY, Wiley.

Duhigg, C. 2012, *The power of habit: Why we do what we do in life and business*, New York, NY, Random House.

Eoyang, G. H., & Holladay, R. J. 2013, *Adaptive action: Leveraging uncertainty in your organization*, Stanford, CA, Stanford University Press.

Family Violence Death Review Committee. 2014, *Fourth annual report: January 2013 to December 2013*, Wellington, New Zealand, Family Violence Death Review Committee, http://www.hqsc.govt.nz/assets/FVDRC/Publications/FVDRC-4th-report-June-2014 .pdf.

Fisher, D., Rooke, D., & Torbert, W. 2003, *Personal and organisational transformations: Through action inquiry*, Edge\Work Press.

Foster, R. N., 2012, "Creative Destruction Whips through Corporate America," *Innosight Executive Briefing*, Winter, Lexington, MA, http://www.innosight.com/innovation -resources/strategy-innovation/upload/creative-destruction-whips-through-corporate -america_final2012.pdf.

Gaventa, J. 2006, "Finding the spaces for change: A power analysis," *IDS Bulletin*, 37(6), 23–33.

Gawande, A. 2009, *The checklist manifesto: How to get things right*, New York, NY, Metropolitan Books.

Gladwell, M. 2005, *Blink: The power of thinking without thinking*, Boston, MA, Back Bay Books.

Glouberman, S., & Zimmerman, B. 2002, "Complicated and complex systems: What would successful reform of Medicare look like?" Discussion Paper No. 8, Commission on the Future of Health Care in Canada.

Green, D. 2008, *From poverty to power: How active citizens and effective states can change the world*, Oxford, UK, Oxfam International.

Heath, C., & Heath, D. 2007, *Made to stick: Why some ideas survive and others die*, New York, NY, Random House.

Heath, C., & Heath, D. 2010, *Switch: How to change things when change is hard*, New York, NY, Broadway.

Heifetz, R. 1998, *Leadership without easy answers*. Cambridge, MA, Harvard University Press.

Heifetz, R., Grashow, A., & Linsky, M. 2009, *The practice of adaptive leadership: Tools and tactics for changing your organization and the world*, Boston, MA, Harvard Business Press.

Heifetz, R., & Linskey, M. 2002, *Leadership on the line: Staying alive through the dangers of leading*. Cambridge, MA, Harvard Business Review Press.

Horn, R. E., & Weber, R. P. 2007, *New tools for resolving wicked problems: Mess mapping and resolution mapping processes*, Watertown, MA, Strategy Kinetics.

Hummelbrunner, R., & Jones, H. 2013, *A guide to managing in the face of complexity*, Background note, London, UK, Overseas Development Institute.

Jentz, B. 2007, *Talk sense: Communicating to lead and learn*, Acton, MA, Research for Better Teaching.

Johnson, B. 1996, *Polarity management: Identifying and managing unsolvable problems*, Amherst, MA, HRD Press.

Johnson, M. 2008, *A typology of domestic violence: Intimate terrorism, violent resistance, and situational couple violence*, Boston, MA, Northeastern University Press.

Johnson, S. K. 2008, "I second that emotion: Effects of emotional contagion and affect at work on leader and follower outcomes," *Leadership Quarterly*, 19(1), 1–19, http://www.sciencedirect.com/science/article/pii/S1048984307001464.

Johnston, K. 2008, "Complexity of thinking and levels of self-complexity required to sustainably manage the environment," PhD diss., Australian National University, Canberra.

Kahane, A. 2010, *Power and love: A theory and practice of social change*, San Francisco, CA, Berrett-Koehler.

Kahneman, D. 2011, *Thinking fast and slow*, New York, NY, Farrar, Straus & Giroux.

Kay, J. 2010, *Obliquity: Why our goals are best achieved indirectly*, London, UK, Profile Books.

Kegan, R. 1994, *In over our heads: The mental demands of modern life*, Cambridge, MA, Harvard University Press.

Kegan, R., & Lahey, L. 2001, *How the way we talk can change the way we work: Seven languages for transformation*, San Francisco, CA, Jossey-Bass.

Kegan, R., & Lahey, L. 2009, *Immunity to change: How to overcome it and unlock the potential in yourself and your organization*, Boston, MA, Harvard Business School Press.

Kegan, R., Lahey, L., Fleming, A., & Miller, M. 2014, "Making business personal," *Harvard Business Review*, 92(4), 3–10.

Keller, S., & Aiken, C. 2009, *The inconvenient truth about change management*, McKinsey and Company, http://www.mckinsey.com/App_Media/Reports/Financial_Services/The_Inconvenient_Truth_About_Change_Management.

Kelley, T. 2001, *The art of innovation: Lessons in creativity from IDEO, America's leading design firm*, New York, NY, Currency/Doubleday.

Kotter, J. P. 1995, "Leading change: Why transformation efforts fail," *Harvard Business Review*, 73(2), 59–67.

Kurtz, C. F., & Snowden, D. F. 2003, "The new dynamics of strategy: Sense-making in a complex and complicated world," *IBM Systems Journal*, 42(3), 462–83.

Licata, A. 2009, *It's not rocket science: Down-to-earth advice on raising stellar kids*, http://www.lulu.com/shop/alice-licata-phd/its-not-rocket-science-down-to-earth-advice-on-raising-stellar-kids/paperback/product-5565389.html.

Losada, M. 1999, "The complex dynamics of high performance teams," *Mathematical and Computer Modelling*, 30(9–10), 179–92.

Marquardt, M. J. 1999, *Action learning in action: Transforming problems and people for world-class organizational learning*, San Francisco, CA, Davies-Black.

Midgley, G. 2000, *Systemic intervention: Philosophy, methodology, and practice*, New York, NY, Kluwer Academic and Plenum.

Mulgan, G. 2006, *Good and bad power: The ideals and betrayals of government*, London, UK, Penguin.

Patterson, K., Grenny, J., McMillan, R., & Switzler, L. 2002, *Crucial conversations: Tools for talking when stakes are high*, New York, NY, McGraw-Hill.

Pelham, B. W., Mirenberg, M. C., & Jones, J. T. 2002, "Why Susie sells seashells by the seashore: Implicit egotism and major life decisions," *Journal of Personality and Social Psychology*, 82(4), 469–87.

Rittel, H. W. J., & Webber, M. W. 1973, "Dilemmas in a general theory of planning," *Policy Sciences* 4, 155–69.

Schulz, K. 2011, *Being wrong: Adventures in the margin of error*, New York, NY, HarperCollins.

Seddon, J. 2008, *Systems thinking in the public sector: The failure of the reform regime . . . and a manifesto for a better way*, Axminster, UK, Triarchy Press.

Snowden, D. J., & Boone, M. E. 2007, "A leader's framework for decision making," *Harvard Business Review*, 85(11), 69–76.

Stacey, R. 2012, *Tools and techniques of leadership and management: Meeting the challenge of complexity*, Abingdon, UK, Routledge.

Stark, E., 2007, *Coercive control: How men entrap women in personal life*, New York, NY, Oxford University Press.

Stevens, I., & Cox, P. 2008, "Complexity theory: Developing new understandings of child protection in field settings and in residential child care," *British Journal of Social Work*, 38(7), 1320–36.

Stone, D., Patton, B., & Heen, S. 2000, *Difficult conversations: How to discuss what matters most*, New York, NY, Penguin.

Sweeney, L. B., & Meadows, D. 1995, *The systems thinking playbook: Exercises to stretch and build learning and systems thinking capabilities*, Durham, NH, University of New Hampshire.

Torbert, W. R. 2012, *Brief definitions*, Boston, MA, Action Inquiry Associates.

Vedantam, S. 2005, "See no bias; many Americans believe they are not prejudiced," *Washington Post*, January 23, W12.

Warren-Adamson, C, 2010, *The usefulness of the complexity paradigm to child and family practice*, Presentation paper, School of Applied Social Science, University of Brighton, Brighton, UK, http://www.brighton.ac.uk/sass/complex-systems/resources/.

Wilson, T. D. 2002, *Strangers to ourselves: Discovering the adaptive unconscious*, Cambridge, MA, Belknap Press of Harvard University Press.

INDEX

Page numbers followed by "f" or "t" indicate material in figures or tables.